HEARTMIND WISDOM

Collection #3

Courageous & Inspiring

Journeys of Everyday People

21 True Stories

Kindness is Key Training

& Publishing Inc.

WWW.HEARTMINDEFFECT.COM

DISCLAIMER

The intention of Kindness Is Key (KiK) is to provide inspiration and 'food for thought' by sharing personal experiences and life-gained wisdoms. KiK believes that the chapters in this Heartmind Wisdom collection are an accurate, honest and personal account of each author's recollections, interpretations and conclusions regarding persons, events and circumstances. However, it is acknowledged that recounted events, circumstances and conclusions are subjective and may or may not be recollected, interpreted or concluded in the same way by all persons.

ISBN – 978-1-77084-719-4

Printed in Victoria, BC, Canada by First Choice Books.

 FIRST CHOICE BOOKS

www.firstchoicebooks.ca

10   9   8   7   6   5   4

A Kind Welcome to Heartmind Wisdom Collection #3

Written by Julie Duciaume

Having VIP admission and front row seats at a pre-screening of the latest Hollywood blockbuster is what it felt like when I was given the privilege of proofreading the chapters in this collection of authentic and remarkable life stories. Reading each one left an indelible mark on my heart, mind and soul. Without a doubt, reading these courageous and inspiring authors' heartwarming stories of triumph will have the same impact on you.

Written by extraordinary everyday people, the stories contain invaluable lessons about love, self-worth, overcoming adversity, personal transformation, spiritual guidance, and intuition.

A percentage of retail sales from the Heartmind Wisdom Collection goes to

MERCY SHIPS CANADA

Mercy Ships, an international faith-based organization, uses hospital ships to deliver free health care services, capacity building, and sustainable development to those without access in the developing world. Founded in 1978, Mercy Ships has worked in more than 70 countries providing services valued at over $1 Billion, directly impacting some 2.35 million lives. Each year up to 1,200 volunteers from over 40 nations—including surgeons, nurses, health care trainers, seamen, cooks, and agriculturalists—pay their own board and room while donating their time and skills to the effort.

Mercy Ships seeks to become the face of love in action, bringing hope and healing to the world's poorest—transforming one life at a time. To learn more about our organization or to donate, please contact:

Mercy Ships Canada

5 – 3318 Oak Street
Victoria, B.C. V8X 1R1
1-866-900-7447
www.mercyships.ca

About the
Heartmind Wisdom Collection

Written by everyday people, the Heartmind Wisdom collection is an engaging, inspiring, and insightful anthology of authentic stories of triumph and transformation.

Published in June 2013, the first collection became an Amazon Top 100 Best Seller and hit #1 in the New Age category. Hundreds attended the launch celebrating the second book. With each chapter in this third collection, you'll dive into the author's journey and resurface inspired and refreshed.

To assist you in finding the stories that will resonate with you, the book is divided into five categories: Bouncing Back, Divine Connection, Healing from Loss, Hope, and Self-Actualization.

Contents

BOUNCING BACK

A JOURNEY BACK TO ME
The Road to Self-Love

Jennifer Marie Luce

"**W**hat have you been doing to yourself?" Joseph asked. "*What the heck?*" I thought. I had just met this man. Who was *he* to ask me such a question? I stammered to speak, but he cut me off. "You have probably been through so many things in your life going by the name Jen."

How does he know? He was correct. Still, I felt defensive and self-conscious. I stared at him, scared to hear what he would say next.

"Each letter in your name is associated with a number, and each number has a particular energetic vibration and life lesson associated with it. You are missing five numbers using your shortened name, which means you have been unintentionally living through some major karmic lessons."

The idea of learning about our numerology blueprint had sounded like fun when a girlfriend suggested it. A few days prior to my appointment, I had submitted my name and birthday to Joseph P. Ghabi, a respected blueprint numerologist. But listening to this man with a notable Middle Eastern accent, I wasn't sure that I wanted to learn any more about what my shortened name meant. Neither could I stop listening.

"Sometimes, you might have fear of failing…a fear of concentration…a lack of management, but all of these things are learnable," he continued. "Sometimes, you might be sabotaging yourself a lot. That we need to stop. Instead of self-sabotaging, it's time to say, 'I'm doing it for me.' Metaphysically speaking, whatever you went through in your life from a young age, you have to say, 'Stuff Happens.' Period! 'Must be something good for me to learn.' First thing is…you need to start using your full name."

Staring at him, I felt as though my whole life had just been exposed and laid out in front of me by a stranger. Many of the things, perhaps all of the things, he'd said were true at least to some degree. However, I wasn't wild about his suggestion that I should go by my birth name, the one Mom used when she was unhappy with me. I liked the shortened, less formal version.

Grudgingly and apprehensively, I decided to attend his weekend numerology course, Consciously Living Your Destiny. Though shocking and slightly embarrassing, the man's overall assessment of my life had been accurate, and I didn't want to continue living a life filled with strife and pain. If going by Jennifer Marie instead of Jen was going to make a difference, I was willing to do it. *Would this mean everything would change?*

Once home, I thought about my name and what my mom had told me about my traumatic birth. The umbilical cord wrapped around my neck, when I showed signs of distress, she had undergone an emergency cesarean section and had lost a lot of blood. Both of us almost died. Though my parents had chosen my name, when they laid eyes on me, they felt it didn't fit. For the first several days of my life, they called me Bright Eyes in reference to my huge blue eyes. Eventually, they named me Jennifer Marie. According to my parents, I was deeply wanted. My mom took the utmost care of me. Until I was old enough to talk, I was "Daddy's Little Girl." My own memories were less Brady Bunch happy.

"Jenny, if you don't eat your food, you can't leave the table."

Not wanting to disappoint my dad, I shrank into my chair and looked down at my food. "But I'm full, Daddy." It wasn't the first time I'd tried to feign my way out of eating something. Sheepishly, I glanced at my mom for support.

"Come on, honey. Please eat a little more," Mom coaxed. "You want to grow up to be a big girl, don't you?"

I pushed the peas on my plate around with my fork, moving them from one side to the other. I didn't like them and didn't want to eat them. I also didn't want to make my daddy angry. When I glanced back at her, I was shaking my head no.

"She has to learn her manners," my father said in his grumpiest of grumpy voices. "What about all the children in Africa who don't have any food? I'm not throwing this away!"

I melted further into the hard wooden chair, no longer feeling like I was *Daddy's Little Girl*.

"Leave her be," Mom said. "She's just a child."

"She's being a poky little puppy!" Dad bellowed. "I'm tired of her taking so long to finish things because she gets sidetracked or can't make up her mind."

"Oh, it's okay for you to be late all the time," Mom snapped. "Why do you call her poky? She doesn't call you names!"

Oh no, I made them fight again. It's all my fault. And why does Daddy have to call me names, especially that one? Though I tried to hold them back, tears welled in my eyes.

"Well, if you're not going to eat, then off to your room! And no TV," screamed my dad.

I ran up to my room. *No TV again. Why did I keep getting punished?* Crying, I scrambled up on my bed and picked up my favorite book *The Poky Little Puppy*. Staring down at it, I thought about the nights my parents read me the story. It was our special time together. But if my being *poky* made my dad mad, then the book was bad too. I threw it under my bed to stay hidden forever. I didn't want to be reminded of how bad I was. I didn't want Mommy and Daddy to fight all the time neither. *Maybe they didn't like me anymore.*

As my mom's belly grew bigger and bigger, she told me that I had a little brother coming soon. At the beginning, I was excited, wondering what it would be like when he arrived. She told me that she would need my help which made me feel good. I loved helping her with cleaning and baking and other fun things.

Then my mom had to go away to the hospital for a few days. I didn't understand what was happening and it made me nervous. What did "him coming" really mean? Everything was already changing and he wasn't even here yet. I wanted things to be the way they always had— safe with Mommy and Daddy.

I was too scared to visit my mom in the hospital, so I met my new little brother for the first time after they came home. It was neat to have him there, so little, crying all the time and squirming about. I felt important helping my mom change his diapers and feed him, but the attention I got wasn't the same. He always came first now.

When he grew out of diapers and became more independent, he started doing sneaky things to get me into trouble. Most of the time it wasn't even my fault, but because I was the big sister, I was told that I should've known better.

In my preteens, as I fought for acknowledgement and respect, the relationship with my mom became strained. I felt forgotten. She had been the person standing up for me in the past, but had become the big ogre disciplinarian. I often got grounded from watching TV and playing with friends, and had my toys taken away for things I didn't do. When the fighting between my parents escalated, so did the arguments between my mom and me. We fought like cats and dogs. At night, I stuck my nose into fantasy books and listened to music to drown out the sound of my parents fighting downstairs.

My parents had separated a few years earlier. When they got back together, their relationship remained tense. I reached for my independence by asking for more responsibility around the house. That didn't turn out to be what I wanted. While I did chores or looked after my little brother, I'd look out the window and see my friends playing. Though I wanted to please my parents and make life easier for them, I resented being trapped in the house. Torn between praise and fun, I was often frustrated and confused.

The changes in my body and the accompanying emotional roller coaster, added to my angst and confusion. As my body developed, I wasn't too happy about having things where there were none before. Not comfortable with the new, ever-changing me, I often sat in the shower and cried. When I tried to explain how I felt about becoming a woman, my brother and dad ridiculed me. Afraid to speak to my family and others about what I wanted or how I felt, I stopped saying much and did what I was told.

Deciding that my mom was too strict, I started lying so I could do what I wanted and get my own way. I wore baggy black sweatshirts and my blond hair in a way that covered part of my face. Wanting to fit in at school, I shortened my name. Jen sounded cooler and more adult than Jenny. In spite of my efforts to hide and blend, I was bullied.

I was picked on for being smart. My hair color made me a walking target for dumb blond jokes. Thanks to my buckteeth, I was called Bucktooth and Bugs Bunny. My last name *Luce* sounded like *loose*, which earned me the nickname Hooker. When I complained to my mom that while I was riding my bike, some boys from school chased me down the street and tried to pinch my bum, Mom sloughed it off by saying they liked me. *Huh?*

No matter how hard I tried to please my parents, their fighting continued as did the arguments between me and my mom. After a while, everything I was doing to make others happy seemed pointless. I became sadder and sadder. Desperate for affection and recognition, I turned my nose further into books and my education. Thinking it might be better if I wasn't around anymore, I contemplated running away or ending my life.

My teacher, Mr. MacMath, saw something in me nobody else did. Even though I was super shy and kept my feelings to myself, he seemed to know who I was on the inside. He had me read aloud, and when I finished early, he asked me to help the other kids with their schoolwork. He made me feel important, valued and happy. Though grateful for his respect and appreciation, I wished that I could feel the same way at home.

In junior high, I discovered boys. At first, this new kind of attention made me feel special. However, when my first so-called boyfriend tried to push sex on me, I realized he wasn't really interested in me. Having interpreted his attraction to me as a sign that I was finally starting to fit in, I was crushed. When he cheated on me, I was brokenhearted. When my second boyfriend treated me the exact same way, including cheating on me when I wouldn't put out, I was devastated and certain that no one would ever love me for me. I was sixteen. Unable to talk to anyone or make the awful feelings inside go away, I seriously contemplated doing away with myself. The sense of control that came with having a plan in place to help end the emotional turmoil that had plagued me for years, felt oddly comforting.

My life improved in high school. Being smart became a positive attribute. I met an awesome guy, became a cheerleader, and joined a few activity groups. At school, I was popular and considered cool. At home, I begged my parents to either stop fighting or get a divorce.

One night, I simply couldn't take their fighting anymore. It was time to voice what I'd long dreaded was the ugly and painful truth. Getting out of bed, I stormed into the living room, tears dripping down my chin as I stood there trembling in my pajamas. "Stop it! Both of you, just stop it!" I hollered. "Please, stop staying together for my brother and me. It's not helping anything. I can't sleep hearing you guys fight."

A short while later, they decided to get a divorce and Dad moved out. Finally, we'd have peace in the house. Then, I got sick with mononucleosis. Once again, just as things started looking up, something or someone pulled the proverbial rug from beneath my feet.

Fortunately, I recovered my health, finished high school, got a part-time job and a car, and started college. Way too soon for my liking, a short while after they divorced, Mom met a happy-go-lucky guy who moved in with us. I didn't like the disparaging way he talked to her. Healthwise, he didn't take care of himself. As much as I was happy that my parents had split up "for the kids' sake," along with their marriage, went my hope for a close-knit family and the foundation of my existence. With little to anchor me, I started smoking and drinking.

While driving home one night, in my mind's eye, I saw an unfamiliar building. With no idea what or where this building was, I didn't give the vision much thought. Stepping into the house, I had the eerie feeling that something was wrong, but everything and everyone appeared normal. Minutes later, my stepfather had a massive coronary heart attack. Mom and I tried to resuscitate him while we waited for an ambulance.

Rushing my mom out of the bedroom to protect her, I watched the paramedics performing defibrillation on him. I was horrified. Still unconscious, he was rushed to the hospital. Mom and I followed in my car. Pulling up to the hospital, I realized that it was the unfamiliar building I'd envisioned.

Once inside, we were told by doctors that he had died at the house, and there was nothing they could do. When I walked into his room, I was shocked to see tubes coming out of him everywhere. Something inside of me snapped and shattered my heart and soul into a zillion pieces. A feeling of absolute hopelessness and helplessness washed over me.

Though I'd tried so hard to save this man, there was nothing I could do. Though I'd done everything in my power to save my parents' marriage, I couldn't. Though I desperately tried to be strong, feel safe and valued, effort after effort, my actions proved futile. My boyfriend of three years ended our relationship. My world just kept crumbling, time and time again. I would never be happy, never have the life I wanted. I was tired of trying.

Out of good-girl options, unable to focus, I quit school, and turned to partying to fill the dark emptiness that haunted me twenty-four-seven.

I smoked and drank excessively. When that didn't sufficiently numb my pain, I cut myself. With suicide on my mind constantly, I entered the psych ward at our local hospital for an extended stay. I didn't learn much; I was too focused on helping everyone else. There forward, I chose men based on my feelings of deservedness— ones who treated me like dirt. The more a man yelled, hit and took advantage of me, the more needed and wanted I felt. When it felt like killing myself slowly was taking too long, I toyed with taking matters into my own hands. One by one, I took pills out of bottles and chased each down with booze.

Groggy, the lights far too bright, I half-opened my eyes. There was a doctor standing over me.

"If you'd been just a few minutes later young lady, you wouldn't be here. You're very lucky. Your boyfriend brought you in just in time."

"Why does my throat hurt?" I asked, glancing about for my boyfriend. He wasn't there. I silently thanked him for saving my life.

"We put a tube down your throat so we could get some charcoal in there to absorb the alcohol and pills you took," the doctor explained as he handed me a cup with chalky liquid. "Drink up. It'll help you feel better."

Horrified, ashamed and worried about what people might think, I wouldn't let anyone visit me during my hospital stay. I hadn't really wanted to take my life; I just wanted the emotional pain to stop.

Thanks to another fight with my boyfriend, and a few too many at a self-pity party for one, I had another stupid mistake to add to my list of traits that made me feel unworthy.

Worried about me, hoping it would help me to stop mistreating myself physically and emotionally, Mom took me to Europe for a holiday. I realized she was scared for me, but told myself that it was too little too late. Though I enjoyed a good portion of our trip, once home, having been half-stoned from prescribed meds, I couldn't remember a lot of what we'd done. It didn't help that I also drank. Regardless, something shifted in me.

After breaking up with my rotten boyfriend, I asked Mom to take me back to the hospital so I could admit myself back into the psych ward. While there, I focused on healing myself, became more patient and allowed myself to just be. When a few friends didn't support me, though it was tough, I severed ties. Some friends, old and new, were incredibly supportive. My best friend stood by me through everything. She gave me a journal and encouraged me to write. Inscribed inside the front cover was: "Use this to focus on the love in your life." I was nowhere near being able to *focus on the love*. Regardless, as dark as they were, it helped to get my feelings and thoughts out of my head and onto paper.

After a successful stint there, I was accepted to the hospital's outpatient psych program. I quickly made new friends with people who got how I was feeling. Through meditation, I accessed my spiritual side and connected with something greater than myself.

Mom's wonderful new boyfriend (who soon became my step-dad) gifted me *The Celestine Prophecy*. Written by James Redfield, the book centered on the narrator's spiritual awakening through a transitional period in his life. Reading it put what I was feeling and experiencing into words that I hadn't been able to express. Through the sense of connection I felt with the narrator, I no longer felt that I didn't fit anywhere. I was finally ready to let down the facades of my false self.

With the support of my psych group leader and friends, I slowly peeled back the layers of masks I'd been wearing since childhood. With the release of each veneer, I took more and more responsibility for my life. By taking responsibility, I regained control and a sense of hope.

Instead of blaming my parents, I tried to understand them. Neither had an easy childhood. In separate conversations, I told Mom, and then Dad, how much I appreciated and loved them, and that I knew they had done their best by my brother and me.

I learned to focus more on the positive things about myself and what I wanted. Though it was slow-going, I did succeed in manifesting a happier life. Thankfully, the times when I felt down or depressed, weren't as tough and the silence wasn't as loud.

I went back to work. Having fully acknowledged that I needed help, I built a hefty support circle. I also habitually practiced meditation and contemplation. Focusing inward and allowing the silence within, it was challenging for me to allow the pain to surface and meet it head-on, instead of shoving it down to become a ticking time bomb.

Feeling stronger, while still working full-time, I went back to school part-time to complete my Associate of Arts Degree in Psychology. A counselor I met helped me begin to align my feelings with thoughts and reduce the bang of past traumas through a relatively new psychotherapy called Eye Movement Desensitization and Reprocessing

(EMDR). Prescribed medication helped me deal with residual depression and anxiety.

As time went by, happier with myself and emotionally stronger, I more easily recognized relationships that were harmful and exited sooner. I excelled at work, quickly moved up the corporate ladder, and started dating a man I met through work. He spoiled me rotten. We traveled, dined out often and enjoyed each other's company. Unfortunately, as years passed, our relationship struggles dampened the joy and fun. From a different culture, his family and friends came first and occupied much of his free time.

Feeling that he wasn't there for me as much as I needed him to be, I often felt left out, abandoned and underappreciated. Of course, he'd try to make it up to me with presents or an extravagant dinner. That just made me feel that he was trying to buy my love.

Taking another position, I threw myself into my work. Shortly thereafter, I became exhausted and unwell. Figuring the culprits making me sick were my workload, eating out and our lavish lifestyle, I kept going. Though I paid closer attention to my diet and exercise, I didn't get better.

In 2006, a few years into our relationship, I was diagnosed with a rare form of ovarian cancer. My exciting life came to a screeching halt. Afraid of losing me, my boyfriend started to withdraw. Having lost my nana to breast cancer a few years prior, I equated my diagnosis with death. It didn't matter that I had an insanely high percentage of being cured, my heart couldn't hear that. I was petrified. My world crumbled again. *Why when things were going pretty good did something always have to happen?*

Chemotherapy caused most of my hair to fall out. To show her support, when I went to have my head shaved, my best friend sat in the next chair and had her head shaved too. Though it helped that we were both bald, much of my identity centered on my once long, blond hair. I couldn't look at my steroid-puffy face and baldheaded-self in the mirror and see the old me anymore, whoever that was.

Throughout my treatments, I fought to maintain my sense of dignity and independence. It was a battle I lost. After being on my own for six years, at age twenty-nine, at her insistence, my Mom moved in with me during my treatments. Having to let go of my pride and be vulnerable was truly tough for me. However, without Mom's loving care and patience, I can only imagine what might have happened to me. She drove me to appointments, cooked my meals, and encouraged me to eat even though nothing would stay down. I was grateful for all that she did, including how gracefully she handled my over-emotional chemo-induced-menopausal moodiness. She truly loved me for me.

My boyfriend did his best to make me feel loved and hopeful. Though I didn't believe him, it helped that he continued to call me Beautiful. Barely able to cope with my own feelings, I did little to help him process his. Several months after the completion of twenty horrific chemotherapy treatments, we broke up. I was devastated. I'd thought he was my soul mate.

Along with him went our plans for the future. Everything else I had planned, no longer felt right. Getting a puppy, Lucy, was my saving grace. When I couldn't even look at myself in the mirror, she showed me unconditional love. Cute with a personality to match, she harnessed everyone's attention, taking the focus off of me.

By the end of the chemo treatments, fibromyalgia had settled into every joint in my body and I walked like an old arthritic woman. Also suffering from chemo-induced memory loss, I had to retrain my brain. I couldn't remember simple words such as pen, chair, and table, which made me feel stupid. Each time this happened, I thought, "My vocabulary was once fairly extensive, what happened?" Afraid that the overwhelming workload and stress of my job had caused or contributed to my cancer, I dreaded returning to work.

I realized that the Universe had knocked me off my feet to get my attention. For me, cancer's message was, "Okay, Jen. It's time to wake up, sweetheart. You recognize that you're not doing what you're meant to do." The trouble was that I had no idea what I was meant to do.

After a year-and-a-half of convalescing, feeling beholden to them for paying my way while I got well, I returned to my old job. Forcing myself to stay focused on my desire for a better life, I quickly fell back into my "old normal" work and life routines.

Initially, I didn't grasp that having survived cancer I was a different person. I kept working hard, but developed an overwhelming desire to give back to the world for allowing me to live. I volunteered to support young adult cancer survivors thinking it would help me heal as well. I felt accepted and appreciated, however, the loss of many people that I was trying to support, took its toll on my health and frame of mind.

In 2009, I went on a river kayaking adventure with other young adult cancer survivors to make a documentary called *Wrong Way to Hope*. I'd never kayaked through rapids before. I quickly realized that there were many parallels between being thrown in a river with no experience and being diagnosed with cancer. Over the course of a week, we did some heavy digging into survivor themes, including transition, isolation and identity.

As part of the documentary experience, I went on a twenty-four-hour solo expedition. For a long while, I sat on the shore of the Owyhee River watching the wind blow through the sage trees and ripple the clear water. The air smelled fresh and sweet. I closed my eyes and felt the tears well up as a peace I had never experienced before washed over me. An eternal knowingness in the form of a gentle breeze swept through me and I heard a whisper at the core of my being say, "I'm here."

My eyes shot open as I searched for the owner of the voice. "Are you God?" I quietly asked. I already knew the answer. I had been searching for this moment my entire life. This sense of being one with all and an unusual familiarity filled me. Whether it was God or what I considered to be a higher power, or Source…the unmistakable Divine Presence or Being was within me and everywhere around me. I wasn't alone. I never had been. I went home from that trip with a new awareness of my purpose to help others. Unfortunately, I quickly got swept back up in the whirlwind of "achieving Jen" and got lost.

I tried my hardest to be the person I had been before: perfect at most things, dedicated, hardworking, a multitasker and an overachiever. I strove for new, more challenging positions, but wasn't getting interviewed. My health still wasn't the best, I took sick leave too often, and my employer didn't consider me "reliable" enough to be entrusted with a new position. After years of persistence, I was finally offered an incredible opportunity helping to lead a high-profile project. It was the chance to shine and get the recognition and appreciation that I had been waiting for. At long last, I had proven myself worthy of something great that would be my own. Someone believed in me.

Having taken Joseph's advice in 2012, I had begun using my full name Jennifer Marie. It was hard to get accustomed to it, but the more I used it, the more confident I felt. Without a doubt, the new name vibration gifted me with a degree of personal power that eventually led to my being offered the position.

It soon became clear that the project was more than I could handle. The expectations were too great, the hours too long, and the workload too heavy. The new me couldn't manage all that anymore; nor did the new me want to manage all that anymore. I asked for assistance from my superiors. It was to no avail. They basically told me that I had to do whatever the project demanded of me. I felt responsible and couldn't walk away from the job.

Words that Joseph had said to me at the numerology course kept repeating in my head, "It's time to stop playing small. People are waiting to hear what you have to say. Do you want to keep them waiting?"

I didn't *want* to keep people waiting, I wanted to build my career *and* touch lots of people through writing, teaching and speaking. The only problem was I didn't have the time, energy or any clue of what path to take.

I heard the Universe again yelling at me, "Okay, Jennifer Marie. We aren't joking anymore! You're not listening hard enough. Do what you are meant to do!" I ran to Joseph for spiritual advice, but I still wasn't hearing what he had to say.

Every day my chest felt so tight from anxiety that I thought I was having mini heart attacks. My body was in constant physical pain from sitting at a desk, sometimes for over twelve hours. I was hypervigilant and jumped at every unexpected sound or movement. Evenings and weekends, I tried to catch up by working from home. I couldn't concentrate when awake and couldn't sleep when I went to bed. Tired and overwhelmed, I didn't have the energy or desire to eat healthy food. Burned out and afraid I was headed for another major health collapse, I had no choice but to go on sick leave.

I felt like a complete failure. I'd let myself and the team down. Unworthiness and shame drifted back into my life like a heavy fog. I didn't deserve *any* of the wonderful things life had to offer—love, abundance or happiness. It took a conversation with my mom for me to fully appreciate an inner-knowing I'd recently identified.

"Honey, what do you mean you don't feel worthy? I don't understand."

"Mom, I am not saying that I am less worthy than anyone else. The problem is that I don't feel worthy. There's something amiss inside of me and I cannot love myself completely and unconditionally."

"I still don't understand," Mom said, sounding loving and genuinely concerned.

"What I'm saying is that I've been fighting for love, acceptance and acknowledgement outside of myself. What I didn't realize until recently is that I first need to foster, experience and celebrate those qualities within myself."

After we hung up, it struck me that it hadn't been enough to *use* my full name, I needed to *live* my full name. To do this, I had to finish clearing past hurts and more deeply connect with my spiritual-self so that I could identify and live my divine purpose.

Trusting the Universe, I began listening to my intuition and paying attention to the lessons behind the people I met and the opportunities being presented. I heard them as possible ways to free myself from past cycles. When introduced to people who could make my dream of becoming a published author a reality, I heard them and acted.

I read books by and listened to famous gurus such as Napoleon Hill, Bob Proctor, Mike Dooley, Lola Jones, Beautiful Chorus and Wayne Dyer. Recognizing that they were powerful manifestors, I paid closer attention to my thoughts and spoken words. What I believed and expressed, would be what I received.

Still recovering from the major fatigue associated with burnout, coupled with dealing with ongoing anxiety, depression and unexplainable physical pain, created an upward battle and conflict with the new perspectives I was learning and incorporating into my life. For the first time, I felt that I was worth the effort it took to transition through this uncomfortableness. For once, I welcomed changes in my life. I wanted to change.

In early 2015, I began Joseph's intensive six-month course Find Your Authentic Peace with the Past. My boyfriend Stefan, who was studying to be a numerologist and healer, encouraged me to take the course. I had progressed enough on my own to allow a wonderful loving man into my life, but wanted and needed to do more healing.

Initially, I was scared but chose to work through my fears. Allowing myself to be vulnerable so that I could fully face past disillusionments and walk through the fire of my doubt, broke me down to my core. It also empowered me and helped me build a foundation for the ever-evolving, newer version of Jennifer Marie.

One layer at a time and on a much deeper level, I began to fully realize what it meant to truly love myself, to truly step into my own power. By examining and redefining what success meant to me, I came to appreciate that recognition and money did not equate with self-respect and true worthiness.

A critical awareness that came to me during the course was the importance of moving away from extremes and toward balance. Going on extended sick leave wasn't a failure indicator, it was a hallmark awakening. An acted upon realization worthy of celebration, not shame and disappointment. I had honored the Universe's nudge away from illness and toward healthfulness.

Near the completion of Joseph's course, I created a list of affirmations. I would honor my personal power by adhering to whispers of my heart, not the screams of my false ego. I would trust in the process of letting go in order to make room for the new. I would have faith that the path to my purpose was unfolding within the same mysteries that shrouded my ability to identify it by more than a feeling.

I graduated from the course recognizing that like the old adage about hard work—nothing worth having is ever easy. My transformation would be a continuing process. I was more than okay with that and content with the strides I had made. Having a new regard for myself, my hopes and aspirations, I'd traded in fear for freedom. I'd accepted that I was a good person, a caring person, a wise person.

Fully aware that perfection is more a hindrance than a prerequisite to helping others, purpose-wise, I will get to wherever I am meant to be, accomplish whatever I am meant to do, one easy and graceful forward step at a time.

"And the day came when the risk to remain tight in the bud was more painful than the risk it took to blossom."

— Anaïs Nin

About Jennifer Marie Luce

Jennifer Marie lives in Vancouver, British Columbia. She is a writer, a poet, an intuitive, an energy healer, and a Tera Mai Seichem Reiki Master. Her love of travel has taken her to seventeen countries and more than a hundred cities. She enjoys helping others identify their paths and turn their lives around. She can be contacted by e-mail at info@heartmindeffect.com.

Jennifer Marie is available to speak to audiences about a number of healing modalities and life challenges. For more information, visit her Facebook page https://www.facebook.com/turnlifearound/ and her blog www.turnurlifearound.wordpress.com.

MORE LONELY CHOICES
Roswyn Nelson

"No, Mrs. Nelson, we can't discharge you until we bring the baby back from the nursery to compare the wrist bands for identification."

My heart broke, again. I had already said good-bye. I had held him, cuddled him, fed him, and given him to the nurse to take back to the nursery. I had dressed, packed my belongings, and made my way down the long, lonely corridor to the discharge desk. Once there, a stern-faced, unsmiling woman told me that I'd have to go through the awful, heartrending process of saying good-bye one more time.

"Why?" I sobbed.

"It's the rule," said the woman in charge. One I was sure was designed to punish me for making the decision to give my precious baby boy up for adoption.

Why and how you may ask, does a person find herself in a situation where she seemingly has no choice but to put her baby up for adoption? Well, let me tell you about it.

It was 1962, and I was in my mid-twenties. I'd had four babies, contagious hepatitis, and a major car accident that had caused severe injuries…all in the course of five short years.

I was mentally and physically distraught. Filled with anger, frustration and disappointment, I was sure my kids and young husband would be better off without me. On the verge of a total breakdown and exhausted, I made arrangements for someone to take care of my children while I recovered. Leaving the small town of Cranbrook, British Columbia, where we lived, I flew to Vancouver.

I needed time to heal, but had no idea of how heartbreaking, gut-wrenching lonely it was going to be, without my family, my babies.

It was a beautiful sun-drenched September day when the plane landed at the airport. Feeling lost, scared and alone, I walked through the busy terminal asking myself, "What will I do? Where will I go?"

Stepping into the perfect, crystal-clear autumn day, my first priority was finding somewhere to live. Luckily, I found a place the same day, and by the next day, I had a job.

A few months later, the kids and their dad moved to Alberta. Our marriage separation was permanent. However, the hope of having my children with me again was never out of my mind.

Two years later, the two youngest came to live with me. Our two-room basement suite was very crowded. Although I realized that raising all four kids by myself would be challenging, I prayed that my two older children would soon join us.

My wonderful landlady, Gloria, became my friend, confidante, and cheerleader. She watched the kids when I needed her to, and I needed her often as I worked afternoons waitressing. It was a good thing that I loved being a waitress because I raised my kids on the tips.

In the sixties, it was a man's world. Women were mostly stay-at-home moms, and single parenting was uncommon. Divorcees were a rarity. A lot of men thought divorced women were easy conquests, and for sure they didn't want one of those "scarlet women" to be friends with their wives. Being a waitress was seen as even more of an open invitation. All that said, I loved the freedom and adventure of working in upscale dining rooms or being a cocktail waitress in some of the better clubs.

One of my favorite places to work was the Lulu Belle on Broadway. When he was in town, Rolf Harris would come in after his gig at The Cave Theatre Restaurant and entertain our patrons with his show from the previous evening. Rolf Harris was a popular singer in the sixties. One of his biggest hits was "My Boomerang Won't Come Back."

Ken Stauffer, the owner of both the Lulu Belle and The Cave, would often invite his staff as his guests to a show at The Cave. One show that my kids remember well starred the illusionist-hypnotist Ravine, who wowed his audiences with daunting and amusing feats of the unexpected. It was entertaining to witness a dozen people asleep and standing on one foot. The starched white linen, wine glasses and silverware on the tables in the dining room impressed my kids, but also scared them to death. All the pop they could drink, made Ken their hero.

Being busy with the kids and work, didn't leave much time for me. One winter day, while walking down the street, I spotted a fellow I'd met the previous fall. He'd mentioned back then that he was going to Mexico soon, so my first question when I walked up to him was, "Have you been to Mexico yet?" "No," he said. "I'm going next Friday. Wanna come with me?" Thus began one of the most exciting adventures of my life, hitchhiking all the way to Acapulco and back. As I wrote in one of my poems, "Never before have I ever seen, the beauty and splendor where I have been. Never again will I ever go, to a country more beautiful than Mexico."

A vacation was just what I needed and the opportunity could not have come at a better time financially. I'd recently received an inheritance from an uncle, and I had a full two weeks' wages coming from an inventory company where I was working temporarily.

One daughter and son still with their dad in Alberta, I made arrangements for Gloria to look after my two youngest boys. My boss gave me the time off and promised to wire my due wages if I needed the money. It was early March and we were off—Wayne, his ukulele and me.

Rides were easy to come by, and we soon made our way to San Francisco. We decided to go for something to eat and a glass of wine at a local nightclub with live music. At the door, the bouncer asked me for ID. Thinking he was joking, after all, I was twenty-seven, I laughed and went to go past him, only to have him grab my arm and demand my identification. Still thinking it was the funniest thing I'd ever been asked, I reached for my wallet. It wasn't there. OMG! I must have left it in the washroom at the last place we'd stopped along the way. Needless to say, the bouncer was the least of our worries.

The next morning, we decided to continue on our way. Wayne had money with him, and I could have money wired to me later. Though aware that losing my wallet created huge future problems, such as not having ID to get into Mexico, we hatched a plan and headed for Mexicali on the Baja Peninsula.

The plan was that we'd walk around town until we found someone who was around my age, height and weight. We'd convince her to loan me her driver's license. Though licenses to drive didn't have photos in those days, there had to be a close resemblance because they did have a detailed description of the driver.

Luckily, we met a young woman named Isabell from Cotton, California and she agreed to help us. Wayne and Isabell waited in a local cantina, while I marched off to the customs office. Just as I was leaving, the illicit driver's license in hand, I turned to Isabell and asked the question that saved my bacon. "Where is Cotton?"

"It's about twenty-six miles up the road," she said.

The customs agent, a typical Mexican law enforcement officer by my criteria, was comfortably rotund, with a huge black Pancho Villa mustache. He wore a big sombrero tilted back on his head. His feet encased in riding boots were lazily planted on his desk and a well-chewed cigar hung from the corner of his mouth. Squinting at me through smoke-blinded eyes, he asked, "What can I do for you?"

"I need a visa," I said, handing him my phony ID.

His feet came off the desk, he reached into a drawer, found the form he was looking for, stamped it March 9, 1965, and handed it to me. As I was taking it from him, his hand tightened on the paper and he asked, "Where is this town, Cotton?"

"Oh," I answered nonchalantly. "It's about twenty-six miles north of here."

"Sí, señorita." He smiled, his big white teeth gleaming, and released the form.

Relieved that our plan had worked, filled with anticipation and excitement, we were soon back on the road. We hitched a ride with a young Mexican couple, Pepe and Malae. Pepe was a border patrol officer in Mexicali and they were on their way to Durango for a vacation.

For some unknown reason, they invited us to accompany them for a few days. Since we had no schedule to keep we agreed.

The trip down the coast to Mazatlán and inland to Guadalajara was spectacular. We drove through tiny villages high in the Sierra Madre, with mile high cliffs, purple haze in the distance and golden light reflecting off mountain tops. We passed herds of cattle roaming on grassy plains.

As we were descending into the valley, our first sight of Victoria de Durango, the capital city of the state of Durango, was like something out of the movies. Twilight was stealing over the countryside as the sun set in the mountains behind us.

As we drove through the city, the fountains alive with dancing water, flower lined streets, the ancient architecture mixed with the new, the Cathedrals with spires reaching the sky held us totally enthralled. Then, like a mirage in the distance, the ranch came into view. Pepe's father was second in command at a government-sponsored cattle ranch where we stayed. His house was ornate and opulent. It had exquisite furnishings, massive rooms, big four-poster beds, and lots of servants to take care of everyone. The John Wayne movie *Rio Grande* was filmed there.

One memorable evening, Malae invited me to a wedding shower for one of her friends. They were all speaking Spanish and one of the women asked me, "Habla Español?" (Do you speak Spanish?). My quick response was "Muy bonito" (Very pretty). A gust of laughter filled the room and you can imagine my embarrassment when they explained to me that I should have said "Muy poquito" (Very little).

A few days later, we left the ranch and continued on our way to Acapulco. We found a room in a quaint little cottage by the ocean for five pesos a day. The sights, sounds and aromas were something to behold. Hibiscus plants, palm trees, white sand and the blue Pacific Ocean took our breath away. The water system consisted of a barrel on the roof of our cabin that caught rain water that was heated by the sun for showering and flushing.

Living among the locals was an unmatched experience. We partied on the beach, watched the cliff divers perform death-defying feats, walked barefoot in the sand, ate coconuts that Wayne shimmied up the coconut palms to get, bought watermelon juice from street vendors, and rode the third-class buses downtown to the markets.

Market sellers, street vendors and crafters used the buses to transport their wares. The cacophony was deafening, and the smell wasn't much better as people transported chickens in cages, long-snouted barracudas under their arms, and iguanas on strings.

And then there was Roberto. Wayne and his good buddy, Gary, had been to Acapulco once before and had made friends with a shoeshine boy named Roberto. We went looking for him and found him at his shoeshine stand. Though he looked like a poor little ragamuffin about twelve years old, he was actually about thirty years old, married, and had a couple of kids. He was so excited to see Wayne that he invited us to his jaw-droppingly gorgeous home for dinner.

Later in the evening, we wandered into the downtown tourist area to listen to the Mariachi bands and enjoy the sights and sounds of the night life. We feasted our eyes on the lights and the expensive gowns, jewelry and fashions of the elite, all under the star studded skies. Wayne's money had run out by then. With the help of someone at a bank, we had found a way for my boss to wire money to me. Then we waited, and waited, and waited. Late on a Friday afternoon, we convinced the bank to call my boss to ask when the money would arrive only to learn that he'd forgotten to wire it.

With no money and none coming soon, we decided there was only one thing to do—hit the road for home and hope we didn't starve along the way. The sentiment expressed by the song lyrics, "Busted flat in Baton Rouge waiting for a train," was nothing compared to us being busted flat in Acapulco praying for a ride to Mexico City.

We were standing on the highway waiting for a ride when a big black Caddy pulled up and stopped. The driver was well-dressed, dapper and spoke only Spanish. There was a picture of JFK on his dash that struck me as interesting. However, as I didn't speak Spanish, I couldn't ask him about it. Wayne knew a smattering of Spanish so he could at least hold his own.

The driver noticed the ukulele and asked if we'd sing something. Wayne, with a cigarette in his mouth, played, and the two of us sang "Michael Row the Boat Ashore." As we finished, the man, who up until that point had only spoken Spanish, said in perfect unaccented English, "You should never smoke when you sing a beautiful song like that." We were very happy we hadn't said anything we shouldn't have in English. He then told us that he worked for the government, had been a friend of JFK's, and that he was working on details pertaining to the assassination.

Mexico City was the next big adventure. Our Caddy driver dropped us on the outskirts of the city as night was falling. We were walking up the street with no idea where we were or where to go, when a taxi pulled up beside us and the driver asked if we wanted to take his cab somewhere.

We explained that we were Canadian and had no money, and a most amazing thing happened. The cabdriver offered to take us to where his personal car was parked and said we could sleep in his vehicle for the night. He'd come back in the morning and take us to the other end of the city so we could continue our journey home. As he was learning to speak English, we could repay him by teaching him more words. Safe, protected and cared for, we slept like babies that night. He came back in the morning and drove to a store, and when he came out he had cold chicken, buns and all the fixings for a picnic. Then he drove us around, showing us Mexico City. Like no tourist would ever see it, we witnessed the city through the eyes of a person who truly loved his home. At one place, he told us that we were looking at the highest building in the world.

"That's not possible," I said. "That building is only three stories tall."

"You're right," he said, laughing. "But it's built on the highest point in the world."

The crowning glory came when he took us to the zoo. It was amazing. I saw my first and only live black panther. We had a great picnic, and then as it was getting late in the day, he drove us to the other side of the city to a bus stop.

As we were getting out of his car, he brought me to tears when he slipped a twenty peso note into Wayne's hand. That twenty pesos bought us an all-night ride on the next bus, with money left over for food. I don't remember the man's name after all these years, but I'll never forget what he did for us that long ago time.

The bus dropped us off in a dusty little village where people grew sugar cane. There was absolutely no traffic. We sat on a curb for hours waiting for a car or any other vehicle to come along.

As the day dragged on, children leaving a nearby school came to stare at us. We assumed that they'd never before seen the likes of us. The children, with their huge brown eyes, bare feet and shy smiles, eventually got brave enough to give us some sugar cane stalks to suck on.

Late in the afternoon, an old truck rattled to a stop beside us and the driver invited us to crawl up into the open back where two chairs had been placed. He said he'd take us to the next town on a main highway where we could hitch a ride. He drove for several miles and then dropped us on the side of a busy highway. Waving and smiling, he did a U-turn and headed back in the direction from where we'd come. We flagged down a bus that let us off on the outskirts of a fairly large town.

Wayne and I were standing with our thumbs out, when a car that had gone by us a few times stopped. The couple in the car ordered us to get in. They advised us that the woman in the car was the mayor of the town and she didn't like hitchhikers messing up the landscape. Thankfully, when we told them we were Canadians, their whole demeanor changed and they invited us to lunch at the mayor's home. Lunch was delicious, and we had an interesting conversation about the extensive art collection that graced the walls of their home.

After lunch, we were delivered to a bus stop with instructions given in Spanish to the bus driver that we were to be taken far away and out of her jurisdiction. Hours later, when the bus reached its final destination, we were let out at the edge of another small village. The sun was going down and it was almost dark.

A dilapidated old truck, loaded to the gunnels with watermelons, came rumbling down the lane and stopped across the street from us. We were apprehensive when three men jumped down and, shoulder to shoulder, walked towards us. Black leather jackets, collars rolled up James Dean style, they stopped in front of us and the leader growled menacingly, "What are you doing here?"

Our hearts were in our mouths. Wayne said in Spanish, "We're Canadian, we have no money, and we're going home to Canada."

Instantly, the welcome mat rolled out. They asked if we were hungry and invited us to go with them to the leader's grandmother's house to eat and to sleep. When I reached up to hold onto the seat to hoist myself into the cab of the truck, I put my hand smack onto a gun. It had disappeared by the time my head came up even with the seat.

They said they'd come back in the morning after they delivered the watermelons to Mexico City and take us to the next town. We waited awhile the next morning, but they didn't come back. So we left. By the end of the day, we were crossing the border at Tijuana.

Knowing that my lack of identification could present a huge problem at the United States border, I was nervous. The border guards asked for my ID at the same time as another one asked me if I had my shots. I said, "I don't get shots because I'm a Seventh Day Adventist." I'd meant to say a Jehovah's Witness, who I believed didn't get shots. The border guard laughed so much as he led me down the hall to get vaccinated, he forgot to ask again for my ID.

Finally, we were back on American soil and the last leg of our journey. A day later, we reached the Blaine border crossing from Washington State into British Columbia. I didn't think that I'd need identification to return to my home country. I soon discovered that there was no way I was getting into Canada without it.

After what seemed an eternity, one of the border guards said, "I can solve this." He turned to me and asked, "Who's the Minister of Highways?" I quickly replied, "Flying Phil!" the nickname earned by Phil Gaglardi, the B.C. Minister of Highways, because of his many speeding tickets. And, that was how I got home with no ID.

My time away having stretched longer than two weeks; understandably, Gloria was furious with me. My kids were far more forgiving and delighted to have me home.

Wayne and I having shared many adventures in Mexico, I was in love with him. It was a dilemma because he was seven years younger than I was. He had his whole life ahead of him and it didn't include a single mom with four kids.

Life went on and everything back to normal, until June when I was "late." July and most of August crawled by. I was petrified that being pregnant would mean that I wouldn't get my oldest two kids back from their dad and that I might even lose the two younger ones.

In late August, I received a phone call from the kids' dad. He asked me if I'd look after the two older kids for a couple of weeks while he and his girlfriend went on a holiday. I said that if I was going to take them for a couple of weeks, I wanted to take them permanently.

He said, "That's the general idea."

The older two kids came home and we were a family again.

I still didn't know what I was going to do about being pregnant. I was terrified, heartsick and alone. Abortion was not in the realm of possibilities for me. We were barely scraping by financially, and I worried about whether it would be unfair to my four kids if I added another child to our family.

Summer rolled into fall, and fall into winter. By then, everyone knew that I was pregnant. Life really hadn't changed much, except that I could no longer work and had to go on welfare. The social worker I had was caring and understanding.

I made the painful decision, another lonely choice, that when the time came, I'd place the baby for adoption. It wouldn't be fair to the new little life, nor to the other four kids to keep the baby. We were already living below the poverty line; stretching the meager dollars further would be impossible. Imagining how sad and left out the new child would feel when the other four went to family events with their father made my heart ache. The baby deserved the best chance to have a good life. If that meant letting him or her go, it had to be.

Everyone stood by me. Wayne was supportive as were some of his friends. Gary, Wayne's best friend, was always on hand to help.

I gave birth to a baby boy at 3:47 a.m. Sunday, February 27th, 1966 at Vancouver General Hospital. Usually, the birth mother isn't allowed to see the baby she's given up for adoption. However, in my case, the social worker was able to waive the rules and I was allowed to see my baby boy. I held him, I fed him, I loved him, and I named him. He was Gary Vernon Nelson. Gary, after Wayne's best friend and Vernon, Wayne's middle name. Too soon, it was discharge day and I had to say good-bye. I went home with a hole in my heart.

The years passed, my four children grew up, graduated from high school, made plans for their lives, and one by one, got married and created homes of their own. They all became successful in business and made me very proud. They gave me beautiful grandchildren, but there was never a birthday that came and went that I didn't think of my lost son.

I registered with Child Finders to no avail. I left instructions with the Department of Vital Statistics that my information was to be shared if requested. In 1992 the closed adoption information laws changed to open registry adoption. If they wished to be reunited, adoptees and their biological parents could register their contact information.

One day in September 1992, the phone rang. A voice said, "This is the Department of Open Registry Adoptions. Is this Mrs. Nelson?" The very next day I received a registered letter with all the information I needed to contact my son.

I sat there holding the envelope, shaking, my palms wet, afraid to open it, yet afraid not to. Finally, I tore it open to find out who my son had become. His adoptive parents had named him Jason and they all lived in Kamloops. All the information I needed to contact him was in my hand including a telephone number.

I so wanted to pick up the phone, but I didn't know what to say. I wanted to know everything about him. Was he married? What did he do for a living? Was he a professor? A doctor? A truck driver? Could he be a druggie? In jail?

When I could wait no longer, I picked up the phone and dialed the number. Several rings later, a woman answered. "Mrs. Maxfield?" I enquired.

"Yes," she answered.

Hesitantly, I asked, "Are you Jason's wife or his mother?"

"His mother," she replied.

"Are you aware that Jason has been searching for his birth mother?" I asked tentatively.

"Oh, yes," she answered. "His father and I have been helping him. Why?"

"I'm his birth mother."

After a brief pause, both of us burst into tears, cried together for a few minutes, and then both started talking at once. For the next hour-and-a-half, we shared stories, details, laughter and memories.

Jason was working in Calgary. When I asked which one of us should call him, she chose to tell him that I'd been in touch. Before we hung up, she promised to send me some pictures.

At six o'clock that evening, the phone rang and I spoke to my son for the first time. My number one question for him was, "Did you ever wonder why I gave you up?"

After explaining that he'd been looking for me since he'd turned eighteen and had found out that there were four older children, he said, "It didn't take a rocket scientist to figure out the answer to that question."

We talked and talked and talked. When he asked about his birth father, I told him about Wayne and where he lived.

A few days later, the package containing the promised pictures arrived. Jason was the spitting image of his father at the same age.

It was Boxing Day, December 26th, while he was home in Kamloops for Christmas that we were finally able to establish a time and place to meet in person.

On the route between Hope and Merritt that I'd have to take from Vancouver, it was snowing heavily with icy conditions and poor visibility. The weather report advised everyone to stay off the highway unless absolutely necessary. I'd waited so long to meet my son that nothing was going to stop me from at least trying to get there.

It was a two-hundred-mile white-knuckled trip, but I made it. My heart pounding with excitement, I made my way around their house, up the back stairs and across the deck. The patio door slid open and there he was.

For a few seconds, we stood there, just looking at each other, and then we hugged and hugged some more. It was heartwarming and emotionally overwhelming to meet and spend time with Jason.

As he had a business trip to Vancouver planned for February, we arranged a time and place for him to meet his siblings. For the first meeting it would just be the six of us, Brian, Rhonda, David, Ken, Jason and me.

We met at the Keg restaurant in nearby Langley. The first words out of my eldest son Brian's mouth when he met his half-brother were, "You sure do look like Wayne." It was a great evening with lots of talk and laughter.

A couple of days later, he met everyone in our family. What an event that was. Jason had been raised in a small family with one brother and a sister. All of a sudden, he had three new brothers and a sister, their spouses, and a bunch of nephews and a couple of nieces. It must have been totally overwhelming for him.

A few days later, Wayne, who lived up the coast at Lund, made the trip down to meet Jason. We all met at the Lougheed Hotel along with Wayne's daughter from another relationship and her boyfriend, and Wayne's best friend Gary.

On his arrival at the reunion, Gary's first response was, "If there was ever any doubt as to who Jason's father was, there's no question now. They're identical." There had never been any question in my mind, but if Wayne had ever had any doubts, he sure didn't any more.

On one of Jason's visits, Ravine was in town so we went to The Cave to see him. We also went to the Lynn Valley Suspension Bridge, and did some of the things I'd done with the other kids when they were little. It was fun to create our own memories.

Eventually Jason got married to Tannis. His parents invited both Wayne and me to the wedding in Calgary where we sat in the front row with them. His adoptive mother got a chuckle out of people craning their necks to see who was sitting with them.

Wayne, still as handsome as ever with his mass of curly black hair now turned silver, looked down at me as we followed Jason's adoptive parents down the aisle after the ceremony, and made me laugh when he whispered, "Who ever said we'd never walk down the aisle together."

As the years passed, Jason followed in Wayne's footsteps and became a welder and took up scuba diving. He also went on a vacation in Mexico. When Jason and Tannis had children, they made Wayne a grandparent too. Jason made several trips to Lund, B.C. where Wayne and his partner, Linda, owned an oyster farm. They spent many summer holidays together, as Wayne shared his love of the ocean and sailing with Jason. Sadly, Wayne passed over last year.

Jason's adoptive parents are still alive and live in Kamloops. Now a single dad, his two wonderful daughters, Kymber and Ayla, mostly live with him. Their addition to the family, brought the total of my grandchildren to thirteen. Currently, I also have fourteen great-grandchildren. Memories of our Mexican adventure still puts a smile on my face. Knowing that if not for my fun-filled escape with Wayne, I wouldn't have Jason in my life now, eases the pain of my lonely choices of yesteryear. Life is good and I am truly blessed.

> *"Our greatest glory is not in never falling,*
> *but in rising every time we fall."*
>
> —Confucius

About Roswyn Nelson

Roswyn is semiretired and lives in White Rock, British Columbia. A people-lover and believer in natural products, she is actively involved in network marketing. Roswyn's favorite pastime is spending time with her children and their spouses, her thirteen grandchildren and fourteen great-grandchildren. She can be contacted by e-mail at info@ heartmindeffect.com.

Roswyn's chapter in *Heartmind Wisdom Collection #1* is "Lonely Choices." The Heartmind Wisdom Collection is available at www.heartmindstore. com and through online bookstores.

NO PAIN, NO GAIN

Joseph Aquilino

On a dark gloomy day on October 21st, 2008, as usual, I arrived at work at six a.m. Two hours later, I was on the floor screaming.

Having worked in retail for all of my adult life, I enjoyed my colleagues and interacting with clients. The day began like every other: clear the sidecaps shelves of merchandise no longer being featured, sweep and mop the floor, check and restock the main shelves. Around eight a.m., I was clearing the shelves of misplaced merchandise when a huge can of tomato sauce fell and landed on the toes of my left foot. The pain unexpected and intense, my knees buckled as I screamed and hit the floor with a thump. Certain my toes were broken and afraid to move, I hollered for help.

Within seconds, two colleagues came to my rescue and helped me get to my feet. Once upright, my toes throbbing and stiff, I limped toward the front counter, intending to tell my boss what had happened. As I approached him, the concern on my boss's face was obvious. The pain caused by walking unbearable, I doubled over and grabbed for a shelf to steady myself and to take some of the weight off my left foot. Seconds later, a colleague pushing a cart loaded with electronic equipment, came around the corner and ran over my ankle and injured foot. Once again, I hit the floor screaming in pain.

My boss rushed to my side. It took a few minutes for me to get my bearings. Combined, the cart and merchandise had to weigh at least 200 pounds. Taking deep breaths, I lifted my pant leg and stared at my throbbing ankle and foot. They didn't appear mangled; hopefully, nothing was broken.

After assisting me to my feet, my boss asked if I wanted to finish my shift or go home. Not one to give up easily and determined to fight through the pain, I chose to stay at work. For the next eight hours, I hobbled about the store, sweating profusely and wincing in pain. By the end of my shift, I was in tears.

Once in my car, worn out, frustrated and anxious, I cried and cursed until my throat and head ached. When able to collect myself emotionally, I removed my left shoe, relieved to see that there wasn't any blood. Alarmingly, my foot started to swell as though it was a balloon being pumped full of air. I took off my sock. The skin was bright red. I rubbed my ankle and the top of my foot; they felt cold. *How could my foot and ankle feel cold on the outside when on the inside they burned like they were on fire?*

Eyes flooded with tears, I headed for home, driving well below the speed limit. Over and over, I questioned my judgment, repeatedly asking myself, "Was it the right thing to stay at work and finish my shift? Was it my own stubborn self's fault that the severe pain wouldn't let up? Why did I have to be such a hero?"

Halfway through what should have been a forty-five-minute drive, the world looped around me as the pain took complete control of my senses. I pulled over and bellowed before bursting into a chest-heaving crying jag. It was another forty-five minutes before I pulled into our driveway.

"What happened?" my father wanted to know as he watched me hop up one stair at a time on my right foot and then drag up my left. After explaining the double-whammy of accidents, Dad assured me that my foot would feel better in the morning. Hoping he was right, after what seemed an eternity, I made it to the top of the stairs and into my room.

Sitting on my bed, I swung my right leg up and then used both hands to pull up my left leg. My foot had doubled in size and was now brown with red spots. *What the heck?* When I touched my foot, it felt even colder and my skin stung. I tried to rotate my ankle but couldn't. Scared that it might be broken, but not wanting to worry my father, I flopped back on my bed and pulled a wool blanket over me. When the blanket touched my foot, a stabbing pain caused me to jerk my leg and scream. I would have to sleep with my freezing cold foot outside the covers.

My heart pounding, sweating and delirious, I rocked my shoulders from side-to-side, trying to distract myself from the pain as I prayed to God for relief, even if that meant making me pass out. Though the pain did not subside, the skin on my entire foot was suddenly aflame with pins and needles. Much like when a younger me placed my frozen hands under warm tap water, my foot felt numb and on fire at the same time; as though my foot was there and not there.

That night and for the next three days, I took over-the-counter pain meds and tried to get some rest. Stoic masters of denial, though it was obvious we were wrong, my father and I kept telling one another that my foot would get better. On the fourth day, Dad said, "Go to the doctor." Aware that I wouldn't be able to bear the pain or exist on almost no sleep for much longer, I did as he suggested.

I made an appointment with a podiatrist. After a brief visual and excruciatingly painful mobility examination, his diagnosis of "contusion with muscle involvement" reinforced my hope that my injuries would heal. His recommendation was that I take one week off of work, followed by limited and light work duties until my foot could bear weight.

A week later, some of the swelling was gone. However, whether sitting, lying or walking, the inside and outside of my foot still burned and throbbed. When I stood, shooting pain shot up my leg and my knees buckled. The skin on my foot ached; a finger touch felt like a fire-hot branding iron.

Putting weight on the pinky-toe side of my left foot was the least painful, so after convincing myself that I'd be able to handle it, I went back to work. Self-conscious of my pronounced limp and aware of the doubting glances of coworkers who obviously thought I was playing up the pain, my anxiety level was through the roof. Some people laughed when they watched me hobbling about. Wishing I were invisible, I tried to concentrate despite the emotional and physical pain. But no matter how hard I tried, I couldn't think straight, often forgetting what I was doing halfway through a task. I'd answer the phone, listen to what the caller had to say and be stumped as to how I should respond. While filing paperwork, I had difficulty remembering the alphabet, let alone the company's sorting system. While clearing merchandise from a shelf, I'd wince in pain and sweat. Even the simplest task took me what seemed like forever.

On the second day of my second week back at work, having witnessed the accident and aware of my stoic efforts and obvious limits, my boss helped me fill out an accident report for Workers' Compensation Board. When I asked to leave early, he sympathetically nodded his consent.

Before leaving work, I called my primary physician to make an appointment. When I told her the reason I wanted to see the doctor, the receptionist informed me that they didn't accept Workers' Compensation patients. Losing control of my temper, I threw my cell phone onto the desk and cursed under my breath. *How could my own physician refuse to help me when I needed him most?* Feeling miserable and defeated, I hobbled out of work with pain searing through my foot and my head hung low.

Through my research on the Internet, I found a clinic on Staten Island that accepted Workers' Compensation claims. It was only a few miles from home and near a physical therapy clinic. Thinking physical therapy would likely be key to my recovery, two days later when I felt strong enough to make it there and back, I went to the clinic. It was a rainy night and the place was packed with people. Thankfully, seeing how much pain I was in, an elderly gentleman claimed he'd prefer to stand and gave me his seat.

Though it was November and cold outside, everyone in the office was sweating. Feeling faint from the heat and the pain in my foot, at my request, the receptionist brought me glass after glass of water. The clinic floor was filthy and the waiting room was disgustingly unkempt. Allergic to the dust, my throat felt like it was closing up as I sneezed and sneezed. I wanted to run, to get out of the room, out of my body, but I could barely walk, which made me feel trapped and scared. Two hours later, after changing positions a zillion times and thousands of deep breaths, it was finally my turn to see the doctor.

Following his examination, Dr. Mani had me follow him to another room so he could x-ray my foot. Although I protested, to ensure a clear and accurate image, the doctor insisted that I keep weight on my left foot so that it was flat while he took the x-ray. Taking a deep breath and bracing myself mentally, I did as he requested. For the first time in my life, the room went black as I literally saw tiny little stars everywhere and bellowed. Seeming to emanate from the far end of a long tunnel, I heard someone call out, "You okay back there? It sounds like someone is being killed." Mercifully, the doctor announced that he was done and I could start making my way back to his office.

Seeming to have a heart of gold, Dr. Mani assured me that I wasn't imagining the pain. Though there were no broken bones, severe tendonitis, bone tissue inflammation and neuropathy were the reasons my foot was still swollen, painful and yet oddly numb. When I asked if my foot would ever function normally again, he said it was too soon to tell and that he would inform Workers' Compensation that I would be off work until there was a difference in my status. For me, it was a good-news-bad-news prognosis. I was relieved that he hadn't recommended I return to work and deathly afraid the pain in my foot would never go away.

Each time I visited Dr. Mani, after examining my foot, he would have me rate my pain level on a scale of one to ten, with ten being unbearable. Over the next three months, my pain level vacillated between eight and ten, matching what would have equaled my anxiety level if anyone had asked.

In January, having yet to pay me a dime, Workers' Compensation sent me to an independent medical examiner. Following his quick examination, Dr. Soren recommended that I return to work on limited duty. When I told this to Dr. Mani, he strongly advised me not to return to work. Knowing that he was right, I adhered to my primary physician's advice. Workers' Compensation responded by denying my claim.

It was a difficult time for me. I felt depressed, anxious, hopeless and useless. Bill collectors called daily and the pain in my foot would not let up. *How much more could my body take? How much more could my head take?* At times, it seemed as though I'd be better off dead.

Tired of being broke on top of being in constant pain, in March 2009, I hired a lawyer. A tall, stocky and brown-haired man in his fifties, my lawyer went to bat for me. He had my claim reinstated and successfully fought for my back pay and payment for my past and future medical treatments. Thankfully, he also dealt with my less-than-pleasant Workers' Compensation adjuster.

Though my financial crisis was over, I continued to suffer physically and emotionally. My ankle and foot remained swollen, and the burning seldom fell below a pain level of ten. The color of my skin turned brown and became dotted with white spots and red spots. Then rashes started popping up around the injury. The tiny blister-like bubbles were itchy and filled with a yellowish-white liquid that oozed out if I scratched them. According to my new podiatrist, the itchiness meant the nerves in my foot were trying to regenerate. Although the blisters were driving me mad, taking his word that they were a good sign, for the first time in a long while, I felt hopeful.

A month later, my pain level and symptoms unchanged, a new neurologist diagnosed me as having *Complex Regional Pain Syndrome* (CRPS). Also known as *Reflex Sympathetic Dystrophy* (RSD), he explained that the condition most commonly presents after a forceful trauma to a limb or appendage and that emotional stress may be a precipitating factor. As there wasn't a single test that could definitively diagnose CRPS/RSD, he recommended that I conduct research on the Internet so that I'd fully understand my condition. He also suggested that I might want to find a local support group.

Through my research, I learned that, though rare, CRPS/RSD can also develop following a surgery, stroke or heart attack and from something as seemingly innocuous as a sprained ankle. The most obvious indicator was that the associated residual pain was out of proportion to the severity of the initial injury.

Though it wasn't fully understood why these types of injuries sometimes triggered CRPS/RSD, experts thought it might be due to dysfunctional interaction between one's central and peripheral nervous systems and inappropriate inflammatory response.

What made most sense to me was the list of common symptoms, most of which I continued to experience. Typically, CRPS/RSD begins with burning pain, the area becomes swollen and inflamed, and the skin becomes excessively sensitive to touch, and hypersensitive to hot or cold temperatures. Dystrophy (tissue and muscle wasting) was a worrisome complication, as was the associated depression and anxiety that led many sufferers to commit suicide.

At the time, there weren't many support groups and I needed help dealing with the intense never-ending pain, my fears, and desperation. Mostly homebound, I reached out to people via social media. I quickly discovered that I wasn't alone. Like me, others were seeking support and relief for what was purportedly a lifelong disease with limited treatment options. Due to the high incident of sufferers who took their lives, CRPS/RSD was referred to by some as "the suicide disease."

Realizing that I had to helm my own recovery ship, over time, I sought and amassed a team of twelve specialists, including an acupuncturist, a life coach and a spiritual adviser. Also on my team were: clinical psychologist Dr. Mark Kleinman, holistic healer Sue Knill-Birkham, and awesome pain specialist Dr. Jack D'Angelo.

The years between 2008 and 2010 were a long, painful and often discouraging uphill-downhill battle. With every new specialist who actually "got me" and what I daily endured, I felt more hopeful. One day, somehow, someway, I'd find a way to either live life fully despite the pain, or science would find a miracle cure. Never, never would I give up. Life was precious and I wanted mine back.

Then, I'd have a bad day that snowballed into a horrible week. Someone would say or do something to hurt my sensitive ego and raw feelings, or my pain medications would stop doing their trick, or I'd learn about someone who'd given up and taken their own life, and I'd freefall into depression. *My life will never be the same. They'll never find a cure. What's the sense in trying?*

During this period, I sought relief through fifteen different medications and tried numerous treatments, including: acupuncture, physical therapy, lumbar block therapy (a series of corticosteroid injections in my lower back) and peripheral nerve block therapy (anesthetic injected into the nerve bundles in my ankle and foot). I also tried wearing pain patches and heat therapy. All offered minimal or no pain relief and barely measurable mobility gain in my foot and ankle.

Thankfully, in the summer of 2010, what my team had been patiently trying to tell and show me began to sink into my pain-riddled, fogged-out mind. Instead of wishing and hoping my disease away, I needed to learn how to live fully in spite of my condition. There forward, I sometimes actually felt happy. When I did, I would do an imagined Irish jig about the room while thinking, "Huh? I'm happy! Break out the champagne. I forgot how terrific and freeing happy feels."

Living *with* the disease, instead of *despite* the disease, I paid attention to my inner-self while I *tested* rather than *resented* my limitations. I learned how to reduce my depression and anxiety by employing techniques such as deep breathing exercises, physical exercises, music therapy and meditation. The Emotional Freedom Technique (EFT) of tapping on the energy meridians just under the skin was effective and far less painful than acupuncture. Reiki treatments helped too.

It wasn't a smooth transition. Sometimes I would dip back into depression with thoughts of, "Woe is me; my life is over. I can't do anything anymore." Gratefully, following an appointment with one of the professionals on my Psychology Development Team, I'd feel renewed and realize I could still be a productive person.

Early in 2012, Dr. D'Angelo told me about an experimental new pain-relief treatment called Calmare therapy. Excited, I went home and researched the treatment on the Internet. Also known as "scrambler therapy" the concept of being able to send a "no pain" message to the affected nerves in my toes, foot and ankle was exciting. Best of all, the process of using electrical stimulation to block pain was non-invasive. Each treatment would take about forty-five minutes while a machine emitted barely detectable amps of electricity into my affected nerves via surface electrodes applied to my skin.

I was a tad nervous about being one of the first guinea pigs for Competitive Technologies, the company that brought the machine to the United States from Italy where it was invented. The butterflies in my stomach, however, were also born of excitement. If this treatment worked, I'd be helping myself and the thousands of CRPS/RSD sufferers I'd befriended on social media.

My first session was with a senior executive from Competitive Technologies and Dr. D'Angelo. Remarkably, by the end of the treatment my pain level dropped to seven. I was sold! The next week, I began a series of nine additional treatment sessions. Following the end of my tenth treatment, without taking any medication, my daily pain level consistently hovered between four and five.

When asked if I'd continue for thirty-five more treatments as an experiment to see if my pain level would decrease further, I cautiously obliged. Normally, a patient underwent a total of ten forty-five minute sessions administered over a two-week period that excluded weekends. I would be one of the first to undergo a prolonged series of treatments. *Would four-and-a-half times the normal number of treatments cause unforeseen complications or result in irreversible consequences?*

During the additional treatments, I prayed before enjoying what gradually extended into between five and six hours of uninterrupted sleep per night. With more sleep, I felt far less anxious. Admittedly, my progression was not in a straight line. Sometimes, my pain level increased. In the beginning, my treatments were sometimes painful.

As part of the trial, the doctor experimented with the placement of the electrodes. One involved a crisscrossing pattern. Another was called the mirroring method where electrodes were placed on both sides of my body to stop the pain that sometimes spread to my good foot and ankle. Electrodes were also placed on my neck and lower back to ensure that the scrambling signals reached my brainstem. The most effective positioning for me was when the electrodes were placed directly onto my injured left foot, ankle and calf.

The itching that fluctuated along with the decreases and increases in my pain levels was challenging. Of course, I wanted to scratch and sometimes did while sleeping. At various points in the trial, my pain level went down as low as two. Throughout the trial, my mobility and physical strength steadily increased. I no longer needed help getting out of or making my bed. I could enjoy an unassisted shower, cut my toenails and do minor household chores. I felt on top of the world!

After the initial trial, I continued with Calmare therapy on an as-needed basis. Luckily, my case with Workers' Compensation was settled in June 2013.

Calmare treatment is now widely recognized as an effective and safe treatment for chronic pain. In gratitude, I am a staunch advocate. Over fifty-million Americans live with chronic, often unbearable, pain. Through my Internet radio shows and social media websites, I continually reach out to and support those diagnosed with Complex Regional Pain Syndrome or Reflex Sympathetic Dystrophy.

Daily, I do my utmost to be a positive light in the world as I continue what I consider to be God's work. Some might say that I continually shove down others' throats the importance of never giving up, trying different treatments until you find one that works for you, and maintaining a positive outlook. They're right! With hope, comes action; with action comes hope. *Sue me for caring!*

If I hadn't tried Calmare therapy, chances are that my life would have turned out very differently. Like most people afflicted with CRPS/RSD, my pain is seldom completely gone. Between treatments, it creeps higher until it becomes abundantly clear that I need a few more sessions. Luckily, the frequency and number of sessions needed for me to maintain a level of pain I can easily tolerate is ever-decreasing. Recently, I actually enjoyed seven consecutive days of being absolutely pain free. Elated that I could put my foot flat on the floor, I went for power walks. This welcomed reprieve gave me hope that a time will come when I won't need any Calmare treatments at all.

I am confident that I'll one day marry, buy a big house and have a few kids. Whether or not the "American Dream" ever comes true for me, I'm grateful for my renewed lease on life. As most sufferers know, depression, anxiety, nightmares, and panic attacks are ongoing symptoms of CRPS/RSD. There are days when these pesky menaces afflict me. But they no longer consume me or knock me down for extended periods. Standing tall, I say aloud, "Get out of my way CRPS/RSD! I've got things to do, people to help, and goals to pursue."

I will forever be a proud advocate and supporter of my sisters and brother who live with chronic pain. I will educate the public and raise awareness by bringing people together in community through Internet radio, social media, and neighborhood gatherings. In just three short years, thanks to my fellow advocates, awareness, support and treatment options abound for those diagnosed with CRPS/RSD. Amen!

About Joseph Aquilino

Joseph lives in Staten Island, New York. His passion is helping the millions of people living with chronic pain. He is also a staunch advocate for those afflicted with Complex Regional Pain Syndrome (CRPS), also known as Reflex Sympathetic Dystrophy (RSD). He can be contacted by e-mail at info@heartmindeffect.com.

Gregarious and wise, in just four years, his popular *Joey Giggles* Blog Talk Radio show has amassed an audience of over 100,000 listeners. Tune into Joseph's show at www.blogtalkradio.com/joeygiggles.

THROUGH THE LOOKING GLASS

Lexia Nash

*"On the Road that I have taken, one day
walking I awaken, amazed to see where I've
come, where I'm going, where I'm from."*

— Dean Koontz, *The Book of Counted Sorrows*

As she sat idle for a few moments, relishing in the beauty of the world, she thought to herself, "I am so lucky to be alive today; how fortunate am I to be sitting here enjoying the dawn of yet another new day." For today she had made it, truly made it. She had survived and finally conquered all the hardship and turmoil that had plagued her for so long. A new leaf was turned, though it had taken many years to reprogram her ways of thinking and discover her true self. It was in this moment that she recognized the significance of the changes that had taken place. It had been a long time coming.

Only a few short years ago, it seemed as though I was living life through the looking glass. Not a thought was given to the grave consequences of my actions, no heed taken as I plunged head first into self-destruction.

The room smelled of mildew. Florescent lights flickered overhead, making their telltale buzzing sound, softly humming below the chatter of the families gathered for a brief visit. In the middle of the room, chairs were lined along gray metal tables. The walls were cold and unforgiving. "I miss you, Mom," I said. "Please come back and visit me again soon. Next time, bring my sister and a couple of dollars too, okay?"

Saying she would, we hugged tightly and said our good-byes. I led her to the security gate. As the heavy metal door slammed shut behind her, I watched her walk down the grassy pathway. Brought painfully back into reality, with every step she took, I felt more and more alone. I was sixteen, in way over my head and caught up in a life that was not my destiny. Yet, it was a life that, at the time, I so badly wanted. Sentenced on remand to youth custody, I was behind bars for six months until my court date. It was not my first time in custody. Hopefully, it was the last.

After my mother left, I thought long and hard about everything I had done to get into my situation. I honestly wanted out. But how could I change? This was who I was. Seldom thinking about the future, I lived from day-to-day. I was aware that my lifestyle was hurting my family. I could see the torment in my mother's eyes and knew my father was worried. My younger sister looked up to me; the last thing I wanted was for her to follow in my footsteps.

The next several weeks were lonely and the days long. Back in court, the crown counsel recognized I wasn't too far gone to change my ways and offered me an ultimatum. I could stay in custody for six more months, or instead be sentenced to a wilderness reform camp on a remote island off the Sunshine Coast of British Columbia. I took the lesser of the two evils. Anything was better than the detention center, and I truly wanted to get my life back on track. My family was carefully optimistic about my decision, hoping I'd return to my old self.

The next morning, I packed all my dreams and meager belongings into two suitcases. Putting on a brave face, I set off to what I expected would be a new beginning. A short ferry ride, followed by an even quicker water taxi trip around the gulf and I was there, miles away from the destruction and despair that had been my existence.

Stepping off the boat, the crisp spring air felt deliciously cool on my face as I breathed life into my lungs for the first time in years. Somewhat calmed by the sound of the water lapping against the shore, I gazed at the beautiful surroundings, and thought, "I can do this. Surely, in this peaceful place of second chances, I'll be able to heal my wounds and learn from my mistakes."

I carried my suitcases up the winding gravel road to the main house and was shown to my room.

Unpacking, I felt nervous about meeting the staff and the teenagers who would be my housemates. Thankfully, over the next few days, I quickly made friends. Most of the teen residents had stories similar to mine. Bonded through our dark and miserable pasts, our sense of kinship was instantaneous.

Justin was the first person I met. "Hi," he said excitedly as he looked over at me from where he was sitting on the living room couch. "You're the new girl, hey."

He was younger than me and had wild mischievous blue eyes. I was betting he had a personality to match his devilish grin. Realizing that he was sizing me up, I shrugged. "Yeah, I'm the new girl." Though Justin seemed nice enough, I wasn't ready to let my guard down. Experience had taught me that being tough was the only way to survive.

Undeterred by my aloofness, Justin smiled wide before saying, "I've been here for a couple of weeks. So far it's been okay."

"What's there to do on this island, anyway?" I asked, flicking my hair back with one hand as I casually reached for a magazine on the coffee table.

"Not much. Everything runs off of generators so we don't get to play video games or watch T.V."

I must have had a look of horror on my face, for he added, "The mountains are pretty cool, I just got back from a hike on the cliffs. If you want, I can show you around for a bit tomorrow."

"Sounds good," I said with a half-hearted smile. "It depends on what's up." Then, feeling guilty for acting tough when he was being so nice, I added, "My friends call me Peaches."

Later that evening, I met two more teens, including Sarah who was about my age and had a vivacious outlook on life. Like a rubber ball rebounding off of a sidewalk, even though she had been through numerous downfalls, she was strong and courageous, seeming to always bounce back. As we exchanged stories, I discovered that her life mirrored mine.

My other new-found friend had nicknamed himself *Prang*. I found it amusing that like me calling myself *Peaches*, his alias was likely part of a ploy to avoid being identified should someone from the streets rat him out. He quickly became my favorite new friend. Caring and genuine, he was the person I turned to when times were rough. With ragged sandy brown hair and gold-flecked hazel eyes, he stood nearly six feet tall. He was lanky, yet strong. Prang had arrived on the Island a few months prior to me, and willingly showed me the ropes.

Having formed a natural bond, Justin, Sarah, Prang and I spent our days adventuring in the forest. I learned more about the island each day. During the still and star-filled nights, over cups of cocoa, we spent our time telling tales from our pasts. Most nights, we played five hundred rummy until our eyelids felt as though a thousand little fingers were using all of their strength to pull the veil of sleep over our eyes.

Like horses trapped in a locked barn, as one mundane day rolled into another, we became restless. Tired with the lackluster routine, my three new buddies and I found a myriad of ways to taunt the staff and get into trouble. Street life was unpredictable, exciting, and varied. Life on the island was blah, blah, blah.

While exploring the deep woods, we came across a cabin hidden among the thick brush and trees. The fisherman who lived there was a kind and gentle soul who made his living selling crabs. Befriending our little group, he told us that he was aware of the minimum-security camp for youth and had lived on the island for many years. Providing us with a small bit of sanity, he taught us how to trap crabs and paid us to help set the nets and bag the catch.

A few weeks after we met, when we arrived at his cabin, the fisherman wasn't home. Surprised and concerned for his welfare, Justin said, "Open the door and holler his name. Maybe he didn't hear us knocking." Peering inside the dimly lit shelter, we called out to the fisherman. He didn't answer. We glanced about, spotting a row of half-full liquor bottles on a shelf.

Acting on impulse, we barged into the house and headed toward the cache. Justin and I kept watch, as Prang and Sarah raced into the kitchen to grab shopping bags. Once the bags were full, we sped out the door and beelined it for the hills.

"What a rush," I said and everyone laughed. We continued climbing up the rocky and thick-forested mountain in search of a spot to drink our stolen goods. Reaching a sea-green mossy area that opened to the sky, we flopped on the soft ground. Feeling free, we spoke boisterously about our brazen deed and took turns chugging the golden liquid straight from the bottle.

The fisherman must have come home shortly afterward, noticed all of his liquor was gone, and marched over to the camp. As dusk darkened the forest, we heard the staff from the wilderness camp calling our names. We'd been ratted out and the search party was gaining ground. The three of us jumped up, tossed the bottles and fled. Dodging this way and that, we sped along the cliff near the water's edge. Knowing the area well, we hoped to outmaneuver the staff. If caught, our fun would be over and our punishment just beginning. Then I tripped.

I stepped on a jagged, sloping rock, lost my balance and in trying to stay upright, twisted my ankle and fell before being launched onto the cliff below. I landed hard on one knee. Instantly, burning pain shot up my leg.

Hot on our trail, the camp supervisors watched me fall. Their main concern switched to my wellbeing. Coming to my aid, two staff members helped me hobble back to camp as my friends reluctantly followed. I felt miserable. We'd been caught, our fun was over, the staff was mad, and I was in pain. On top of that, I felt guilty for betraying the fisherman.

The very next day, ashamed and distraught, I decided to escape. I could no longer handle being hindered by their rules. Having noticed a large piece of Styrofoam stored behind the main camp house, I hobbled as fast as I could and found it. Heading for the beach, I threw it in the ocean and flopped on top of my getaway raft. Fueled by a fear of getting caught, I made good pace through the icy water. My arms ached as I bobbed over waves and the island grew smaller.

About halfway to the mainland, it dawned on me that I wasn't going to make it. The ocean now a swirling angry pool, I thought, "I'm going to drown out here and no one will know where to find my body."

Panicked, I glanced about the gray ocean and spotted a small boat. Waving frantically, I hoped they would see me. As the vessel chugged closer, my cheeks flushed red hot. *What was I thinking climbing onto a giant piece of Styrofoam and attempting to make it five miles across the ocean?* How embarrassing.

I thanked the man who helped me onto what turned out to be a water taxi. Shivering and soaked to the core, I told him the truth, including where I had come from. He immediately took me back to camp.

For the next few weeks, I begrudgingly did the extra chores assigned as my punishment for being part of the liquor escapade and for attempting escape.

Every so often, the staff would take one of us teens to the mainland either to help with shopping or to spend a couple of nights at the camp's lodge and have family visit. My punishment complete and having been on my best behavior for a month, I was allowed to go.

Perched on top of a cliff and overlooking the ocean, staying at the lodge was considered a privilege. My buddies had told me that there were two bedrooms for teens, and another bedroom that served as sleeping quarters and an office for staff. Unlike on the island where water had to be boiled for the bathtub, the lodge had a shower. There was also a television and a landline for calling family.

I'd been on the island for three months and this would be my first overnight stay on the mainland. Dad would be my first visitor. Arriving at the lodge, excited and eager to see him, I was reminded of how I felt during the many times my dad and I had sat by a lake waiting for a fish to bite. When I finally heard the familiar sound of his old brown Mazda truck, I raced to the door. Running down the stairs, I flew into his open arms. *He hadn't changed a bit.*

After locking me in a bear hug, he smiled in a way that said he noticed the glimmer of light in my eyes. He could see that my true self was re-emerging from the empty soul I had been for the past few years. After asking if I was hungry, we headed for a nearby café to have lunch.

Studying us, the waitress said, "You two have the same eyes, you must be related." Proud, I announced, "He's my Dad." Following his lead, I ordered what he ordered—beef dip, fries, coleslaw and a coke. As we ate lunch, we reminisced about past adventures and happy times. Every story recounted made me miss my family and childhood friends more and more. Though tasty by restaurant standards, each bite increased my craving for Mom's home cooking and Dad's special Ukrainian dishes. When dusk settled into the sky, my heart sank. On a curfew, it was time to head back to the lodge.

A rush of nostalgia grabbed hold of me as I climbed into his truck and closed the door. The dream catcher that hung from the rearview mirror scattered the setting sun's burnt orange rays about the interior and across my dad's face. The familiar scent of sweet grass filled my nostrils as Dad cranked up his favorite Traveling Willburys CD. Overcome by happy memories of wilderness adventures with him and my younger sister, tears welled in my eyes. *How long would it be before I saw him again? How long would it be before my mom and sister were allowed to visit?* My heart ached.

Back at the lodge, I felt lonely and lost. Everyone and everything seemed foreign. Seeing my dad made me resent living with near-strangers. But going home wasn't an option. I'd already caused my family enough pain. With that thought, I suddenly couldn't stand being separated from my street friends.

That night in bed, I planned every detail of what I was sure would be my grand escape. By morning, I knew exactly what I had to do. Excited, over the coming weeks I could barely concentrate. Mundane tasks such as chopping wood, cooking, and cleaning the main house became unbearably boring. Constantly scheming, I was only interested in what would ensure my safe and permanent exodus.

One afternoon while hiking with Sarah and Prang, I casually shared my escape plans. An adventure of this magnitude too enticing to miss out on, both begged to go along. Two days later, the staff told me that I'd be accompanying them on their mainland shopping trip, and that I should be ready to leave at seven a.m. the following day.

As part of our plan, Prang went to bed early, saying he wasn't feeling well. Sarah and I stayed up playing rummy with the staff. Claiming the greasy nachos we'd had for dinner had upset her stomach, she quit the game early and went to bed. My mind wound tight with anticipation, I didn't sleep a wink.

The next morning, between bites of cold cereal, I casually mentioned that I had checked on Prang and Sarah and that both were still unwell. The kitchen staff said that they'd look in on them later. In truth, at dawn, my good friends had crept out of the house and were now hiding like migrant stowaways in the hull of the supply boat.

A half hour later, two staff and I made our way to the water's edge. Jumping aboard the boat that was rocking ever so gently against the morning's lazy tide, I hollered, "I'll get the life jackets." Fearing they'd see inside, I only partially opened the hatch door. Smirking, Prang quickly passed me three lifejackets from inside.

Checking a grin and turning towards the staff, I cheerfully said, "I got 'em!"

The twenty minute trip to the Sunshine Coast seemed to take forever. When we docked at the marina, I took my sweet time getting off the boat, making sure the staff climbed off first. When they were ten feet away, I unlocked the hatch door, hopped off the boat and sauntered up the dock. A few seconds later, I called out that I'd forgotten my money and jacket and would catch up with them.

Suspecting nothing, they called back, "No problem; we'll meet you there." I watched to make certain that they kept making their way toward town. Running back to the boat, I climbed aboard and whistled. Sarah and Prang leapt out of hiding. Quicker than racehorses headed for the finish line, we fled into the hills, toward the highway. *I wasn't about to get caught again.*

A few seconds later, the staff yelled, "Hey! What are you doing?!" I glanced back. Their hands on their hips and mouths open wide, they looked shocked and terrified as they realized what was happening in that moment of chaos. Ignoring a twinge of guilt, I kept going.

Feeling free and powered by adrenaline, we three fugitives ran a mile up the hill toward the highway. Ignoring the effects of the marathon our bodies had just gone through, once there, we stuck out our thumbs. Our first ride was with an eccentric woman on an acid trip. Rock and roll music blared out of the radio as she talked to herself. Uncertain if she even knew we were there, my friends and I exchanged worried glances. A few miles down the road, I hollered, "Pull over here! I want out. Now!"

Once safe, we laughed our heads off. Next we were picked up by a van full of elderly church ladies who sang us gospel songs and blessed our souls. Thankfully, they took us all the way to Sechelt. Knowing the description the staff gave the police would include what we were wearing, we headed for the hospital and changed into the clothes that were stuffed in our knapsacks.

We walked the two miles to the terminal and caught the next ferry to Horseshoe Bay. Back on familiar ground, Sarah, Prang and I wished each other luck, and said good bye with the hope that we would see each other again.

The seasons drifted one into another, and with each change in weather, my life altered course. Though always intent on cleaning up my act, I tended to blow with the wind. Many months were spent in downpours with me having little or no control. Sometimes the sun shone brightly, and I'd take a right turn. Then the fog would roll in and I'd be back on a path of self-destruction once more.

A few short weeks before my eighteenth birthday, my court ordered supervision over, I met with my probation officer to complete the paperwork. Plopping onto a tweed chair, I peered across his mahogany desk. Smirking, I said, "Hey, Ian. Bet you can't wait to get me off your caseload."

Leaning forward in his big black leather chair, he warned, "You know, if you get into trouble again, you will be headed for adult prison." I already knew that. But hearing him say it, shook me at my core.

"You still have your whole life to look forward to, you know? Continuing down this road would be a big mistake for a bright girl like you." I liked Ian. He'd been my P.O. for four years. No matter what trouble I got myself into, he was always respectful and kind. What he said always carried weight with me. Today, his words lifted a weight from my shoulders. I was done with risking my freedom for a bit of fun.

He continued counseling me with his words. While I sat and listened, I thought of the years spent getting to know him and all the guidance he tried so hard to give. Then, it dawned on me. There had to be more than this turnstile life I'd chosen, going around in circles with no end in sight. Looking him square in the eye, I vowed, "Don't worry, Ian. I'm out of the system. You won't be seeing me in your office again."

Ian smiled and stretched out his hand to congratulate me. The expression in his eyes indicated that he believed I was finally ready to change. I believed in me too. Having aged-out of the youth system, I made a pact with myself to be true to my word. In that instant, I released the carefree, could-give-a-darn attitude that had shackled my demise. Skipping down the steps, I finally felt free.

Finding a harmonious rhythm wasn't easy. Over the next few years, I dealt with many ups and downs. Strangely enough, it was the "be tough, or die" lessons learned on the street that gave me the fortitude to face and handle what came my way. What played through my mind during difficult times were the trials that I had overcome.

Ties long ago severed, I never saw Sarah or Prang again. Whenever talking with teens in search of guidance, I share what I learned from the mistakes I made—though throwing caution to the wind can be fun and seem freeing; in truth, it leads you away from your true self and toward a life that is not meant to be yours. Have fun, of course, but don't have so much fun that you get lost and trapped in a world from which there is no return.

Though I suspect they often wanted to give up on me, my family never did. Their faith in my abilities eventually transferred to me. I now thoroughly enjoy spending time with them creating new memories.

In my early twenties, I reconnected with a childhood friend who is now my husband. Rather than ever remind me of the errors of my ways when I was younger, he encourages me to be the best I can be, celebrating each of my achievements with heartfelt pride. Together now for almost ten years, we have formed a solid bond of trust and will grow old together. Life is busy and filled with future plans and abundant dreams.

It had been a busy week, so today, I decided to treat myself to a morning coffee at the cafe next to my house. As I received my drink at the counter, I closed my eyes and inhaled the fragrant aroma seeping through the lid. My mouth watering for the sweet liquid inside, I took a seat by the window and basked in the morning light of the summer sun. It felt wonderfully warm on my face.

Taking a long sip from the cup, I savored my coffee and all that was good and right with the world. A movement in the mirror to the right caught my attention. In the reflection, I saw a busy coffee shop full of people who'd taken a break to enjoy the same fix of caffeinated pleasure that I was soaking up. Watching them, I noticed their smiles and gestures as dozens of conversations murmured around the room.

Then I spotted her: A bright-eyed woman with long blond hair, the sun playing through the golden strands that cascaded down her back. The two bouncing and playful young boys she had with her were talking away about their day, the fun they had enjoyed earlier that week, and how they looked forward to their weekend adventures. Their laughter lit up her face. One could see the love that she had for them, the joys they brought her, and the pure delight she had when they called out, "Mommy."

Just as I saw her, her eyes had caught mine. In that moment, we looked deep into each other's souls, through the looking glass once more, but now reversed. It was her looking out at me that day. Seeing myself in that coffee shop mirror, a double image of who I was and who I had now become, my heart swelled.

Smiling as I watched my two handsome young sons, I thought to myself, "I am so lucky to be alive today; how fortunate am I to be sitting here enjoying the dawn of yet another new day." It was in this moment that I recognized the significance of the changes that had taken place. It *had* been a long time coming.

About Lexia Nash

Lexia lives in Burnaby, British Columbia, with her loving husband Mike and their two adventurous sons, Rory and Miles. When younger, she was a volunteer corporal officer, and taught cadets in the Navy League program at the H.M.C.S. Discovery base in Stanley Park, Vancouver.

Figure skating, horseback riding, wilderness survival camping and her lifelong love of reading have all greatly enriched her life. She is passionate about raising her children to appreciate the beauties nature has to offer. Every day is a perfect opportunity to take the road less traveled. She can be contacted by e-mail at info@heartmindeffect.com.

TO CANADA, THE PROMISED LAND

Arnold Vingsnes

"**Y**ou gotta punch him back, like this." Bobby Simpson demonstrated a quick left followed by a right hook, stopping short of my face. "You gotta stick up for yourself."

I'd never punched anyone. *I was stronger than I looked. What if I hurt them?*

I was eight years old and my family had just moved to Canada from a remote tiny island in Norway. Bobby was a classmate and lived down the street. Saying I sounded funny, he enjoyed teasing me as I struggled to learn and speak English. His mocking didn't bother me. Without Bobby's friendship, adjusting to my new home country would have been scarier, lonelier and bloodier.

Nearly every day after school, the bully directly across the street from my house lay in wait for me. The first time I encountered him, I rounded a corner and spotted him standing with his arms crossed chest-high and a smirk on his face. As I tried to pass, he lunged at me hollering, "Hey, you stupid import, go home! Nobody wants you or your family here!"

When he knocked me to the ground, I curled my body inward and shielded my head with my arms. After a flurry of fists and kicks, he relented and left me lying on the sidewalk sobbing in pain and disbelief. It took me a minute to get up. When able to steady myself on my feet, I ran for home and up the stairs to my room. *Why did we have to move to Canada? Everything was good in Norway.*

I missed the ocean, our house and the wilderness. Many times, while lying on my bed, I'd close my eyes and pretend I was back there. Located among a smattering of other islands in the North Sea, winters on Ertvågsøya were bitterly cold and hurricane stormy. Even though our home was somewhat sheltered, when winter descended, it did so with a fury. When the wind blew, it blew. Screeching through the gnarled stunted shrubs, the storm threw itself directly at our home. At times, it seemed as though the house actually ached...creaking, moaning and groaning as though it wanted to depart its foundation and hurtle up the valley with the storm.

At the mouth of a cove and directly behind a small protective cliff sat our little island home. There was little insulation, so whether the wind was taking a rare rest or not, during the winter we kept a wood fire burning in each room's small potbellied stove. Once the house was dark, the fires would goof off and go to sleep. The first kid up had to stoke the fires awake and then jump back in bed before they froze to death. Being found dead in pajamas was an unthinkable fate.

Mom cooked on a large cast iron stove that readily gobbled its fair share of wood. We had electricity but not a refrigerator. The potatoes, carrots and turnips our big garden gifted us in the fall were stored in the root cellar below our house. Mom cooked and canned most of the fruit and berries we picked. The only store was a twenty-minute brisk walk from our house. It didn't have refrigeration either, so meat-wise, it only sold cured cold-cuts and canned meat. Our main grocery store was the sea. It provided us an abundance of delicacies, most of which were caught by me.

Though the sea seldom welcomed me with smooth sailing, most mornings I set out in a fifteen-foot rowboat to collect the bounty from our crab traps and hook a fish or two. I always hoped to catch salmon but cod, haddock or flounder were the typical catch of the day. Rarely, we ate lamb or chicken purchased from a neighboring farmer. Our staple diet was fish, fish and more fish.

Without indoor plumbing or a well, water for drinking, cooking and bathing was carried from the creek located about a thousand feet from our house. On bath day, bucket after bucket of creek water was needed to fill the big galvanized tub sitting atop our sturdy kitchen table. After heating some of the crystal clear, icy water on the stove, beginning with my younger two sisters, we took turns scrubbing ourselves clean. Our clothes were washed in a huge cast iron pot that sat by the creek. Once a week, Mom scooped water into the pot, lit a fire under it and using a long-handled stick, stirred our clothes clean before rinsing them in the creek.

Our primary mode of transportation was our feet. There were no taxis or buses and our family didn't have horses or a car. It was a half-hour walk to the nearest neighbor's house. Shine, rain or blizzard, we walked an hour each way to school. The only person with a running car was my grandfather. The storekeeper had a vehicle too, an old 1930's truck with a hand crank. Its running days long passed, the forlorn relic just sat there recalling happier days and missing its youth.

Much of the spring, summer and fall months were dedicated to preparing for the winter. Dad mostly away working and my sisters too young to help, I felled trees, chopped firewood and dried sod. Everything wood was stored in our tiny barn, which also contained our outhouse.

During winter, it took some fairly urgent need before I put on my boots and coat and headed for the shockingly cold outdoor facilities. No matter the time of year, nighttime visits were best avoided. After the sun sank to the other side of the world, the gnarly, stunted trees morphed into a forest of dangerous zombies with hairy, waving arms that could reach out and grab you. They were particularly frightening when the moon broke through the branches and lit their grotesque, dastardly faces. Thankfully, we all had bedpans.

During the summer months, I loved heading out by myself to explore the ocean or wander through the forest and up into the mountains. Occasionally, a friend or two would join me. My mother had no idea what I was up to most of the time, which afforded her a false sense of peace and gave me a sense of freedom.

Many times, our family dinner caught, I'd row about the shoreline in hopeful pursuit of newly washed ashore treasures. On days when the wind took a vacation, I'd pull in the oars and relax, content to be entertained by the movements, sounds and sights of nature. I thoroughly enjoyed being on or near the ocean.

When the mountains called to me, I'd hike through the forest and climb one of the narrow and somewhat treacherous ravines. Once perched high on a cliff, I'd peer down into a gully below or gaze out at the little islands dotting the ocean. Without industry, traffic or large wildlife, the only sound that broke through the still silence was the deep -throated engine rumble of distant ships that were barely discernable on the horizon. Wondering what they might be carrying, where they came from and where they were going to, I fantasized about traveling to faraway lands. *Maybe I'd one day be the captain of a ship.*

The absence of street and industry lights made exploring the night sky an exhilarating adventure. Many a summer's eve, I lay on my back, staring heavenward for hours as flickering and falling stars brought the universe to life. Within minutes, I'd feel as though I was being swept into space, the sense so intense that I'd grab hold of the grass to prevent my body from flying off into the vast unknown. Lying there, gripping the earth in a death clutch, I sometimes toyed with the idea of letting go so that I'd be swept up into the beckoning galaxy of alien secrecies. Only when I flopped myself onto my stomach did I feel safe enough to let go of the earth. It was a strange, overwhelming and incredible sensation.

Though we had electricity, we didn't have a telephone or television. We did have a radio that was constantly on and tuned to Radio Luxemburg, the only station we could get. Perhaps it was some talk show on the radio that sparked our family's exodus to Canada. More likely, it was Grandpa.

Prior to the Second World War, my grandfather went to America to seek his fame and fortune. What he did there remains a mystery, but he returned with money in hand, and built a shipyard at the mouth of the cove. By the time I was born, there wasn't a trace of evidence that anything industrious had ever existed. During the Second World War, a fierce storm carried off the buildings and most of the equipment; what remained fell into Nazi hands. The shipyard was never rebuilt. After the war, Grandpa made his living building custom ordered boats.

My grandparents' glorious, manor-like yellow house sat on the rise on the other side of the creek. Behind the house lay an expanse of pines stretching up the length of the hills and bordering mountain as far as the eye could see. It was a pretty sight. Intrigued with the dusty models of hulls and the shipbuilding machinery in their old red barn, I often imagined the huge lumbering lathes, humungous drill presses and the assortment of mystery equipment brought back to life in a cacophony of sounds and undulating motion.

My father was a fisherman. A year prior to us immigrating, he worked at an aluminum smelter in Norway. Seldom home, when he moved overseas to pave the way for us, his absence wasn't a big deal. Canada was enjoying a postwar boom, but lacked the manpower to drive it. Dad quickly found work at the aluminum smelter in Kitimat, British Columbia. Within a year, he saved enough money to fly us to our new home. November 1958, Mom, my sisters and I boarded a plane for the first time in our lives, all of us excited about moving and eager to join Dad.

I can only imagine how Mom must have felt when we landed. A lone adult in a foreign land, unable to speak the language, three children in tow, all of them gawking, pointing and asking a million questions. After somehow managing to convey to a taxi driver where she wanted to go, we headed for the Hotel Grosvenor in downtown Vancouver, B.C. All of us were enthralled by the vehicles that buzzed this way and that. There were buildings everywhere and streetlights lit up the city like a Christmas tree. Seeming to be in a hurry, people passed one another without stopping to say hello.

Once in our hotel room, Mom switched on the television for my sisters and me to watch while she figured out how to order something for us to eat. Though we didn't understand a word, we were mesmerized by *The Ed Sullivan Show*. A day earlier, the idea of watching a big box with moving pictures and sound coming out of it was unimaginable. When a buzzer sounded, Mom opened a small door in the wall and there were our meals. To us kids, Canada was the most magical place in the world.

The next morning, we flew to Kitimat. Three hours later, Dad picked us up in his 1956 Ford Fairlane. The forest receded behind us as we drove up a long hill with a creek on one side and a cemetery on the other. Towering ten-foot-high snowbanks flanked the roadway. Though there were houses, a small shopping mall and a large hospital, there weren't any tall buildings and barely any traffic. "Where's the city?" Mom asked. "You're looking at it," was Dad's reply as he made a left turn and moments later pulled into the driveway of our new home. I could tell that Mom was disappointed by the size of the town.

A welcoming waft of warm air shuttered out the cold as we entered. I scouted the house for potbellied stoves but couldn't find any. In the bathroom, I tested the faucets on the sink and bathtub and flushed the toilet, happy to see that everything was in working order. I wandered to the kitchen and opened the door of the fridge and then the stove before heading for the living room. Maybe every house in Canada had a magic box with images and sound. Sadly, ours didn't. On the "didn't have" plus side—no piles of firewood in every room, no buckets for carrying water, and best of all, no bedpans.

Without many Norwegians residing in the area, we were on our own to figure out the local customs and currency. Within a few days of arriving, Dad at work, Mom took my sisters and me grocery shopping. Together, we wandered the aisles, picking up boxes and cans and speculating on what might be inside. Though some had pictures, none of us could read the labels or figure out how much each cost. Mom was astounded by the variety of fresh produce and meat, but when no one came to help her, after saying that she was worried about whether she had enough money to pay for things, she insisted we leave. We left the supermarket empty-handed.

Hungry after a long day's work, Dad wasn't happy that supper wasn't on the table. After grumbling a bit, he went to the store. A while later he returned and plopped a frozen TV dinner on the kitchen table. Curious, I studied the box. It had a picture of mashed potatoes, peas and sliced meat. Talking to Mom, he said, "Just take it out of the box and put it in the stove." Appearing bewildered, Mom asked, "How will this one little package feed all of us?" Dad responded, "It expands when you cook it! There'll be plenty to feed us all!" Of course that didn't happen, but how was he to know.

Within a week of arriving, our younger sister Elin too young to go to school, Mom enrolled my sister Anita and me in Kildala Elementary. We were surprised when they placed us both in the same grade. Not understanding the school system, when we talked to Mom about it, she just shrugged her shoulders and assured us that all would be okay. Shy and unable to converse with the other students, my sister and I kept to ourselves. Apparently that was the wrong thing to do because they soon shuffled Anita into a class with younger kids. I eventually caught on that they wanted us to learn English, which wasn't going to happen if we only talked to one another.

The principal was a beady-eyed man who ran the school like a jail-house warden. He never announced his presence when he came into our class. Instead, he'd sneak in the door behind us and just stand there. The teacher could see him, but we couldn't. It didn't take me long to figure out that when our teacher started acting nervous, the principal was in the room. For good reason, I became nervous too.

Although I never figured out why, the principal hated me. After standing at the back for however long he pleased, he'd saunter up behind me and bring his knuckles down hard on my head, his blood-red ring just short of piercing my skin. No one, not even the teacher, would say a word as I winced in pain. Afterward, he'd stand at the front and insist the entire class sing "Row, Row, Row Your Boat."

Obviously afraid of him, none of the teachers in the school ever stood up to the principal. Deciding they were a spineless bunch, I lost respect for the lot of them. But that wasn't the only reason I hated school, often pretending to be ill so I could stay home. Living directly across the street from our house, there was no way I could avoid the prejudiced bully or his continued beatings. Whenever Mom asked about my latest bruised shins or bump on my head, I'd claim to have tripped and fallen. She must have thought I was the clumsiest kid on the planet.

One day, something snapped inside of me. I no longer cared if I killed the stupid, mean oaf with the big mouth. It was time to wipe the smirk off the jerk's face. Charging at him, I fisted him in the nose with a powerful left, then right hooked his jaw. The kid went down; Bobby had taught me well. Dropping to my knees, I straddled his waist and gave him a couple more good punches. He didn't fight back. I got up and left him on the ground holding his bloody nose.

With no idea what to expect, the next day after school I was heart-thumping ready for a good fight. Instead of the opponent I was anticipating, the bully's dad came charging out of their house, bellowing obscenities and racial slurs between hollers that he'd teach me not to beat up his kid. Stunned witless, I wasn't sure whether to run or fight back. Dad solved that conundrum. He came barrelling out of our house, hands fisted and hollering his own list of insults and profanities. Not a punch was exchanged as the bully's dad quickly backed down and hightailed it for home. Neither of them ever again tangled with Dad or me.

Little by little, life in Canada became more bearable, sometimes joyful. Bobby, his black lab Queenie, and I regularly ventured into the tall-treed forest and climbed the foothills of the white-capped Coast Mountains. Often spotting wildlife, including skunks and racoons, we kept out of their way and they left us alone. From an island devoid of large wild animals, any hike that included spotting a black bear or deer was one to talk about at the family dinner table. Though often homesick for Norway, fishing, exploring the shoreline and rafting the Kitimat River helped stymie my longing to return to a simpler way of life. Whether building a fort, complaining about school, or fantasizing about where we'd one day travel, Bobby and I knew we'd forever be the best of friends.

Though my childhood trials and traumas are buried in the past, I haven't forgotten how it felt to be a sometimes welcomed, sometimes shunned or discounted foreigner. Feeling a kinship with new immigrants, I'm curious about their native land and the reasons, hopes and dreams that led them to Canada. Unlike Bobby, God rest his soul, I never mock anyone trying to master a new language.

About Arnold Vingsnes

Arnold Vingsnes lives in Abbotsford, British Columbia. A champion of the everyday man, Arnold has held prominent union and management positions. The scope of his career rare and extensive, he is a sought-after contract negotiator, speaker and teacher.

Arnold has a daughter, stepdaughter and one grandchild. He is currently working on a series of short stories about his life and travels. He can be contacted by e-mail at info@heartmindeffect.com.

Arnold's chapter in *Heartmind Wisdom Collection #1* is "Escape from the Green Room" and his chapter in *Heartmind Wisdom Collection #2* is "The Freedom Voyage." The Heartmind Wisdom Collection is available at www.heartmindstore.com and through online bookstores.

DIVINE
CONNECTION

A COLLABORATIVE JOURNEY OF HOPE & MIRACLES

Katharine Fahlman

"Hope smiles from the threshold of the year to come, whispering, 'It will be happier.'"

—Alfred Lord Tennyson

Raised in a Christian family, my belief in a higher power is solid. I know that God works in conventional and mysterious ways. He also works in what some might view as *impossible* ways.

My grandmother read tea leaves. From the time that I could talk, I often sat across the table from her, awed by what she could tell from the remnants of a friend's or family member's cup of loose leaf tea.

Curious about people's varying beliefs, as a young girl, attending a variety of church services became a passion. What I noticed was that no matter their religion, when leaving church people seemed happier and walked taller.

There was no doubt in my mind that church was a magical place and that Grandma was a magical woman. Still, I wondered two things: Why was what the tea told my grandmother of such interest to people? And, what exactly happened during a church service that made people feel more confident and peacefully happy? It was many years before I fully understood that the answer to both questions was the same.

This curiosity stayed with me into adulthood, so when I read a story in a local newspaper about a nurse, Susan, who participated in Full

Moon Celebrations, I contacted her. When we met, my suppositions based on her profession proved to be true—she was credible and kind.

A few days later, under the silver cast of a bright full moon, I stepped out of my comfort zone and into the midst of a large gathering of mostly women at a neighborhood park. From the moment I arrived, the experience was breathtaking surreal.

Thank goodness, not one head displayed a tall pointed hat and everyone appeared to be "normal" as we held hands and formed a circle. Adhering to rituals rooted in aboriginal cultures around the globe, we closed our eyes and took deep breaths to center ourselves.

Carrying a bundle of burning sage, the organizer called upon the elements and the corners of the earth to protect our sacred space. From the east, she called in air. From the south, fire; from the west, water. After calling on the element of earth from the north, she invited all of us to let go of whatever no longer served us—harmful habits, negative thinking, guilt, physical pain, addictive relationships, and anything that shadowed the lightness of our being—by releasing them to our collective mother, Gaia.

Afterward, we dipped our hands in purified water to cleanse the old and welcome the new. Through meditation and prayer, we connected with our higher-selves, spirit and animal guides. While we chanted, the sound of lightly tapped drums and softly played Tibetan singing bowls soothed our souls and minds. Once totally centered in peace and love, we breathed life into our goals, dreams and desires by calling on the potent energies of the brilliant overhead moon.

I left the ceremony feeling happily peaceful and centered; yet, dizzily excited. Never before had I felt such serene contentment in conjunction with absolute joy. When Susan invited me to attend the Spiritualist Church in Burnaby, British Columbia, I eagerly accepted.

Though I didn't realize that spiritualists practiced mediumship, there was no mistaking the sense of belonging that engulfed me as I sat in the beautiful little chapel. I knew that I'd come home, had found my people.

While savoring my morning tea the next day, I thought about Grandma and how she eagerly shared her psychic gifts with everyone. One face after another flashed through my mind's eye as I pictured those who'd shared tea with her, all of them eager to learn which of their hopeful dreams and aspirations would be revealed by the leaves. It was while sitting in my kitchen reminiscing about my wee, darling Scottish grandmother that I vowed to share my psychic abilities with the world. When young, I knew things that I shouldn't know, which made me appear wise beyond my years. When Mom and Dad were discussing how they could afford our new home before our current one sold, I said, "Why not rent out this one?" I was thirteen. Astonished and impressed, my parents did as I suggested. Grateful for their praise, I never revealed that it wasn't really my idea, but more an "uninvited thought" or "silent whispering" that popped into my head and out of my mouth.

There were numerous other sudden knowings and sage wisdoms that snuck into my head and slipped past my tongue. However, like a news reporter, I kept my source a carefully guarded secret. Heaven forbid my relatives refer to me as they did my cousin who openly shared her visions and knowings. Contrary to what they said, my cousin did not "take spells"; she simply knew things and envisioned future happenings that couldn't be logically explained.

Having met people at the Spiritualist Church who eagerly and openly shared their gifts, I shed my cloak of self-doubt and secrecy and embraced my God-given ability to foretell the future. From that day forward, life became a rollercoaster ride of mind boggling experiences. Realizing that doing so would complement my tea leaf reading sessions, I studied and then added reading oracle cards into the assortment of divining instruments I could offer others.

Faithfully and excitedly, I regularly attended Sunday services at the Spiritualist Church. Observing the mediums who communicated directly with and shared messages from the spirit world was enlightening and heartwarming. Many times, after receiving a message from a deceased relative or friend, the recipient would simply nod while tears dripped into cheek creases formed by his or her wide smile.

Watching the interaction between the mediums and congregation reinforced what I'd suspected since childhood—divine whisperings and sudden-knowings often emanate from departed loved ones who watch over and guide us from the spirit world. For the next several years, I took every mediumship course offered and graciously accepted mentorship from the masters.

Having been the recipient of a miraculous healing, when a friend suggested I study Reiki, I leapt. Familiar with the Japanese technique of "laying on hands" and aware of the healing powers of "life force energy," adding Reiki Master to my list of ways to help others heal seemed a natural next step. People came to me for answers; each healing modality and metaphysical skill I mastered, better equipped me to help them. Years before, I suffered from excruciating back pain. Unable to walk without screaming, the majority of my day was spent in a wheelchair. During a family reunion in Saskatchewan, a cousin trained in reflexology offered to treat me. With nothing to lose, I agreed to a series of treatments during our weeklong stay.

When I climbed unassisted into the passenger seat of our motorhome, my husband Dwayne beamed. After winking and patting my knee, he loaded my wheelchair into the back. Once home, the chair went into storage and I became a certified reflexologist.

Aware of the exponential power of group prayer and collective psychic intention, I joined a healing circle. Though we rejoiced in numerous healing victories, the most profound and provable happened when the growth of a friend's unborn baby was hindered by the positioning of the umbilical cord. As she was in the hospital and not due to deliver for a few weeks, our healing circle met regularly to send mother and child healing energy as we envisioned her delivering a healthy baby.

Aware of when we were meeting, our friend kept her eye on the baby's heart monitor. Whenever we met, the baby's heartbeat fluctuated wildly. Having prepared her for the worst, when our friend's doctor determined the baby's remarkable improvement, he said, "I'm not sure what happened, but your baby is doing fine." Our friend delivered her miracle baby boy without further complications.

The more I studied and participated in the various metaphysical modalities, the more I understood the umbilical cord between science and religion. My most enlightening lesson happened while I was attending a workshop taught by Harold McCoy in Fayetteville, Arkansas.

It was a warm summer day, and dozens of us were gathered in a small church for contemplative prayer and meditations that would prove the existence of guardian angels. I'm not sure why, but as the teacher explained the process, my old friend skepticism reared its doubting little head. "Not going to happen," my logical-self rationalized as my higher-self argued, "Maybe it will. Keep an open mind."

After explaining that, on his cue, our respective guardian angels would materialize behind us and touch our shoulders, the teacher guided us through a meditation summoning our divine protectors. When the teacher loudly proclaimed, "Now!" I felt gentle pressure from a pair of long-fingered large hands, one on each shoulder. Instantaneously, I was enveloped in absolute unconditional love.

Tears flowing, my heart swelled as a vision appeared in my mind's eye. Nine feet tall, carrying a glistening sword and donning large silvery-white wings, I recognized my guardian as being Archangel Michael. This wasn't our first encounter. He'd made his presence known to me once before during an alarmingly turbulent airplane flight when I was fervently praying that we'd make our destination. Knowing the name of the angel to call upon when in peril, and whom to thank when I survived, warmed me inside and out.

In 2008, while chatting over morning coffee, a psychic friend told me that my husband was coming into a lot of money. Trusting my friend's abilities and word, I said, "Great! His business must be about to pick up." A few weeks later, Dwayne won a substantial lottery!

Knowing that we were meant to do something special with our windfall, after selecting a team of credible seers, we hosted a series of psychic fairs throughout British Columbia. We were well-received in every community. Toward the end of our three-month tour, I fully realized the correlated effects of Grandma's tea leaf reading and traditional church services. It was a realization that both warmed and broke my heart.

People went to church to celebrate, honor and learn more about their beliefs. Through the sermon, they found answers and solace. They left feeling hopeful and reassured that the soul is eternal. That's why they walked taller and appeared peacefully happy after a service.

Our clients shared similar motivations and aspirations. They came for readings in search of solutions to challenges and conundrums. Connecting with loved ones via mediums, shored their hope that life is eternal and that the departed were just a veil away. Through our guidance and knowings, they found answers, solace and hope. That's why our clients also walked taller and appeared peacefully happy after a reading.

What saddened me was that although psychics and mediums provided invaluable earthly and spiritual guidance, the metaphysical sciences were underappreciated and often ridiculed. Apparently, I had another question that needed answering—why?

The birth country of many of my ancestors and steeped in Spiritualist history, Scotland was high on my bucket list of must-visit places. While there, I took a third eye development class at a small church. The two-day course included experiential lessons in a variety of metaphysical modalities. In the aura drawing and analysis class, I learned how to better assist clients with unblocking portions of their energy fields that had become obstructed through trauma or illness.

The "ribbon reading" exercises were fun and enlightening. By reading energy vibrations, we practiced deciphering what the ribbons were trying to convey via a person's choices from a collection that varied in color, material, texture, opacity and length.

The "describing spirits" class heightened my awareness of the minute physical characteristics of those who came to me from the eternal side. During the exercise portion, the room buzzed with excited energy and chatter as we described and then relayed spirit messages, one medium to another. Always eager to provide my clients with as much information and "proof" as possible, I left the workshop feeling elated.

However, it was while visiting Stonehenge in Southern England that I experienced the most memorable event of our trip. Built in stages, the first of which began over 5,000 years ago, Stonehenge has long been a sacred place where Celtic Druids gather to celebrate the solstices. Many times while performing a psychic healing session for a client, an older woman with scraggly gray hair, a hooded and tattered ankle-length dress and worn boots, would appear in my mind's eye. Each time, she materialized from the center of the same Stonehenge monolith and then systematically sprinkled what appeared to be fairy dust among the ruins. Having envisioned her ritualistic sprinkling numerous times, her fairy-dust path was embedded in my mind.

Curious about her and whether my assumption was accurate that she visited me during healing sessions because she wanted to guide and teach me, I found the familiar monolith from which she always appeared and retraced her steps. I was able to feel her potent presence throughout the path, but didn't see her. She never again appeared in my mind's eye. I eventually came to the conclusion that she had passed on her healing powers to me and her job was done.

Several months after we returned from Europe, Dwayne and I visited Chichen Itza on Mexico's Yucatan Peninsula. The energy surrounding the ancient El Castillo pyramid dominating the center of the sacred archeological site was palpable. Walking among the ruins, it was easy to feel why centuries before the Mayas had chosen this site to build a temple to the snake deity Kukulkan.

When viewing some of the pictures we'd taken with our digital camera, I noticed a huge orb in front of a photo of the main temple. Familiar with the opaque circular specters that often appear in digital photographs, I was intrigued. Curious as to what he might say, I showed the photo to a Mayan I had befriended. He claimed that the orb was the spirit of the rain god Chaac who used his lightning ax to strike clouds and produce thunder and rain. My Mayan friend's supposition seemed plausible as Chichen translates into English as "at the mouth of the well."

It was fall 2010. Around the world, some people were already concerned that the long-count Mayan calendar—which spans roughly 5,125 years starting in 3114 B.C—would reach the end of its final cycle on December 21, 2012. After many conversations with the locals, I realized what the doomsayers were missing. At the end of thirteenth and final Bak'tun (cycle), the long-count calendar reset back to day one to mark the beginning of the next 5,125 years. The world wasn't approaching its end, but rather a new beginning. I left Mexico with a deeper appreciation for the Maya's belief in the Cycle of Life and filled with hope that this new beginning would bring the world into a higher vibration of humanitarian consciousness.

An exchange with a border guard triggered my understanding of why the metaphysical sciences are sometimes mocked. I was crossing into Washington State when he noticed the "Tranquil Touch Services – Body, Mind & Spirit" sign on my car. "Do you have any of those with you?" he asked, pointing at the sign. It took me a moment to realize what he meant. His expression serious as he looked at me, I was a bit nervous as I answered, "All of them, I hope."

His comment jarred a memory about how I'd hesitated when I opened my first commercial account and the bank manager asked what kind of business I'd be doing. Fingers crossed that he wouldn't mock me, I said, "Psychic mediumship." He nodded, filled in the appropriate spot on the form and then said, "Great! My wife will likely come to see you." Relieved, I gave him a few business cards.

That was when it struck me that it didn't matter why some people danced to a drum of doubt. Some people didn't believe in God; therefore, it made sense that some people didn't believe in the equally unseen world of metaphysics. My job as a psychic medium was to provide services to those who did believe and sought my help.

Generally at a vulnerable crossroad, each of my clients hung on my every word. What I told them or didn't tell them could forever alter their lives. It was in my early twenties when it dawned on me that tea leaf reading was more than a family parlor game. Telling a young girl that her life would be filled with illness, divorce and death almost derailed my future as a psychic. She was devastated. The crestfallen look on her face was a lesson I never forgot. People sought hope, not despair. My role was to relay the positive and tread gently when forecasting anything potentially disturbing or debilitating.

From my grandmother's materialized predictions onward, I have witnessed phenomena after phenomena, and miracle after miracle. Hundreds of people have sought my guidance, encouragement and support. My purpose is to share my knowings and utilize my healing skills in a way that inspires the hope my clients need to move forward in their lives with confidence and clarity.

In this world is a many faceted and complex universe.
All beings are serving a higher purpose at multiple times.
Life may change, but continues beyond infinity.
The ubiquity of energy brings presence of truth and light.

— Katharine Grace

About Katharine Fahlman

Katharine and her husband live in Surrey, British Columbia. As a wife, mother, grandmother and business woman, she relies on her intuitive abilities to help her make decisions, anticipate situations and connect with people on the eternal side. Posted above her bed is a sign that reads: "Good morning. Know that today you are in good hands. You can relax. Thank you for your trust and understanding." She can be contacted by e-mail at info@heartmindeffect.com. Website: www.tranquiltouchservices.ca

Katherine's chapter in *Heartmind Wisdom Collection #1* is "Bankrupt! What I Learned about Life" and her chapter in *Heartmind Wisdom Collection #2* is "Journey of Courage." The Heartmind Wisdom Collection is available at www.heartmindstore.com and through online bookstores.

A JOURNEY OF FAITH

Robert Johnson

*And we know that all things work together
for good to them that love God, to them who
are called according to his purpose.*

—Romans 8:28

"Are you sure you don't want me to go up with you?" my friend asked as I was about to jump out of his car and go into my oral surgeon's office.

"No, it's okay. The surgeon is just removing a keloid scar and said I have nothing to worry about. My mom will pick me up afterward," I answered, sounding cheerier than I felt.

Saying doctors never knew anything for certain, my dentist had convinced me that like the first growth in my mouth, this one might be cancerous too. I trusted his judgment when he recommended the new growth on my inside right cheek be removed and biopsied.

I was sedated and unconscious during the procedure. As he had promised he would, when I awoke, the surgeon showed me the marble-sized, irregularly-shaped tiny red ball. My heart sank. It looked the same as the growth they'd removed a year earlier. My T-cell lymphoma was back.

I'd been healthy my entire life when my parents said in unison, "You should go to the conference!"

"You're young! You should enjoy yourself while you can," Mom added.

Understanding that "while you can" translated into "before you get married," I smiled. Like me, my mom was likely looking forward to when I would meet a nice girl and settle down to raise a family.

"Yes, Robert," Dad agreed. "Traveling to Thailand is a great opportunity for you. You will be with people around your age and your interests will be similar."

Encouraged by family, friends and members of my church, I decided to take a prolonged vacation and attend the World Youth Conference. A few weeks later, I left for my six-week trip, a Thai/English dictionary tucked in my backpack.

It was an interesting adventure. I met people from all walks of life, including a group of Israelis who had just completed their mandatory military service and were vacationing in Thailand. During the first few weeks, a group of missionaries doing God's work in a small village approached me about teaching English to a class of between twenty and thirty children. I was wary of taking on such a task. However, when they insisted I could do it and convinced me that they really needed my help, I agreed to do it. All of the children eager to learn English, I found teaching them an enjoyable endeavor.

One day, my most attentive student was absent. I asked the program coordinator if she knew why he wasn't in class. When she shared that some of my ten-to-twelve-year-old students had to work until two o'clock in the morning, I was shocked. Apparently, they needed to help their families earn enough money to survive. Although aware that children in some countries made terrific sacrifices to go to school, witnessing what Canadians in my country would view as child labor, my heart ached.

While in Thailand, I had a dream. I saw an all-encompassing white light ahead and heard God say, "Be a missionary." The voice and vision vivid and real enough to wake me, I sat up in bed and blurted, "Me a missionary? I don't think so!" I had no desire to do such a thing. Besides, what skills did I have to be a missionary? I downplayed the significance of my dream, rationalizing that I dreamed about being guided toward becoming a missionary because I was teaching English to young children I truly cared about.

Upon returning to Vancouver, British Columbia, I went to the hospital to visit a friend's father who was dying of cancer. I was surprised and impressed as I watched this man doing his best to cheer up his visitors. Aware that he only had days left, he appeared and sounded happy, not sad. After asking me to come closer, he whispered in my ear, "I think God is asking me to tell you to go to your church and become a missionary." I dismissed the message as hallucinations of a dying man.

When a friend I hadn't seen for a long time shared that she was a missionary working in Vancouver, I decided to spend some time with her and her team to see what being a missionary looked like. I was drawn to their way of life and I decided to pray about the unimaginable possibility of becoming a missionary. Taking the Bible in my hands, I opened it to a random page. It was a passage about Apostle Paul sacrificing himself for Jesus. Unnerved, I decided to try one more time. The passage detailed how Paul had endured terrific hardships for Jesus. Though he had been beaten, imprisoned, and wore raggedy clothes, he stood fast in his belief and service. The picture painted wasn't wonderful. I was overcome by a fear and a silly yet powerful thought, "Lord, I don't want to wear raggedy clothes." In that instant, I heard the Spirit of God say to me, "If you are going to follow me, you'll follow me in good times and bad times." Simultaneously, a feeling of peace came over me and I knew I'd found my calling.

My learning curve as a young missionary was steep. After graduating from Bible school, I was offered a position as an assistant to a pastor. Though drawn toward becoming a medical missionary, the call to be out in the field was strong. I accepted the position and moved to Michigan in the United States. For the next four years, I worked with people in Michigan, Indiana and West Virginia studying the Bible and teaching church members how to share their faith.

In 2010, I accepted an invitation to teach Bible classes in Australia. While there, I studied to become a medical missionary. During my practicum, my team and I went to Fiji where we helped other missionaries tend to the locals on one of the islands. At one village, I met a three-year-old boy who'd injured and couldn't move his arm. His father asked if I could help his son. After assessing him, my instinct was to massage his shoulders and pray over him. At the end of the session, the little boy ran off all smiles to show his family that he could move his arm.

While treating him, I wasn't aware that the boy hadn't been able to do anything with his arm for some time. The whole village came out to meet the miracle missionary, claiming that the love and healing of God had come through me to fix the child's injury. Feeling blessed, I knew in my heart that I was fulfilling God's purpose for me on this earth.

Life was wonderful. I was happy, at peace and thoroughly enjoyed my work. The only thing missing was a loving partner, one who shared my faith and understood the missionary lifestyle. However, moving from country to country, I wasn't in one place long enough to nurture a relationship.

Occasionally, I returned to Vancouver, British Columbia to spend time with my family. While there, my father and I often went for walks together. As we approached our family dentist's office one Thursday afternoon, I decided to go in and say hello. After greeting me with a big smile, the receptionist offered me an appointment that had just become available.

After a bit of chitchat, my dentist examined my mouth. Appearing concerned, he asked, "Rob, how long have you had this lump on the inside of your right cheek?"

"I first noticed it on my way to the Solomon Islands about six months ago," I answered. "When in Australia, I had a doctor there look at it. He said it was most likely a cyst, nothing serious."

"It might be nothing," he agreed, with a partial smile. His tone and expression turning serious, he added, "I still think you should see an oral surgeon while you're here visiting."

Though I thought he was being overly cautious, I went along with him and was booked for a biopsy after the weekend. The oral surgeon removed the lump and sent it to the lab for testing.

Shortly after the surgery, I went back to the United States to continue with my missionary work. While in Houston, I met the president and vice-president of Eden Valley in Colorado, a renowned natural healing center primarily attended by the terminal ill. They invited me, at no cost, to go through their program to further advance my education as a medical missionary. I was excited to be part of this Godly mission to help people conquer terminal illness through faith, healthy eating, exercise, hydrotherapy and massage.

A few days after my arrival at Eden Valley, my oral surgeon called. The biopsy confirmed that I had T-Cell lymphoma. Shocked and with no idea what he was talking about, I started asking questions. Rather than answer me, the oral surgeon said it was best if I consulted with a medical professional at Eden Valley. At his request, I gave him the center's fax number and the name of one of the doctors.

After hanging up, I went numb. It was late in the evening when I met with an Eden Valley doctor. Sitting across from him and staring at his moving lips, my ears strained to listen as my brain struggled to understand. Unable to make sense of most of what he said, after he finished speaking, I asked him to repeat what he'd just said. The doctor attempted a sympathetic smile that didn't manage to find its way across his lips before saying, "Rob, you have an aggressive form of cancer."

My oxygen supply blocked by the lump in my throat, I nodded.

"Most people die within eight months of being diagnosed."

My eyes darted left and right. I could not digest what he was telling me.

"My recommendation is that you cancel your missionary plans. Your goal now is just to stay alive."

"What?!" I asked, certain that the pounding in my chest was distorting my hearing.

"You should call your family, Rob," he said, his demeanor somber. Having delivered my death sentence, he stood up. It was time for me to leave.

Not knowing what else to do, after meeting with him, I did as the doctor suggested and called home and spoke to my sister and my mom. Neither of them knew what to say. We only spoke for a few minutes.

When I finally dragged myself to bed, I fell asleep. However, hours before dawn, I awoke with a start. The initial shock having subsided, reality set in. I was going to die within a year.

Getting out of bed, I reached for my Bible and dropped to my knees. I desperately wanted to pray but didn't know what to say. I randomly flipped the pages of my Bible, landing on Psalm 120:1 — "In my distress I cried unto the Lord and He heard me." Feeling God with me…loving and caring for me…giving me permission to cry, I sobbed and sobbed.

By the time the sun lit the sky bright blue, I realized that by the grace of God, I was in the right place to get the spiritual and medical help I needed. Rather than ministering to others, I would undergo treatment.

After consulting with the Eden Valley medical team, though nervous, I trusted that the prescribed hydrotherapy would successfully energize my immune system, increase my white blood cell count and kill the cancer.

Three or four times per week, I sat in a bathtub as medical professionals raised my body temperature to 102 degrees Fahrenheit for twenty minutes. To prevent brain and cell damage, I was given oxygen and my head kept cool via the steady application of cold wet towels.

Like all patients at the center, I adhered to Dr. Gerson's nutrition proto-col—juicing and raw vegetables only. At my home church, people fasted and prayed for me.

Before my next round of treatment, the Eden Valley doctors suggested I return to Vancouver to rest and visit with loved ones. While at home, I received the results of a PET/CT scan that I'd had in Colorado. There wasn't a single indicator of cancer anywhere in my body. God had healed me. It was a miraculous happening that I eagerly shared with everyone.

Asked to speak to the congregation at my church, I looked forward to thanking them for their prayers and fasting. Standing before dozens of smiling faces, I said, "I think God has healed me. No…God healed me. Praise the Lord!" As I claimed my miracle, I felt the full truth of it from the tip of my toes to the top of my head.

The doctors at Eden Valley said my results were unexpected and extraordinary. On their advice, once back at the center, I resumed hydrotherapy treatments as a precaution. However, I did not need them…I was cured…I was the recipient of a miracle.

After one year of being cancer free, my body had produced a brand new, marble-sized, irregularly-shaped tiny red ball. As I climbed into Mom's car, I wondered how it was possible that my T-cell lymphoma had come back. God had healed me. His command was final. Had I done something that upset Him? I was a good person, ate well and took care of myself. I didn't drink or smoke. I knew lots of people who lived unhealthy lifestyles and they weren't sick. It wasn't fair.

Confused and scared, when we arrived at Mom and Dad's place, I headed for my room and stayed there for the entire day. Between prayers and unending questioning, I stared at the ceiling and wondered whether God had really healed me. And, if He had, why did the cancer come back? During the second day of self-exile, my weathered leather-bound copy of Ellen G. White's book *Education* caught my attention.

A practicing and faithful Adventist, I accepted the author's premise that the ultimate goal of learning is to understand more about our Creator-Redeemer and to reflect that understanding in our personal lives. Perhaps the answer for my resurfaced health predicament was within its pages. Picking it up, I read, "All who in this world render true service to God or man receive a preparatory training in the school of sorrow. The weightier the trust and higher the service, the closer the test and the more severe the discipline. Study the experience of Joseph and Moses, and of Daniel and of David."

Encouraged, I studied the Old Testament. What impressed me most was that everyone endures hardships as part of preparing for their life's work. Equally heartening was that their difficulties inspired each to work unselfishly for good. It was then that I knew—my cancer had returned because God was preparing me for my life's labor. He hadn't sentenced me to die; He was with me.

As soon as possible, I went back to Eden Valley. As if returning from an exciting adventure, I was welcomed with open arms. Shortly thereafter, I resumed my hydrotherapy treatments with the absolute expectation of being cured. A month later, I flew back to Vancouver for follow-up scans and blood tests. The results proved what I already knew in my heart. Once again, I was cancer free.

Though my oncologist repeatedly suggested I have radiation therapy, I didn't. I felt great and was committed to staying healthy. I traveled to a health center in New York and received hydrotherapy and other natural treatments in exchange for working there. Six months after having the second lump removed, while visiting my sister in Houston, I discovered a new lump on the right side of my mouth.

My cancer was back for a third time. Not having given up completely, I traveled to a healing center in Georgia and worked in exchange for receiving natural treatments once again. At the end of the year, I felt healthy but the lump was still there. I decided to take time off and dedicate three months solely to my healing.

The lump still there, I returned to Vancouver. This time I closed the shades to the outside world. No longer a miracle star shining a light on God, I felt that I had failed everyone—my family and friends, the missionaries and health professionals at Eden Valley, the people in my church who'd prayed and fasted, those who'd supported me financially as I trained to become a medical missionary, my dentist, and oncologist. It was a long list.

Stripped of hope and clothed in despair, I realized that I wasn't as emotionally strong as I'd once believed. Accepting my frailties, I allowed myself to be discouraged, angry and disappointed. Questioning God's intentions and methods, for the first time in my life, I almost made a major decision out of *fear* not *faith*—perhaps it was time to give up on natural and spiritual healing and undergo radiation.

Giving up was a foreign concept for me. One way or another, whenever faced with adversity, I'd been able to turn things around and find a positive outcome. However, the lump in my cheek a constant reminder, feeling bested by cancer, I grieved the future I'd never have—no wife, no children, no more missionary work.

For the next few weeks, to numb my gloomy resignation, I watched the basketball playoffs on the television. At the end of another wasted day, I'd feel more depressed. Then, I'd worry that being depressed was bad for my health and that I was making my cancer worse. When there were no more questions to ask, no more tears to cry, I prayed, but God was silent.

Eventually, I came to the conclusion that making no decision was worse than making a wrong decision, and booked an appointment with the oncologist to discuss undergoing radiation treatment.

Concerned about me, my family encouraged me to join them at our church's annual Camp Meeting in Hope, B.C., which I did. Spending time in nature with the sun shining and surrounded by caring people, I felt happier, stronger and hopeful. Praying together, I again felt close to God. For the first time since discovering the new lump, I faithfully awaited a sign from Him as to what my next step should be. If God didn't unveil His plan for me, I'd undergo radiation. A course of action in place, I felt more at peace.

At camp, I met a young missionary from Malaysia. For hours on end, we discussed various medical treatments and my options. Impressed that I'd twice been cured of cancer, he encouraged me to continue with natural, faith-based healing. His positivity infectious, I left camp with a renewed sense of hope.

A few days later, the young missionary called to invite me to a healing center in Malaysia where he worked. I'd undergo treatment in exchange for working as a medical missionary there. The contract was for eight months and began in two weeks. I couldn't believe my ears and almost dropped the phone.

Was this the sign from God to give natural treatments one more chance?

Earlier in the week, I'd received a call from the cancer clinic saying that my appointment had been rescheduled to a later date. Unbelievably, it was rescheduled to the same day I would leave for Malaysia. I took the rescheduling of my appointment as confirmation that I was to take the missionary assignment in Malaysia.

I opened up to a friend one morning while sitting in her backyard. As she listened, she asked questions that allowed me to see my situation in a new light. She also advised that I go to Malaysia and have fun. *Have fun?* No one had ever told me to have fun. Remembering how I had cherished the assignments in Fiji, the Solomon Islands and Australia, my spirits soared. Going to Malaysia to continue my work as a medical missionary was the right decision.

Four years have passed since the doctor at Eden Valley gave me eight months to live. I remain eternally grateful for my first and second miracles, and I am looking forward to the third. In the meantime, I will continue doing God's work.

About Robert Johnson

Robert is from Vancouver, British Columbia. He travels the globe as a medical missionary with the Seventh-day Adventist Church. He has served in many countries including the United States, the Solomon Islands, Australia, Fiji, and most recently in Asia. Robert's most joyful activities are working with youth and teaching others about the Bible. He can be contacted by e-mail at info@heartmindeffect.com.

IN A WHISPER

Julie Duciaume

Why didn't I listen to the whispers warning me? The messages had been strong enough to get my attention. Why hadn't I acted in a way that would protect me, not place me in harm's way?

It had been a long day on campus and I was heading home to study. Although it was early evening, it was already dark. Scrounging through my backpack for loose change, I smiled appreciatively at the coins that would be my bus fare home. Thankfully, I didn't have to endure the forty-minute trek across the Interprovincial Bridge from Ottawa to Hull. Also known as the Alexandra Bridge, crossing it on foot, I would indubitably arrive at my destination covered in frost. It was mid-winter and the temperature was -4°F.

I dreaded the times when I was too broke to take the bus. While walking, the bitterly cold humid air would cause a buildup of frost. Halfway home, miniature icicles would form on the scarf over my nose and mouth and on my eyelashes. If I wore mascara, the frost glued my lashes together. When they thawed out, I looked like a character from the Rocky Horror Picture Show. Living off the proceeds of a meager student loan and on pitiful wages from a part-time shift at a coffee shop, I was ecstatic whenever I found enough change for public transportation.

That night, grateful for a warm bus ride home, I settled into a window seat. The bus was already half full when it pulled up in front of the Department of Justice where a dozen or more civil servants were waiting. One of the first people to come aboard was a man, likely in his mid-twenties. Average looking, the only thing that stood out about him was that he wasn't wearing work attire like everyone else.

A second later, I heard a whisper, "He is going to sit directly behind you." Alarmed, I twisted around to see whether the seat behind me was empty. It was. I watched the man's feet as he walked by and swung himself into the seat behind me. *Why had he chosen that seat when there were plenty of others?*

Leaning my head against the window, I peered out at the dancing snowflakes, noting how brilliant and animated they seemed when we'd pass by a street lamp. Hungry, I contemplated what I'd make for dinner before tackling the text books. After a while, I moved my head away from the window and sat straighter. When I turned to look out the window again, the reflection of the man behind me caught my attention. He was staring at the back of my head. The intensity of his stare unnerved me. Ignoring the sudden shower of creepy shivers that came over me, I looked around the now crowded bus.

I heard a second warning whisper: *He is going to ask you a question.* A split second later, the man tapped me on the shoulder and I turned to face him. Smiling, he politely asked if I knew where a certain bar was located in Hull. I nodded and said, "Of course. It's just down the street from my stop." The second I spoke, I realized my mistake. The man now had a reason to disembark with me.

On high alert, I tried to think. My destination was still a few stops ahead and the bus was now standing-room only. If I disembarked before the man behind me, I'd be able to put some distance between us. I stood and started inching my way through the crowd. When I reached the exit, the man was already there. Worried, I rationalized that I was safe because there were lots of people around. I headed for home, aware that the man was a few steps behind. When we reached the street where he needed to turn left, I faced him and pointing leftward, said, "The bar you asked about is that way." I then turned right.

Unsure whether he'd follow me, I hurried toward my home a few blocks away. I had to cross an empty and poorly lit parking lot to get to the duplex I shared with my cousin. I decided it was safer to circumvent the dark lot instead of cutting across it. Though it would take longer, like a humongous shadow, the lot was the perfect place for an attacker to pounce.

Once on the sidewalk, I sensed that the man was a few feet behind me. I whipped around, arm jutted out, my upturned palm facing him and bellowed, "STOP! Turn around and walk away!"

A mere two feet away, the man froze, obviously stunned.

Suddenly, a tidal wave of calming energy enveloped me. It felt as if an invisible wall of spiritual protection had come between me and my potential assailant.

"I just wanted to ask you to come have a drink with me," the man said.

"No!" I roared. "Turn around and walk the other way!"

"I just..."

I cut him off, pointing behind him as I yelled, "Go away!" Like a wolf abandoning his prey, the man turned and walked away.

Christmas Eve 1994, having rented a car, my boyfriend, Robert, and I left Edmonton, Alberta early in the morning and headed for my sister's place in Nelson, British Columbia. The scenery through the Rocky Mountains was breathtaking. As the passenger and self-declared tour guide, I enjoyed pointing out wildlife and providing historic and geographic commentary. A few hours into our drive, far more tired than I should have been, I asked Robert if it would be okay if I took a short nap. He assured me that he was content with listening to his cassette tape of Dire Straits' album *Communiqué* and encouraged me to nod off.

Tilting the passenger seat all the way back, I laid down and pulled my winter coat over my torso and head. Comfortable, my eyes shielded from the bright sun, I felt a little guilty. I should be keeping Robert company, not sleeping. But I couldn't resist my tiredness or argue with the whisper that said it would be okay for me to nap for a little while.

Within seconds, I was lulled to sleep by the song "Portobello Belle." Deep in dreamland, it felt like I was wrapped in a warm and nurturing cocoon that was far away from the vehicle. I could no longer hear Robert singing along to Dire Straits' music or the hum of the engine. It was as if I was encased in a protective clear bubble as I floated among sporadic white clouds and weaved between mountain peaks.

I woke up with a start. "Portobello Belle" was still playing. Confused, I wondered if I had only been asleep for a minute or whether the cassette was replaying a second time. I also couldn't understand why Robert was freaking out.

"We were just in an accident!" he exclaimed, looking at me as though he couldn't believe that I wasn't upset.

Nonplused, I waited in the car while Robert went to talk with the driver from the other vehicle involved in the collision. Glancing about the interior, I noticed a large dent protruding into the passenger door, exactly where my head had been resting. The point of impact was just shy of where my right ear would have been. Yet, I hadn't heard or felt anything. It was as if I wasn't there when the accident happened.

How was that possible? In my dream, I'd been floating in another realm, a peaceful place where no harm could come to me. Had I actually been temporarily transported to another sphere? If I'd been awake, I would most likely have tensed up at the anticipation of the crash, perhaps sustained injuries. Instead, contrary to my usual habit of staying awake to keep the driver company, I'd given in to my overwhelming desire to sleep and the whisper in my ear that said it would be okay.

Le Château was the first stop on our shopping spree. Spotting a chic pair of turquoise linen-cotton pants with an elastic waistband, I squealed when I found a pair in my size. Nothing satisfied my friends, sisters and me more than a fabulous and unique fashion find. Snatching them off the rack, I hurried to the change room and tried them on. They fit perfectly and were amazingly comfortable. However, as I made my way to the checkout, in my mind's ear I heard, "These pants won't hold up to a swift tug. Maybe you should instead find a pair with a zipper or drawstring." Paying no mind, I exclaimed to the store clerk, "I love these. I'll take them!"

The next day, I wore my modish new pants to school. Fifteen, self-conscious and shy, I blushed through the numerous compliments my classmates made on the color and style of my pants. Like most young teens, although I wanted to stand out and be recognized for my individuality, I wasn't totally comfortable with an onslaught of attention.

As the bilingual high school I attended had only five hundred students, all of us either knew or recognized one another. During lunch in the cafeteria, we'd gather with like-minded peers in areas or at tables that had been previously claimed as belonging to our individual groups. On the day I debuted my turquoise pants, I ordered a hotdog for lunch. While standing at the condiment counter, my back to the crowd, I heard the nearby grade twelve boys cheering and chanting, "Do it! Do it! C'mon, Danny, you can do it!"

Dismissing the importance of their silliness, I concentrated on squeezing mustard onto my hotdog bun. I was reaching for the relish when someone grabbed onto and pulled my pants down to my ankles. Realizing that my underwear had gone down too, I gasped and turned red. My buttocks exposed, the cafeteria fell silent. Mortified, without facing the crowd, I pulled up my clothing and bolted out of the cafeteria.

Desperate to get as far away as possible, I ran out of the school and down the street. Hot tears flooding, I cursed Danny for being cruel and myself for making unwise choices. *Why hadn't I listened to the voice that warned me of this possibility?* Once home, my father demanded to know why I'd left school early. Sobbing, I recounted how the grade twelve boys had egged Danny into pulling my pants down. Infuriated, Dad called the principal. Danny was suspended from school for three days.

Not wanting me to wallow in self-pity, my parents insisted I go to school the very next day. Still mortified, I kept to myself and avoided eye contact with most everyone. Talking with my closest friends, I learned that my being pantsed by Danny was a hot topic with students and faculty staff. I wasn't surprised. However, I was shocked when his cousin stormed up to me and said, "I hope you're happy! You got Danny suspended!" Her insensitivity didn't cut deep; the vast majority of my classmates were supportive and empathetic.

My turquoise pants remained my favorite. With the incident weeks behind me, I decided to again wear them to school. This time, I listened for foreshadowing whispers. There were none.

Having walked nearly a kilometer in Edmonton, Alberta's bitter winter weather, my good friend Coco and I were grateful for the heated glass enclosure in the center of the bus loop at Jasper Place Terminal. Inseparable, we spent almost every weekend having sleepovers at each other's places. We'd just left her house and were headed for mine.

Our bus wasn't due to depart for twenty minutes. To pass the time, we chatted and people watched. Unexpectedly, as one man walked through the terminal doors, an alarm bell sounded for a few seconds. Glancing around, I noted that no one else seemed disturbed by the bells. *Was I the only one who heard them?*

When our bus arrived, Coco and I climbed aboard and headed toward the back. Spotting two vacant bench seats, we sat down. While my good friend was chatting my ear off, I noticed that the seat across from her was occupied by the man who'd walked through the door at the same time that the alarm bell sounded. He looked harmless. Nevertheless, I kept an eye on him.

As the bus left the terminal, the man pulled out a newspaper and began reading. Further convinced that he was harmless, I chatted with

Coco. However, as much as I tried to forget about him, an eerie feeling caused me to occasionally glance his way. The third time I looked his way, I noticed that he was leering at me over the top of his newspaper. His glazed eyes were locked on me as though he were mentally undressing me. I felt violated and scared.

Just then, I noticed that his newspaper seemed to be moving of its own volition and not in sync with the motions of the bus. Lowering the paper so I could see his face, the man flashed me a lascivious grin. It was the creepiest smile I'd ever seen. I was considering what action I should take, when the newspaper pages separated and revealed his dirty secret.

Screeching, "Oh, my God!" I leapt out of my seat and ran toward the bus driver. After explaining what had happened, I asked the driver to kick the man off of the bus. Meanwhile, the man had rung the buzzer and exited the bus. By the time I returned to my seat, Coco had figured out what had happened. She'd seen the man zip up his pants before making his escape.

During the remainder of the ride home, I inwardly chastised myself for dismissing the warning bell. If I hadn't, when I noticed the man sitting across from Coco, I likely would have insisted we change seats. If the man had then followed us, I would have immediately reported his unwanted attention to the driver. Instead, I'd convinced myself that there was nothing to worry about. It was a mistake I vowed never to make again.

Today, I always listen to and heed what I believe are divine whispers and forewarnings from the Universe. Though some people dismiss this spiritual intervention as being mere coincidence or gut instinct, my experiences are too plentiful and vivid to ignore. Not that my invincible teenage-self didn't try to do just that. I often poo-pooed warning signs, erroneously thinking that nothing bad would ever happen to me.

It doesn't matter whether one attributes such pre-emptive whispers as stemming from guardian angels, spirit guides, or intuition. After all, the Latin root of intuition is *tuere*, meaning to guard or protect. For me, intuition is a knowing deep in my heart without proof or intellectually knowing the reason why.

Now that I pay attention, I receive messages in a variety of forms. I still sometimes hear whispers or bells in my mind's ear. Occasionally, the flash of an image or several frames of a movie will appear in my mind's eye. Other times, it's an all-encompassing feeling or inexplicable emotional or physical response that alerts me to danger. Regardless, whenever the Universe intervenes, I pay attention.

In hindsight, there is not one instance where I did not receive a warning message prior to an encounter with danger. In some cases, to my detriment, I failed to recognize or acknowledge the signs or whispers immediately, or not at all. Women are often taught to be polite and attentive to others; however, to remain safe, we must also listen to our higher selves and not brush off a nagging feeling that someone means to do us harm.

Though I was able to finesse my way out of danger, I regret that I never reported the man who stalked me or the exhibitionist on the bus. In my defense, had the police asked me for a description of any of the perpetrators, I would have described each of them as being average height, build and looks. There was nothing that stood out about any of the men other than a feeling that something was "off" about them.

Realizing that left unreported, perpetrators fly under the radar and rarely get caught, I now make a practice of jotting down details when people or incidents give me a funny feeling. Unless there is a good reason to do so, I don't report my observations to the police. However, if needed, I have information that could help capture a crime suspect.

Wanting to help other women, for a time, I volunteered as a support worker with a police sponsored Victim Services program in the greater Vancouver area. I noticed that though many of the women had experienced incidents similar to those I'd encountered, they had reacted in a variety of ways and found various healing mechanisms.

Unfortunately, living in a large metropolis and having been a frequent user of public transit, I've witnessed my fair share of men with an affinity for exposing themselves. After the initial feelings of vulnerability and violation subside, I use humor as a coping mechanism, sometimes joking that I have a neon sign on my forehead that intermittently lights up with "Flash Me!"

Having managed to walk away from each unpleasant situation relatively unscathed, my intuition has become a trusted friend. In her Life Class Lesson 11: Your Life Speaks to You in a Whisper, Oprah Winfrey explains that "If you don't get the whisper, the message gets a bit louder. It becomes a pebble (a problem), then a brick (a crisis), then a wall falling down on you (a full-blown disaster)." Listen to the whispers.

About Julie Duciaume

Julie lives in Surrey, British Columbia with her husband and daughter. Her life is driven by her passion for animals, health, social justice, and human rights issues. Wanting to share the love she lavishes on her own animal companions, Julie volunteers at a local shelter where she cares for small animals and provides adoption counseling. She is a fundraiser for the Surrey, B.C. SPCA. Her favorite pastimes include walking in nature and creating cards. She can be contacted by e-mail at info@heartmindeffect.com.

Julie's chapter in *Heartmind Wisdom Collection #2* is "Tofu, Tears & Tenderness." The Heartmind Wisdom Collection is available at www. heartmindstore.com and through online bookstores.

SCORPION IN MY BED

Maytawee

Chiang Mai is set at the base of majestic jungle mountains and surrounded by sacred temples that date back 500 years and earlier. This *Land of Smiles* is protracted by a moat and ancient stone walls. Its culture naturally moves in a rhythmic flow that, when joined, captures one's tender heart, opening the gateway to unexpected bliss. Day and night, one's senses are awakened by the sweet and sour smells emanating from market flowers and street debris, and by the melodies of monks chanting from the temples. The city's ancient architecture and mystical eye candy provide the perfect ambiance.

It is common in Chiang Mai to be awakened at 4:30 a.m. by neighborhood roosters, the original inventors of the alarm clock. My first morning there, as I abided to their crowing and began to dress, something within me longed to visit the nearby temple. Slipping on a pair of pressed white trousers, my mind's chatter protested, beckoning me to go to bed and stick to the planned agenda for this trip. In response, my conscious-self declared to this mind intruder that, from this moment forward, there would be no more plans.

Watching my torn-up agenda fall into the garbage, piece by piece, I was overcome by an incredible sense of freedom and a sense that I was at the dawn of an experience that held the promise of soothing my soul with peace. My body responded with a rush of playful energy as I swiftly gathered the last of my things, flung them into a knapsack and made my way down the stairs.

As I opened the door, I was immersed in the sweet scent of flowers and warm air. Stepping out onto the sidewalk, I noticed how narrow the path was, fitting for only one person. Recalling Buddha's teachings that "the path to enlightenment is to be taken alone in the here and now," I mused that navigating the irregular footing of red clay bricks, dirt and concrete would be my first lesson. If I slipped, I would likely land in the direct path of oncoming traffic, mere inches away from the curb.

A tuk tuk (a souped-up Thai-style golf cart) zipped past me carrying a well-dressed Thai woman likely on her way to the morning market. A shadow to my left captured my attention and revealed an elderly woman preparing her daily meal in her outdoor kitchen. Youthful and requiring no chairs, she rested her buttocks on the back of her legs. At her side, a tattered dog waited for its morning meal. We greeted each other Thai-style, no words necessary, simply a deep connection through nodding while looking into each other's eyes and sending beams of joy to one another. A burst of gratitude came over me for this brief innocent connection.

As I turned the corner, a temple emerged before me like a mirage in a desert. Its carved and painted pillars of blue and gold perfectly inlayed with one-inch diamond cut mirrors stopped me in my tracks. A "Wow!" crossed my lips. Drawn like a magnet, I entered the building to get closer to the chanting monks. Heeding to the posted sign, I slipped off my shoes and added them to the array of footwear piled outside the door. Amused by the petite slippers surrounding my seemingly large Birkenstocks, I was reminded that I am considered big in Thailand, unlike at home where I am the one labeled petite.

I began my ascent up the stairs and felt shivers run up and down my spine as the monks' chant filled my ears. Small beads of sweat gathered at the base of my neck before finding a pathway down my back and coming to rest in a puddle at the curve of my spine. I accepted this as a metaphor for the flow that I wanted to experience in my life.

The white marble floor felt cool on my feet, a nice contrast to the thick tropical air. Entering, I couldn't deny the profound power that the thirty-foot golden Buddha commanded as it cast a gaze over the group of people seeking and observing continual teachings of humility. I bowed in reverence.

The rows of orange robed monks chanting bass-tone prayers appeared like a surreal movie scene. A voice within told me that I'd been here before, yet my mind argued with the impossibility. The smells, sounds and ambiance all felt oddly familiar. I'd never thought about whether karma was real or not, but in this moment, I had a deep sense that I was experiencing a karmic connection of some sort. It was confusing. Everything that was happening I'd experienced before, but at separate times. Tears welled in my eyes as my hands simultaneously moved into a prayer position, allowing me to merge with the sacred sounds.

A soft voice at my ear pulled me back into the present as I heard myself being invited for tea. Opening my eyes, a young monk's face came into focus. Smiling, he gestured with his hand toward the garden. Nodding, I replied, "Yes, thank you. *Ka*," voicing an acknowledgement in Thai. At the exit of the temple hall, my sandals were placed perfectly at the door for me to easily slip into. *What a kind and thoughtful gesture of honor.*

Entering the garden, the scent of Jasmine embraced me as I wondered what would be the tea protocol. I clearly understood that no woman could touch, hug or shake a monk's hand. A little nervous, I acknowledged that my Western tactile ways would not work in this culture. A smiling monk offered me a cup of lemongrass tea from a silver tray, a perfect complement to the Jasmine aroma.

Tall in comparison to the others and wearing white trousers, I stood out like a beacon. To my relief, I noticed an empty chair and took a seat in an attempt to blend in. A few shy monks walked past, unsure of how to approach me, just as I was unsure about how to act around them. Our mutual nervousness was as real as the humidity surrounding us.

To my left, a young monk approached, smiling as he asked in broken English, "Do you know of the Buddha's Dharma?" I returned his smile, relieved and grateful that someone was talking to me. "Ka." His eyes met mine as I continued, "What I know is that nature is the dharma. We are part of it, connected to all things." The wide-eyed surprise of my new monk friend, followed by a few Thai words, brought on a throng of orange robes. Beaming smiles and sparkling brown eyes encased me and filled the space around me with joy.

A young monk at my feet, about ten years old, asked, "Do you know of Karma and living in non-suffering?" I took a deep breath to allow the answers from my heart to come forth. In respect for the arising stillness, not a word was spoken. A reflection of my personal studies with Eckhart Tolle and Mooji began to surface. "Yes, when we rest fully in the moment, we are gifted with what life is presenting to us now. This gift is unique to us, given only in this moment. This is why we cannot judge anything. For it is what it is. In this acceptance, we are set free from suffering, even if emotional or physical pain is present. By not adding any mind or *monkey* mind to this moment, we are meeting it with pure love. From this space we can overcome all things and suffering is no more."

As I spoke, I noticed an elderly monk making his way over to our group. Aware that his eyes were fixed on me and that he was following every word I said, I spoke slowly, making sure I was genuinely expressing what I knew to be true. Again, there was silence for a brief moment before the elderly monk spoke to me in a powerful tone, "You have been here before and taught all these monks in another lifetime as a monk yourself. Now you are meeting karma with karma." Then, for an hour or more, we all sat together in stillness. No words necessary. Reconnecting through our hearts.

The next morning, I heard Fah, my new monk friend, calling from outside my bamboo hut. "Maytawee, come now. We must go now!"

Looking through the cracks of the bamboo wall, I spotted him in the garden below, moving around like a feather in the wind. "Maytawee you are invited to come and meet Master Monk. He lives in the jungle temple. He is a revered monk and only accepts people at his temple that have had karma with him. This is a great honor. Come now and bring an overnight knapsack."

I yelled back, "What? What are you talking about?"

Fah repeated, "Come now. We must go now."

I jumped to my feet, gathered a few things and rushed to acquiesce his request. My initial thought, "This is crazy!" was followed by, "Just accept each moment as it comes and allow this auspicious journey to unfold."

Fah waited for me next to his typical-Thai-car ordained with dents, one bumper and two pieces of wood holding up the front seat. Safety belts were nonexistent. Settled in our seats, we both placed our hands on the dash, laughing and sending a prayer that the car would start again. Amen. Our mutual prayer was answered as it revved up on the first try.

We didn't talk much as Fah maneuvered his way through traffic. From time to time, I gazed in the side mirror, watching the moated city of Chiang Mai slowly disappear behind us. Fah's voice pulled me back from my inner-ponderings as he began to tell me about the eighty-two-year-old monk we were about to meet. Master Monk had never before invited a foreigner to stay at the temple.

I felt an uneasiness in the pit of my stomach and uncertain that I wanted to be the first foreigner accepted to stay at the temple. Promptly, my mind slipped into "what if" thinking. *What if I got sick? No one speaks English. What if something happened to me in the middle of the jungle?* After a few additional fearful ponderings, realizing that I was probably freaking myself out unnecessarily, I took a deep breath and decided to concentrate on the beautiful scenery around me. My gaze and thoughts turned toward the rows of rice fields, the roaming water buffaloes and Thailand's beautiful sky. I was blessed to be on this adventure, trusted that it would unfold perfectly.

After several hours of driving and light conversation, Fah pulled off the highway onto a red dirt road. We were immediately in the jungle. The thick dense air hung off of the vines that brushed the car as we passed, their collected dew dripping onto the road. The exotic sounds of birds greeted us. It was as if we had departed from our world through a vapor barrier into a place where time stood still.

As if not to disturb the stillness, Fah whispered, "The temple languages are Pali and Thai. Pali is the original language of Buddha. There is little to no English spoken here, but you will do fine."

Returning his whisper, I asked, "Are you sure I will do fine?"

He patted my hand as if saying, "Quiet now."

A surge of fear ran through my body. Trying to reassure myself with the thought that I was only a call away from help, I frantically looked for my cell phone. *What have I gotten myself into?* Staring at my phone, I heard myself call out, "There is no reception!"

Fah smiled. "Yes, isn't that great! There is no running water or electricity either."

In an instant, the fear inside me increased to the point where it became all-consuming, like a pestering mosquito that I couldn't swat away. While doing my best to breathe calmly and orient back to trust, it crossed my mind that if I'd only followed my original plan, I would not be in this situation.

After several more turns, we entered a large cleared area. Three women dressed in white welcomed us. Their smiles emanated a tender love that quickly washed away all my fears. An oval-faced woman with deep brown eyes opened my car door. Introduced as Noot, her tender gestures warmed my heart; her loving kindness reminded me of Buddha's core teachings.

Stepping out of the car, my eyes wandered to the temple nestled on the riverbed of the mountain valley. Bamboo bridges provided a pathway to the main hall. Similar to my experience upon entering the Chiang Mai temple, I was overcome by a feeling that I'd been there before.

Noot took my hand to guide me across a bridge. As we touched, deep down, I knew that she was a sister from lifetimes ago. Overcome with emotion, I looked at her. Her knowing expression told me that she felt the connection too.

Entering the main hall, I noticed that the Buddha statue was much smaller than the one in Chiang Mai. Buddha's eyes were softer, more dreamy and meditative. As we passed by, one-by-one, we bowed to Buddha. Glancing just ahead, I noted the elephants carved into a beautiful teak door. Awed, my body inched closer as I felt my curiosity bubble up. *What was waiting for us behind the door?*

Noot opened the door and I stepped inside. It took a moment for my eyes to adjust to the bright light. To my surprise, there were no walls, only a woven bamboo roof for protection from the sun and jungle rains. At the far end, facing east like Buddha, was a large chaise lounge adorned with many colorful pillows and gifts. We were each invited to sit on one of the handmade Hill Tribe pillows on the floor.

Not sure why we were bowing at the chaise lounge, my eyes were drawn to look closer. A man dressed in an earth-toned robe sat in the middle of the pillow fest. An inner-smile flushed through me at the sight of this slight man with a round face and eyes that resembled the charming extraterrestrial character in the movie *E.T.* Speaking in Thai, Noot addressed him as Master Monk.

Fascinated and seemingly suspended in time, I was unable to move an inch as I waited for our personal connection. His globe-like head turned my way. We locked eyes and met through the windows to our souls. My body filled with a joyful madness I'd never before experienced. I felt crazy and happy, and did not want the sensation or moment to end. In an instant, he looked away, taking with him my new emotional drug. I wanted to run away; yet, at the same time I felt complete, even blissful. Tears emerged as I looked for more interaction with him.

An hour passed without further connection with Master Monk. At peace to sit in his presence, I closed my eyes, dropping deep within and allowing the jungle ambiance to sweep me away. At one point, Noot placed her hand on my arm. A while later, when I slowly opened my eyes, Master Monk asked me, "What is your day of birth?" Coming out of my blissful state, it took me a moment to ponder this earthly fact. Unable to recall which day of the week I was born, I shrugged my shoulders. Noot answered in Thai, and a younger monk interpreted what she had said, "Sunday." Master Monk smiled and said, "Good." A few moments later, Noot guided me out of the room. (I later learned that in Thailand there is a Buddha posture for each day of the week. The day one is born is one's Buddha day and corresponding personal birth Buddha.)

In an adjacent room, Noot and I stood in front of a large teak armoire. Like the door I'd admired earlier, it was beautifully carved. She opened the armoire doors, exposing rows of perfectly folded white clothing. As Noot began selecting articles and placing them against my body, I felt like one of the paper dolls I'd played with as a child. Aware that most of the clothes were too small for me, I chuckled. In a playful tone, Noot whispered, "Chang." She had good-naturedly called me elephant. Only five-feet-four-inches tall, I wondered if I'd ever get used to being viewed as a giant. Nevertheless, I was honored to be seen by her.

Once Noot was satisfied that she'd found my correct size, we headed toward the hillside where several small huts were located. As we passed a beautiful Buddha statue, we bowed in unison, our hands folded as a symbol of the surrender of one's self and the desire to benefit all beings. Pointing to the top hut, Noot said, "Bann," meaning small house. I surmised that this was the area where the monk-nuns stayed.

As we made our way up the hillside, noticing that it took Noot two steps for every one of mine, I smiled. *Was this how tall people in North America felt when walking next to me?* What a strange sense of power.

As I entered my bann, out of nowhere, my mind decided to remind me that no one at the temple spoke English, which quickly escalated into a series of thoughts. *What if I get sick? Is the water here from the river? That can't be safe. What have I done? I could die here. There are no phones, no connection to the outside world. This is madness.*

All the bliss I'd experienced a minute earlier evaporated into the thick jungle air. I began to sweat as my eyes rapidly darted around my little hut looking for some type of safe feeling or assurance. My chattering brain, or my *monkey mind* as the Buddhists call it, intensified, yelling, "Maytawee, what have you done?!"

Unable to catch my breath, I turned to Noot. Seemingly aware that I was frightened, she flashed me an assuring smile. Stepping onto the porch, she bowed and said, "Sawasdee Ka, Kuhn Maytawee." I recognized what she had said as being the term used in respectful goodbyes and greetings. Though I did not want her to go just yet, I returned the bow.

Standing on my tiny porch, I watched Noot depart. Encouraging myself to take a few deep breaths, my body started to relax. Not sure what to do next, I turned my attention to my new home. It was a four-foot-by-six-foot room with a dirt floor. There was a small side table about twelve inches from the ground and a matching chair. Spotting a rolled-up bamboo mat, I assumed it was my bed. There were also two wool blankets, a tin cup and a spoon. Definitely not the Taj Mahal experience I longed for at that moment.

Along the front and right sides of my new abode were two small windows about the size of a Kleenex box. The screens were old and ripped, the holes large enough for any size of bug to enter. Located between my hut and my neighbor's hut, I discovered something that was clearly meant to be the bathroom. It was anything but inviting. A hole in the floor served as the toilet. A scoop and a large blue plastic bucket filled with what appeared to be river water served as a shower.

I began to unpack by placing my toothbrush in the tin cup. To my surprise, I heard myself sigh as I thought, "Okay, this is home now." Though I knew it would be a wasted effort, I pulled out my cell phone, compelled to check for coverage. No reception bars. I turned off the power for good, and made a conscious decision to embrace the moment. Accepting that everything that was known and familiar was behind me, at least for a while, I committed to immersing myself in my new world; especially, if it meant that I'd enjoy more bliss and peace being with Master Monk.

The white robe Noot had gifted me caught my attention. One by one, I took off my colorful worldly clothes. A profound knowing came over me: What was...was and will be no more. The white robe represented a clean slate for me. I tenderly glided my hands over it. Touching my robe connected me with a deep yearning to dedicate myself in sacred service to God. My journey toward becoming a monk-nun had begun.

A while later, the tea bell emanating from the temple hall rang, and was followed by a gong sound that traveled across the huts and trees, blessing the jungle. I stepped out onto my porch to witness the flow of orange and white robes joining together. The beautiful sight touched me. There was so much love and dedication all held lovingly in this temple container amidst the vast jungle. I made my way down the hill to join them.

Little words in Thai were shared while a monk-nun handed me a cup of tea. As I learned to settle into my new routine of sitting and observing, the warm tea provided me with the perfect ending to my day of new beginnings. The temple courtyard looked magical in the evening's light as massive leaf shadows danced above us, brushing away the day. I was at peace.

Weeks passed and turned into months. Energy spent in my early days worrying about my discomfort was redirected toward learning and living the teachings, transforming my mind and body to experience freedom. Master Monk said that I'd been a monk side-by-side with him numerous lifetimes before and had come back to complete my training. Other monks concurred. Given how at home I felt in such an unusual and unfamiliar place, I accepted this belief.

Some monks thought I'd depart within a few days of my arrival since no Westerner had ever been there before, let alone lived a jungle monk's life. Through Master Monk, I shared with them how I'd felt like leaving several times, but that something greater than me required me to remain in the teachings at Buddha's feet.

During my stay at the temple, every moment was spent in service to Buddha, God and Spirit, living in the seeking and understanding of truth. Daily meditation practices began at four a.m. While sitting still at Buddha's feet, in Master Monk's presence we chanted sacred prayers. One of Buddha's teachings is to overcome the body, realizing we are not the body, but something greater, so we sat for hours on a cold stone floor in one position. At seven-thirty a.m., we separated to shower. The cool river water from my blue plastic bucket continued to bring up my longing for hot water. Learning to move our attention from pain to peace—as we accept what is—was another body teaching. At 11:30 a.m. when the gong rang, it was time to depart and seek our one meal for the day.

Trusting that God provided, we ate only what the local villagers offered. If they offered rice, we ate rice. Should no offers be made, we would not eat that day. With the exception of one day early in my lesson of faith in the great provider, I was amazed at the abundance of food offered.

Much of our day was spent in study and reflection. Occasionally, I met with Master Monk for new lessons and insights. In the afternoon, we either rested or practiced slow-walking meditation, allowing the body to absorb the finite shifts and changes that spirit invokes. I was often assigned to sweep the temple floor as a meditation. Everything we did was a meditation.

Each day, we also made personal offerings to Buddha, the monks, and the Buddha within. My favorite offering was the flower ceremony where we gathered lotus flowers and gently bended each petal into prayers of glory, thus awakening a continual flow of gratitude, love and kindness, the core teaching of Buddha.

After five months of living at the temple, I chose to take an oath of silence. One prepares to live in silence by taking an afternoon rest. As I took the steps up to my hut, I felt an incredible amount of energy surrounding me as though someone was with me. When I arrived in my room, my mind was prepared to rest in a full REM state. Kneeling down on my cotton mat, I pulled back the covers and readied to crawl under them. Just as I was about to settle into the bed, something caught my eye and I jumped to my feet. As my eyes focused, I spotted a black jungle scorpion circling in the center of my mat!

A curdling scream bellowed out of me and echoed through the temple as the kitchen clangs ceased. I raced outside onto my porch and started yelling, "I have a scorpion in my bed. Please, come help. Help, please!" I looked down at the temple grounds, expecting everyone to come running in response to my call. There was no reaction at all. Enraged that not even one person was moving, I called out again, "Please, come help me." No response.

Fear and anger filled my body while my reasoning mind remembered that no one understood English. I jumped up and down, waved my arms and yelled in a high-pitched tone, a clear sign in my culture to come to a person in need. Still, there was not a single response from a monk or temple helper. I was so confused that for a moment I forgot why I was yelling.

According to Buddhist beliefs, death is not the issue, it is the attachment to the monkey mind that is a problem. The monks watching me jumping up and down and yelling, likely assumed that I was experiencing monkey mind. With no need to respond, they continued their practice. I was full of fear and maddened. *How could not one person come? Didn't they care about me? I was in danger. I had a killer beast in my bed!*

Sweating from fear, I ran toward the hillside and down the steps toward Master Monk's chambers. Passing Buddha with only one bow, my mind reasoned that since I was in crisis, he wouldn't mind that I didn't properly acknowledge him. I burst through the carved door, my eyes fixed on the chaise lounge as I looked for Master Monk in his pillow garden. Hastily finding and sitting on my pillow on the cool stone floor, I bowed to my leader in acknowledgment and said, "Sawadee ka, Master ka." Remaining in my humble bow, I felt the shortness of my breath, the pounding of my heart, and the beads of sweat that dripped off my forehead onto the stone floor.

Master Monk popped his head out of the colorful pillow fest and beheld me with his deep brown eyes, sending me a look of tender love and kindness.

My body relaxed a bit. It took me a few moments to adjust and bring my focus back to the reason why I was at his feet in the first place. When fully present, I exclaimed, "There is a scorpion in my bed. It's black and right in the center. I am preparing to take the oath of silence and must rest. Please, can you send someone to help me?"

Master Monk sat back, took a breath and closed his eyes. I knew he'd have the perfect answer and find the right person to help me. Waiting, looking at this little man in meditation, it occurred to me that I didn't know his age. His wisdom seemed very old and his body looked young. My mind drifted off into a story speculating about his age.

When Master Monk opened his eyes and leaned forward, I responded by leaning toward him. Feeling safe and at peace, I awaited his wise words.

Talking slowly, he said, "Out of two hundred monks in this whole temple, your bed is the only bed that has a scorpion in it."

I felt my face contract into a questioning expression. *What?*

Master Monk continued, "We have karma with everything, good and bad. No one at this temple at this time has karma with a scorpion as you do."

Feeling fear slowly creep back into my body, I pointed out that the situation was dangerous.

His response was, "If you feel the relationship with this scorpion is bad, then you have the karmic gift to find out why."

Did he just send me back into the den of the killer? Is he insane? Does he even realize that my Western body could very well die if bitten by this beast? Does he not fear that if I did die here, the temple could have a lot of problems? I was shocked, frozen and confused. Master Monk's face and posture were completely relaxed. None of what concerned me was of concern to him.

When I didn't leave, he said, "Now, dear one, go find out what karma you have with this scorpion." Smiling, he fell back into meditation.

Humbled, I departed slowly. Something within me chose to trust Master Monk and follow his guidance. Walking back to my hut, I felt as if all eyes were on me. Ascending the stairs, I envisioned the scorpion waiting for me, ready to start war. I began to prepare myself mentally. Since the scorpion had its natural weapon, I too must find one.

Assuming that a monastery must have some object that would make a good weapon, I glanced about and spotted a straw broom. *This will do the job!* While testing its strength, I realized that the flimsy broom wouldn't even kill an ant. Nonetheless, I determined that combined with my Scottish warrior grip, it would have to get the job done.

I stepped on my porch, fully convinced that this beast would kill me unless, as a life-saving measure, I killed it first. Undoubtedly, a jungle scorpion's bite would be deadly. I lifted my broom, ready to attack.

Suddenly, my heart began to race and a strange sensation started coming over me. I felt forced to stop and take a breath. As I did, I became aware that my agitated body began to slow down. The warrior cry faded away, revealing a profound realization as my attention dropped within. My body began to shake, not with fear, but rather as if trying to shake off something, like a duck shakes water off its back. Tears flowed as my mind frantically tried to understand.

I sank to the ground as my inner-voice proclaimed my madness for choosing to be a killer. Without loving forethought, I had jumped into warrior mode, ready to destroy my enemy. But, who was the real enemy? Clearly my killing thoughts were not from loving compassion, which Buddha says we are. It became clear to me that the enemy in this situation presented itself as the judging fearful ego, the one that constantly lives in the past and future, presenting fear and desires as the only reality.

What was this scorpion to me? Why was it in my bed? Something within me declared this was a good day to die; a perfect day to die by letting go of my fearful ego so that I could truly see what I was looking at with fresh new eyes. From my core I gathered the courage to open my heart and look—not with my mind, but with loving compassion. With a conscious breath, I stood up and stepped forward into the doorway of my hut.

A heard a voice from within: *You are it and it is you. There is no separation.* Looking at the center of my bed, I noted that the scorpion's tail was flat, indicating it was at rest. This beast was not readied for war. Like me, my bedmate was looking for a dark warm place to rest. It had no interest in a fight. Out of all the temple monks' beds, my cozy bed was the one that most attracted this creature of God.

Tears of tenderness began to stream down my face as I looked with childlike eyes at its black indigo shell with hues of purple. The beauty of this creature touching me deeply, as I fell to my knees in gratitude. An abundance of love flooded every cell of my being. So much love, I lay on the floor giving thanks for this connection, for this love free from the mind and fear of death. At peace, I happily gave the scorpion my bed. In that very moment, he made his way home out of the window.

As I awakened to the sounds of the evening tea bell, I noticed the world looked new. Colors, smells, even how I felt in this body was somehow softer. Since my experience of unconditional love, my interest in the outer world diminished and my attention was now directed within. Resting in Buddha consciousness, my bliss was captured in every breath.

Entering the tea hall, Master Monk signaled me. I was humbled to sit at his feet. He placed his hand on the table and then lifted it, leaving behind a Buddha necklace. His words brushed over me softly, "You have been a monk many lifetimes and will complete the lessons of monkhood in this lifetime. You will have learned to live in non-suffering, experiencing deep peace." Pointing to the necklace, he continued, "This necklace will protect you as you will be of great service to others." He placed the triangle Buddha necklace over my head. That day of learning my life lesson was now complete.

I had received one of my greatest blessings. My monk journey would continue. In gratitude, I offered a prayer to Master Monk. *"I am a light that reflects all things. I am God's magnificent masquerade. I am earth, wind and fire; here by the grace of air, I enter my soul. We meet in the sweet fragrance of our souls' perfume. Filled with love to be blessed with every breath taken. I am you – you are me."*

We are here to cross paths while on our individual and unique monk's journey. This is why you are reading this. This is you in me and me in you—forever lasting love. Maytawee

About Maytawee

Maytawee lives in Kelowna, British Columbia. She is an ordained Buddhist Monk-nun, a minister of divinity and sought-after keynote speaker and writer. With a focus on The Buddha Within, her workshops include: Fast Track Energy Release, Ajna Light Brainwave Healing and Mandala Sacred Dance Movement. She can be contacted by e-mail at info@heartmindeffect.com or via her website: www.maytawee.ca.

HEALING
FROM LOSS

ADMISSION OF GUILT

Sudipta (Keya) Banerjee

Guilt startled me awake. After twenty-eight years, I still couldn't forget what I had done or forgive myself. Remorse and regret permeated my nightmares, haunted me during quiet times and stole every beat of peace from my heart. I had failed my friend, made a terrible mistake. *How long would I have to bear the cross?*

Bishu and I settled happily into married life. We both had jobs and lived in a spacious house in our hometown of Kolkata. As was the custom in our Indian culture, after Bishu's father passed away, his mother came to live with us. All of us eager to hear the pitter-patter of tiny feet running across the tile floors, shortly after our fifth wedding anniversary, I greeted Bishu at the door and gave him the wonderful news.

"Bishu! Our wishes are coming true!" I said, all smiles.

"Really? Are you certain? How blessed we are! This is a time for celebration."

Bishu, my mother-in-law and I got busy preparing the nursery. It was a fun time. The house was full of love, anticipation and laughter. Bishu and I were so happy. Luckily, I personally blossomed during the pregnancy and was able to work until the last minute.

Finally, our daughter Gina was born. She was perfect. As I watched my husband hold and look adoringly at our tiny miracle from God, all memories of my painful labor vanished. Now we were a complete family.

Anxious about what had been on my mind for a while, reaching for his hand, I said, "We have to think about what's going to happen when I go back to work, Bishu. I only get three months maternity leave. Who's going to take care of our baby? I don't feel right leaving your mother with all the responsibility. After all, she's already brought up her own children."

"Don't worry, Keya. We'll figure it out. Let's get you and our baby home. I am sure a solution will present itself."

After my husband left the room, I was approached by one of the hospital workers. "Excuse me, ma'am," she said. "I didn't mean to eavesdrop, but I heard you say that you are looking for an aya to take care of your precious little baby and help around the house. Would it be too forward of me to offer you my young daughter's services? She would make a perfect aya. She loves babies, is eager to please and needs a job."

We agreed that her daughter would come to visit me after the baby and I were settled at home.

A few days later, when the woman's daughter presented herself at our front door, she smiled shyly as she said, "Hello. I am Laxmi."

"Yes, your mother sent word that you were coming today. Please come in."

She followed me into the sitting area and waited for me to invite her to sit down. Pleased by her good manners, I said, "Tell me a little about yourself."

Laxmi went into an animated discourse about her capabilities with babies. She was fourteen years old. The eldest among her siblings, she took care of them and their dwelling while her mother worked. Her duties had changed and she now needed to earn some money to contribute to her family's income.

I took an instant liking to her. She seemed innocent, sweet and lovely. She was dark complexioned, and unusual for an Indian female, she had curly hair which made her attractive in a special way. I asked her about her schooling and she said she attended classes Monday to Friday from 4 p.m. to 7 p.m. This worked perfectly with my teaching schedule. I'd be home just in time for Laxmi to leave for school. I couldn't have hoped for a better arrangement. We agreed that she would move in with us and start work immediately.

Nice and early the next morning, Laxmi presented herself at our door, eager to begin her duties. Unfortunately, my mother-in-law refused to allow Laxmi near the baby. There was no reasoning with her. She put her foot down, saying that she was Gina's grandmother and would take care of her.

Undeterred, Laxmi did the household work and made herself useful any way she could. She became indispensable to my mother-in-law, heeding her every wish. Vibrant, energetic and always smiling and complying, she was a joy to have around.

Laxmi was like a little sister to me. While on maternity leave, I took her under my wing, often tutoring her in the evening when she came home from school. She held her own in languages, history and geography. However, she was a lost cause when it came to mathematics. As soon as it was time to work on her math homework, she'd disappear or make up a thousand excuses for why she couldn't sit down with me. Knowing I was a caffeine addict, as a distraction, she'd sometimes ply me with cup after cup of coffee.

My wish was for her to graduate from high school. But no matter how hard I tried to get her to study, she simply wasn't interested in school. When I went back to work, things got busier and staying on top of Laxmi's school work slid to the back burner. When she didn't finish her schooling, I felt responsible. I had failed miserably as a tutor.

Time flew by and we were soon celebrating Gina's fourth birthday. Now eighteen, Laxmi seemed content to take care of our family and never talked about her own future. As I cared about her, it bothered me that she didn't seem interested in dating or marriage.

Bishu's hard work earned him a promotion in the New Delhi office of the company where he worked. I was not happy about moving to such a big city. Nevertheless, Gina and I would go wherever Bishu took us. As we packed our belongings and said farewell to family and friends, I wondered about whether we should take Laxmi with us.

When she heard that we were moving, Laxmi's mother came to talk with me about her daughter's future. She said that it was time for Laxmi to find a husband and that it would be best if she moved back home. Agreeing with her, the decision was made not to take Laxmi to New Delhi.

As soon as her mother left, Laxmi dissolved into tears and begged me to take her with us. She insisted she wasn't interested in marriage and that her place was with our family. Confused about why she did not want a husband, or even a boyfriend, I questioned her about it several times. She was adamant that she would never marry. In the end, I decided to take her to Delhi.

Secretly, I was relieved she was moving with us. The more she took over the household chores, the lazier I became. The best helper anyone could have, I had become totally dependent on her.

Settled in New Delhi, with my husband, daughter, mother-in-law and Laxmi, the next two years were happy and hectic. Bishu excelled at his job and sometimes traveled for business. I found work with the Delhi schoolboard. Gina started kindergarten and was glad to make new friends her age. Without hesitation and always with a smile, Laxmi continued to look after our family and the house. My mother-in-law continued to interfere in everything.

Laxmi and I enjoyed each other's company. Before making dinner we often chatted over a cup of Chai tea. Once it cooled down, many evenings we took Gina for walks. On weekends, we shopped together.

After we'd been in New Delhi for two years, Bishu extended one of his business trips and went to visit his sister's family who lived nearby. While there, his sister approached him about taking his niece home with him so she could spend time in the big city. As Minu had recently finished her master's degree, her mother felt it would be good for her to expand her horizons. Bishu eagerly agreed. Having Minu in our home would be fun for her and us.

We welcomed her into our home with open arms. Within a short while, Minu found a job and made new friends. Enjoying her new life fully, it became apparent that she had no intention of returning to her parents' home. Not pleased, I questioned Bishu, saying that I never thought we were offering her a permanent home. Poor Bishu. He didn't know what to say. In India, it's natural for extended family to live together. Realizing there was not much either of us could do, I resigned myself to having Minu live with us for however long she wished.

One morning over breakfast, my mother-in-law said, ""Keya, we need to talk."

Nothing good could come out of this. "Yes, Mother."

"Now that Minu is living with us, things must change. You have always been too friendly with Laxmi. She has become your companion. This is not correct. She is only the maid. Minu is your niece and should be your companion, not Laxmi."

"But, Mother, Laxmi is family," I rationalized. "She has been with us for years."

Shaking her head, my mother-in-law insisted, "Laxmi is the maid, not family. Minu is the one who should go everywhere with you."

I let the subject drop. There was never anything to be gained from arguing with my mother-in-law; especially, now that Bishu was never home long enough to witness what was going on. He'd started his own consulting business and was away from the house more and more. When I tried to talk to him about it, he listened for a while before saying that he was too busy to deal with this kind of petty family problem.

Laxmi resented it when I started asking my niece to do things with me. Obviously hurt, her sunny disposition turned stormy. She challenged what she saw as my decision to set her to the side after all the years of us being buddies. I did not know what to do. Laxmi was right that the new arrangement wasn't fair, but I couldn't tell her so without starting a war with my mother-in-law. I felt guilty and powerless.

Minu wasn't an angel. She discredited Laxmi whenever she could. When there was an altercation between the two young women, Minu always came out the winner in her grandmother's eyes. In the end, the situation worsened to such a degree that my mother-in-law decided to send Laxmi back to her home town of Kolkata.

When I told her, Laxmi started crying and begged me to let her stay. Feeling guilty and sorry for her, I tried to reason with my mother-in-law. But the animosity between Laxmi and Minu did not go away. Poor Laxmi had to suffer. My mother-in-law demanded that I personally escort her back to Kolkata where she belonged.

A few days later, Laxmi and I took the train to Kolkata. She refused to talk to me and I didn't know what to say to her. Both of us miserable, we sat in silence for the entire trip. Mindlessly watching the scenery pass by, guilt churned in my stomach as sadness filled my heart. My time with Laxmi was over.

Her mother came to greet us at the train station. As they were walking away, Laxmi turned, her brown eyes filled with sorrow as she gave me a look that said, "I thought you were a fair person, how come you did this to me?"

Within weeks of taking Laxmi back to Kolkata, my family started to crumble. Minu got married and moved out. A few months later, my mother-in-law had a stroke and died. Shortly thereafter, Bishu was diagnosed with pancreatic cancer. Night and day, I stayed by my wonderful husband's side until he died one year later.

My family disintegrated into ruins, I wondered if it was my fault. If I'd had the courage to stand up to my mother-in-law, would things have turned out differently? If I hadn't been heartlessly unfair to Laxmi, would we all still be living as a big happy family?

Lonely, lost and grief-stricken after Bishu passed away, I was uncertain about what to do. When Gina was nine, having promised my husband that I'd make certain his daughter had the best life possible, I decided to move to Canada. In 1991, I visited my mother and family in Kolkata. While there, I went to Laxmi's house.

Her mother was friendly. Laxmi came out of the house but wouldn't look at me. She just stood there, without saying a single word. Saddened that Laxmi had not forgiven me, I didn't go back to see her. But I did continue to visit her in my nightmares.

Her sorrowful brown eyes haunted my sleep, always relaying the same guilt-niggling question, "I thought you were a fair person, how come you did this to me?" After begging her not to look at me that way, I always awoke with a start. Staring into the night, alone and full of regret, I wondered, Will Laxmi ever forgive me? Will I ever be able to forgive myself?"

When I retired from teaching in 2013, I considered moving back to Kolkata so I could be closer to my mother. Each time I spoke to her by phone, I worried. She was ninety years old and showing signs of depression and forgetfulness. Though my siblings visited her often, I felt that I should help out too. But the idea of moving to India was overwhelming. Settled in Vancouver, British Columbia, I had a condominium, a cat and a daughter who needed me. After assuring me she'd be okay without me, Gina suggested that I try it out for a few months and then make a decision.

Once in Kolkata, Mom and I moved into an apartment that I rented in a new and secure complex. While setting up our new home, I thought about Bishu's and my move to New Delhi. With every relived moment, I saw Laxmi's face. She had taken such good care of Gina…of me…of our family. We had repaid her by sending her away.

That night's nightmare was the same. But this time when I awoke with a start, I decided to do something about it. After breakfast the next morning, I set out to find Laxmi. Her neighborhood hadn't changed much and I easily found Laxmi's mother's house. Before I had a chance to knock on the door, Laxmi swung it open and ran into my arms. We both cried and laughed at the same time.

"Laxmi, I'm thinking of moving back to India to take care of my mom. Would you come and stay with us?"

"Yes, I would," she said, smiling in a way that made her appear much younger than her forty-nine years of age. "I often dreamed that you would come back for me. Now, you are here."

After selling my condo, my cat Misha and I moved to India. Mom, Laxmi, Misha and I are an unusual and loving family. I'm grateful that, together, Laxmi and I were able to right a terrible wrong—me by having the courage to admit and right a mistake I'd made years ago; and Laxmi by forgiving me with a gracious and open heart.

About Sudipta (Keya) Banerjee

Sudipta lives in Kolkata, India. After living in Canada for twenty-eight years, she moved back to India to spend time with her mother. Sudipta is a retired high school teacher. She holds a Master in Physics and in Education. Sudipta has traveled extensively. Her dream is to explore East Africa. She can be contacted by e-mail at info@heartmindeffect.com.

Sudipta's chapter in *Heartmind Wisdom Collection #1* is "There is Always a Solution." The Heartmind Wisdom Collection is available at www. heartmindstore.com and through online bookstores.

LOVING & LOSING JARED

Susan Berger-Thompson

Dedicated to my precious boy Jared.
Mommy has held you in her heart since
before you were born and will forever.
Someday, I will also hold you in my arms.
I love you.

Twenty-two days after my tiny son Robin was born, I was allowed to hold him. Tears streamed down my cheeks as I touched his bare skin for the first time. Still less than three pounds, he looked fragile, breakable. Tiny shoulders less than three inches across topped his thin arms, which were no bigger around than my index finger. His thighs were the size of my thumbs. A mere skiff of blond hair graced the top of his elongated skull. His adorable wee nose and mouth invited my loving kisses, which I showered on them while cherishing his newborn scent. He was the sweetest little darling I'd ever seen.

As I bonded with my baby, half of my soul was in Heaven. The other half was in hell, mourning the loss of his twin brother Jared. Born two months early, their lungs were not fully developed. Jared had fought his way into the world but wasn't strong enough to hold on. For months on end, I replayed how events had unfolded, and wept.

My father died when I was three-and-a-half. My mother kept a roof over our heads, however, compared to the kids we went to school with, our family was poor. Uneducated and angry about her hard life, Mom struggled with her own feelings. When it came to nurturing her offspring, she simply didn't have the know-how. As a result, I ached for love, often lamenting for my father who was purportedly a gentle and loving man.

Turning to my dolls for comfort, I happily assumed the role of mother. I showered these little plastic beings with affection, often dreaming of the day I would have real children. I did a lot of babysitting during my teens, and especially enjoyed looking after babies.

During puberty, I was overweight, unattractive and shy. I often felt worthless. Thankfully, the summer between grades eight and nine, I lost weight and began to feel somewhat better about myself.

I met my (now ex) husband Keith in March of 1973, mere months before graduating. We married a year later. I was eighteen; he was nineteen.

A short time after our first anniversary, I became pregnant, and was devastated when I lost the baby in my first trimester. Soon pregnant again, I miscarried a second time. I cried for days. *Will I ever have the children I so desperately want?* During my third pregnancy, I prayed that I'd be able to carry this baby to full term. Once in the second trimester, I happily anticipated motherhood, shopping for tiny clothes and readying a nursery.

During the wee hours of the morning on January 9, 1977, I restlessly wandered the house. When Keith awoke in the morning and asked what was wrong, I told him about the cramping in my stomach that was getting worse as time went by. We called the hospital and they said at seven months pregnant I should not be having cramps.

We quickly drove to the hospital, where I was admitted to the maternity ward. A large machine was wheeled into my room to check the baby's heart rate. The nurse suddenly looked confused and left. She soon returned with another nurse who then listened to the baby's heartbeat.

"Did your doctor ever say you might be having twins?" the second nurse asked.

I shook my head while exchanging an incredulous glance with Keith.

"Well, I'm fairly certain I heard two heartbeats," she said, smiling.

Relieved that nothing was wrong, the news took a minute to register; when it sank in I was thrilled. Two babies to love was even better than one. Keith and I chatted excitedly after the nurses left the room. "I always knew that I'd be the one of my dad's kids to have twins," I said, reminding Keith that my father had been a twin.

"I guess you'll have more shopping to do," Keith responded, already sounding like a dad.

"Do you think our babies will be okay?" I asked him, fingers crossed that he'd say yes.

"The doctors know what to do," Keith assured me. "I'm certain twins are born prematurely all the time." Somewhat relieved, in between labor pains, I pictured myself proudly pushing my babies in a double stroller.

Our family doctor was on holidays, so his locum was called in to be my primary physician. In his mid-thirties, the man had a soothing bedside manner. I liked and trusted him right away. Once he was sure that I was going to deliver two babies, he explained he would call in a gynecologist as there wasn't an obstetrician in our town.

Talking with me, not down at me, the young doctor also said the main concern would be that the twins' lungs would be underdeveloped. It was likely that they'd spend the first few weeks in incubators. He assured me that a pediatrician had been alerted and would be called in to look after them as soon as they were born.

Crying often…from pain…from worry…from excitement, my mood changed as often as I rolled from one side to the other. Keith was brave enough to let me know I was getting moodier and crankier by the minute. After again checking my vitals, the gynecologist told me he was ordering an epidural, a needle in my spine that would numb me from the waist down. My contractions unbearably painful, I looked forward to relief.

When I'd been in hard labor for over twelve hours, the gynecologist broke my water, thus speeding up the process. At 1:18 p.m., Jared Anton was born, weighing three pounds three ounces. Following quickly at 1:31 p.m., was his twin weighing two pounds thirteen ounces. It took us a day or so to name our second baby since we had only decided on one boy's name.

We were ecstatic with these beautiful creatures who were whisked away to incubators within seconds of being born. I barely got a glimpse of their tiny, perfect faces. Weary but happy, my work done, I glanced around the delivery room and joked that there was barely room for me. As multiple births were uncommon, there were a lot of doctors and nurses in the room observing the teaching experience.

Unable to get out of bed until the epidural wore off and I could feel my legs, it was later that evening when Keith wheeled me down to the Neonatal Intensive Care Unit (NICU). To protect our very vulnerable twins from germs, we had to put on gloves, gowns and masks.

Gazing adoringly through the Plexiglas at my precious, pink, naked babies, my heart thrummed with love. They were mine to cherish. I was the luckiest woman in the world.

"Aren't they beautiful," I said to Keith as I slipped my gloved hand through the hole on the side of one incubator and into what looked like a flexible spring tube covered with plastic.

"Yep, they sure are," he agreed, slowly putting his hand into the other incubator.

"Lying on even their tiny disposable diapers dwarfs them more, doesn't it?" I said, gently stroking Jared's head.

Keith drawled, "Oh, I think they are pretty tiny no matter what they're lying on."

Liquid love spilled from my eyes and ran down my cheeks. After several minutes, we switched places so we could each stroke our other son. The incubators were labeled "Twin A Thompson" and "Twin B Thompson," as were their ankle bracelets. Their lungs tiny and weak, when they occasionally cried, they sounded like baby kittens. Their breathing was rapid and shallow and we could barely hear them. Except for occasionally wiggling their arms or legs, they were fairly still. Each had a dedicated nurse twenty-four hours a day and would until they were out of danger.

Walking into the NICU the next morning, we were startled to see both babies were on ventilators. Anxious, we asked a nurse if something was wrong. She explained that our sons needed a higher saturation of oxygen and assistance with airflow so that they didn't have to struggle to breathe. Pushing our worries aside for a few moments, my husband and I discussed possible names for Jared's brother.

"How about Keith?" suggested my husband with a grin.

"Maybe *Keith* should be his middle name?" I countered. "I really like the name Robin."

Keith nodded and the decision was made; "Twin B" was henceforth to be Robin Keith.

I was discharged on day three. I left thankful that the babies were doing a bit better and that their ventilator oxygen level had been decreased a small amount. Thereafter, I haunted the hospital, visiting my sons for hours each day and wishing I could take them home.

Five days after their birth, the unthinkable happened. The phone rang in the middle of the night. It was the pediatrician; our precious

Jared was dead. "No, no," I screamed, unable to believe what I'd been told. *Please let it be a nightmare, God.*

The devastated look on my husband's face wouldn't let me deny the truth. Totally broken, sobs ripping from deep in my heart, I keened for hours. Our precious baby son was gone. *How could this happen to him and to us?*

The day after Jared died, while we were visiting Robin, a nurse asked my husband and me if we wanted the hospital staff to take care of our baby's body. Grief stricken, Keith and I looked at each other and nodded.

Sorrowful days dragged into weeks, as I wondered if the acute and relentless heartache would ever subside. If not for Keith's strength and Robin needing me, I don't know if I would have survived the agonizing loss. My world was dark, hazy and painful. I couldn't focus. My energy nearly nonexistent, I could barely function. Visiting Robin somewhat eased my pain. However, being at the hospital also reminded me of losing Jared, and teeming tears often blurred my vision and fell silently onto the NICU floor. Thankfully, for a few moments at a time, I was able to set aside my grief and simply receive my remaining son's love as I stroked him through the tiny opening in the incubator. Giving Robin my love was easy. I adored him. However, I secretly worried that we might lose him too.

I don't know if working and taking care of me helped or hindered Keith's grieving, but I will always be grateful for his stoicism and for having his loving arms to fall into during my many crying jags.

One day when I arrived to visit Robin, the pediatrician was there. Answering my unspoken question, he nodded and said, "He's okay." Simple words that sent joy through my heart. I knew what he meant was that Robin was no longer in danger and would grow healthier and stronger every day.

Though he received the bulk of his nourishment via a feeding tube, Robin slowly gained weight. When his breathing improved, he was taken off the respirator. Watching the nurses introduce him to oral sustenance was fascinating. At first, they dipped what looked like a large Q-tip in the formula and let him suck on it. He eventually graduated to a syringe full of milky liquid.

It was Robin who coaxed my first heartfelt smile in a long while, when around week five, he was finally able to eagerly suck his formula from a bottle. I grinned so wide my cheeks hurt. Robin was strong and would be mine to love for a long, long time.

Then came the momentous day when Keith and I finally got to hold and cuddle our baby boy. It was as scary as it was thrilling. No bigger than two pounds of butter laid end-to-end, we feared he'd somehow slip through our fingers and fall, or that we'd hold him too tightly. The nurses assured us that he wouldn't break and he didn't. After that day, we were able to cuddle him and feed him whenever we visited.

At nine weeks old, a couple of days past his original due date, Robin came home, weighing in at slightly more than five-and-a-half pounds. As happy as I was having my beautiful baby with me, my joy was shadowed by the loss of Jared. Awareness of the futility didn't stop me from searching for explanations, reasons for why he died. I felt guilty for having been intimate with my husband a few hours before going into labor. I smoked cigarettes throughout my pregnancy. *Was that why the twins were born tinier than their father's hands? If I'd gone to the hospital as soon as I felt cramps, would the doctors have been able to stop the contractions? How was it that my family physician missed that I was having twins? If he had detected two fetuses, was there anything different he or I could have done?*

As the weeks passed, the hours I wept each day slowly diminished. Still, I feared that no amount of healing time would wash away my pain. When Robin was four months old, I became pregnant. Surprisingly, I had no fears about this pregnancy, and anticipated a healthy full-term baby. Though I still mourned the loss of Jared, caring for my new daughter Brandie and her toddler brother filled my days and most of my heart. As months turned into years, the joy of raising my children slowly eased the pain of losing Jared, and he was less often forefront in my thoughts.

Though the guilt lessened in time, it was years before I could totally banish the self-blaming thoughts and accept that Jared's death was no one's fault. Often on my mind, I wondered where his little body had been laid to rest. I was unable to get concrete answers from the hospital or local cemetery. Some of what I learned led me to the conclusion that he had been incinerated. I felt horrible that at the time of his death I didn't have the emotional or mental wherewithal to arrange a proper burial for my son. The image of my child being disposed of in such a crude manner continues to haunt me.

Nowadays, in Canada where I live, parents are required by law to make any necessary burial arrangements for their children. Thankfully, young people bumbling their way through the loss of a newborn, as Keith and I were doing back then, will never have to feel such remorse born of ignorance.

My mother passed away in 2002. Knowing that she'd be pleased, we immortalized Jared by including his name and particulars on the back of her tombstone. It brings me some comfort that when people pass by, they will know my son lived and was loved.

It has now been over thirty-nine years since the early morning phone call from my baby's pediatrician shattered my heart and soul into a zillion pieces. Unfortunately, married young and unable to weather the many other storms that came our way, Keith and I divorced in 1985.

Jared's birth and life was a precious gift that I was only able to savor for five days. The tragedy of his death taught me that life is precious and fleeting, and that what is most important is to love deeply. Bad things happen to everyone, and when that everyone is me, I know I am strong enough to survive.

When I look at my two beautiful children, I often feel Jared's absence and try to picture Robin's carbon copy standing next to him. I wonder what his personality would have been like and how difficult it might have been to tell the twins apart. When I think about or watch any of my five gorgeous grandchildren, I wonder how many children Jared might have had. All these years later, it still saddens me, that on this earth, he has never felt my embrace or experienced my love. He has never sat with our family and reminisced, never known the giddy joy of a first love, or been awed by the beauty of a sunrise or sunset. Always, I wish my son were here.

JARED

Tiny one, so much loved
Mother sends you kisses
and many hugs.

So many times I pray
you are with your Grandmas and Grandpas,
snuggling.

Forever in my heart,
often on my mind,
always missed.

About Susan Berger-Thompson

Susan lives in Prince George, British Columbia. Spending time with her children and grandchildren is her greatest joy. Her love of writing and art began in her teens. She can be contacted by e-mail at info@heartmindeffect.com.

Her chapter in *Heartmind Wisdom Collection #1* is "Dying to Live." The Heartmind Wisdom Collection is available at www.heartmindstore.com and through online bookstores.

MORE THAN AN INCH

Joyce M. Ross

Though a good-natured kid, when it was important I could throw a tantrum worthy of an Oscar.

Kneeling in front of an overstuffed living-room chair, I bellowed down the hall for the umpteenth time, "I wanna see Nana!"

"Well, you can't. Children aren't allowed in the hospital." Standing in front of the bathroom mirror, Mom puckered her lips and kissed a Kleenex.

Flopping my face into the cushion, I went back to screaming throat-stinging loud and pounding the seat of the armchair with my fists as I thumped the tops of my feet against the hardwood floor. All of me hurt. But I didn't care. I had to see Nana.

"Why do you want to see Nana so badly?" my mother asked, alerting me that she was now standing next to me and what my siblings I referred to as the duck chair.

Thinking there was a chance I'd get to see Nana, I glanced up, wiped at my tears, and went mute. I had no idea why I had to see Nana.

Mom collected a photo of our family that was tucked into a frame that had a tiny plastic fern on one side and resembled a rather slim aquarium minus the fish. After kissing each of us kids on the head, she left.

Sadder than I'd ever before been, I got off the floor and curled up in the overstuffed armchair that Mom had recovered in a material adorned with the Mallard ducks Dad said were good eatin'. My eyes burned like there was soap in them; my ankles ached and felt like I'd been skating in wrong-sized skates all day; and my red, swollen fists throbbed like my heart had jumped half in each one and was trying to get out so it could mend itself back together like Humpy Dumpty.

Nana died the next day.

When I was nine years old, my father lost his boat building business as a result of the crooked actions of his so-called partner. My parents sold the three-bedroom house Dad had built on Lake Nipissing in North Bay, Ontario, and moved our brood to the outskirts of Victoria on Vancouver Island, British Columbia.

Far less than rich, the six of us moved into a well-ventilated shack with one decent-sized bedroom and one walk-in-closet-sized bedroom. We three girls got the big room. My brother slept on a foldout couch in the living room. Mom and Dad made do with the closet.

Though my eldest sister and I took turns picking fights with and trading pals, as the years rolled by, Crystal was the neighborhood friend I valued most. She had mesmerizing green eyes the size of chestnuts and shoulder-length curly hair like Shirley Temple's. I'm not sure why I liked her best; I just did.

The weird thing about Crystal was that her family lived in a small apartment that was attached to the funeral parlor where her dad worked as the director. As soon as she could do so without us getting caught, she took me downstairs to the dimly-lit gray-walled showroom where a couple of dozen satin-lined coffins were waiting, lids open, for someone to sleep in them for eternity. They looked comfy enough, but I couldn't decide which would suit me best. Maybe the one lined with blue satin; blue was my favorite color.

When we met, though I knew about death because Nana had died and because our dog Mike had been put to sleep after he got a bone lodged in his throat and no one could get it out, I wasn't entirely certain what death was all about. One thing that I did know for sure was that eventually whomever or whatever you loved went somewhere forever, maybe Heaven.

Mom and Dad did their best to help us kids understand that dying wasn't necessarily a bad thing, which was why Heaven was only a possible final destination. Mom was raised Catholic and occasionally mentioned some places called hell and purgatory, where you didn't want to go but would if you misbehaved too much. Then there was the whole business of Armageddon and judgment day that I learned about at a Saturday afternoon Jehovah's Witnesses Bible school picnic.

I went to the picnic because Mom wanted us to learn about different religions and because I thought it'd be fun. Which it was, except for the scalding sun beaming down on my hatless head and the foaming dark-brown liquid with bits of white stuff floating around in it that they served in a tall glass at lunch. Certain it had either gone bad or was poison, even when the other kids drank theirs, there was no way I was gonna drink mine. When I later told Mom about it, she said it was an ice-cream float.

As President John F. Kennedy had been shot and killed by a maniac when I was seven years old, I also knew that no matter how famous or important you were, there was no escaping this trip to *Never, Never Want To Go There Land*. At the time, I was in grade two and had made friends with a classmate who'd emigrated from the United States. We were both too young to fully understand the significance of the tragedy, but that didn't stop her from crying when our teacher told us about it.

For the next several days, everyone talked about how sad it was that the U.S. President had been shot. People felt bad for his wife and kids. Even the man who lived inside our radio was upset and talked about it a lot. We didn't have a television, but if the pictures on the front page of the *North Bay Nugget* were an indicator, the people in *TV Land* were probably sad too.

When preteen age, after the nice lady I was babysitting for was killed in a car crash, fear of dying had settled into my gut like a bunch of glued-to-gether rocks. She'd left at 7:00 a.m. in the morning and had driven up the island for some reason and was planning on going to the car races at Western Speedway that evening. She and her two children lived two doors away from my family. Theirs was the nicest and biggest house out of five that made up what my older sister and I had dubbed *the boondocks*. I often babysat her toddler-aged daughter while she and her preteen-aged daughter went somewhere.

As her mom was about to go out the door that morning, crying and screeching, the toddler wrapped her pudgy little arms around her mother's legs and clung on. Her mother and I were surprised.

I enjoyed babysitting the little girl and she seemed to really like me. Her mother often went out, so neither the woman nor I could figure out why the little girl was suddenly so upset. When her mother closed the door and left, the toddler threw herself on the floor and sobbed and sobbed.

Two hours later, I called her uncle and asked him to come over and help me calm her down. He couldn't quiet her either. When he tried to pick her up, like she had with me, she flailed her arms and screamed.

Eventually, the poor little dickens fell asleep on the floor and we put her in bed.

When her mom didn't come home at 11:00 p.m., I called the same uncle and asked him to spend the night with her so I could go home. In the morning we received the bad news. The nice lady had been killed in a car accident on her way down island. Apparently, a drunk driver had swerved into her lane and hit her car head-on. The impact had caused the steering wheel to snap in half and pierce her heart. I cried for hours. Everyone in the boondocks was sad for weeks.

By then, I'd learned about reincarnation. Shocked by the nice lady's death and life's unpredictability, I spent numerous hours trying to decide what living creature I'd like to be on my next trip to earth. At first, I was partial to becoming an evergreen tree like the ones that towered over the golf course across the street from our house. Trees lived for hundreds of years, got to play outside day and night, and could see for miles. I knew this because I'd once scurried up the branches of a cloud-tall pine until I was so high that my friends below appeared smaller than Crystal's hamster's pencil-eraser-sized pink and hairless babies. Going up the branches was hurry-up-and-get-there fun; coming down was take-your-time, heart-trying-to-thump-its-way-out-of-my-ribcage scary.

When it dawned on me that trees were stationary, I decided to reincarnate as a seagull. They could fly and liked junk food as much as I did. It sometimes takes me years to catch on, so by then I had a job, my own place, and a couple of new best friends—Patricia and Patricia. So that they both didn't answer when I asked a question, I called them by their nicknames, Patti and Trish.

To make sure that God, or whoever put the stamp of approval on one's passport back to earth, was hyperaware of my decision to reincarnate as a seagull, when I was visiting the store where Trish worked and spotted a gigantic framed picture of a gull flying high in a brilliant blue sky, I bought it and hung it on a wall in my apartment.

Patti, Trish and I weren't angels. Beginning with thinking it was a ton of fun to help the teenage boys from the Belmont Park navy housing complex turn over their neighbors' garbage cans, and ending with underage drinking, we were brats. In between, there were games of spin-the-bottle and truth-or-dare where we took turns kissing each of the Belmont Park boys.

Like most teenagers, we took a lot of dumb risks. We hitchhiked day and night, and let friends drive us around when they were stoned or drunk. During the summertime, we snuck out late at night to smoke cigarettes on the pitch-black golf course. All three of us survived, but not all of our friends and family did.

Rick from the navy housing complex died in a car crash. Sharon, one of our friends at Elizabeth Fisher Junior High School, rolled her car off the highway, landed upside down in a ditch and drowned. Patti's dad got sick and died. A few years later, her mom died from cancer.

From 1974 to 1980, I worked with troubled teens at the Victoria Youth Detention Centre. During the six years I worked there, at different times, after they were released back into society, about a half-dozen teens who'd spent time in the center were killed in car accidents or committed suicide.

Beginning with Nana, each death broke my heart. They were all good people worthy of a spot in Heaven. They were all deeply loved and their families and close friends would miss them for a very long time. But not the rest of the world.

Unlike when President J. F. Kennedy was assassinated, following each of their deaths, there were no radio or television reports, no newspaper headlines or lengthy write-ups about the contributions each had made to society. Instead, buried toward the back of the local paper, each one's life was marked with an inch-long announcement that included the dates of his or her birth and death, the names of immediate relatives and the location of the funeral service.

When young and there forward, I viewed this inequality as an injustice. How could one person's life be less important than another's? Dead or alive, why did the media celebrate one being and not another? Everyone deserved to have his or her contributions recognized, rejoiced and remembered. Newspaper-wise, the space needed to properly honor each one was far more than an inch.

After I quit the detention center, I moved to Toronto, Ontario, where my older sister was studying law. During a discussion with my Aunt Nina about my having to find a job or go back to school, she asked, "What do you want to do for a living?" Without forethought, "I want to be a writer!" popped out of my mouth, surprising her and me.

After reading a zillion *True Romance* magazines, at age fourteen, I had penned a short story and sent it off to the publisher. Crafting poetry was delightful child's play and I thoroughly enjoyed studying English in school. Past that, I wasn't consciously aware that I wanted to be a writer. Obviously my subconscious mind had been keeping secrets from me. Either that, or some extraterrestrial being had been flying overhead on its way somewhere, overheard our conversation, and when Aunt Nina asked her question, it chose a random card out of the earthly occupations deck it kept in its bag of tricks and slotted it into my conscious mind. Regardless, my mind and soul were all aboard the become-a-writer ship that set sail in my heart.

Over the next year, I lived off my savings and diligently worked at becoming a romance novelist. One manuscript off to Harlequin, I banged the second out on the old Olivetti electric typewriter that once belonged to my mother. Bottles of liquid White Out and reams of paper consumed my budget while writing consumed me. The next year, I took a part-time job as a cocktail waitress at Peter's Backyard Restaurant and Bar. During the day, I wrote. Evenings and nights I carried trays of drinks over my head as I smiled and excused my way through a packed room of partiers. When Harlequin rejected my first novel, I pouted in bed for a couple of days; when they rejected the second, I quit writing.

After my sister completed law school, the two of us moved to Vancouver, B.C. A waitress at the Bayshore Hotel, where I worked, introduced me to the Mary Kay Cosmetics business opportunity. Shortly after achieving pink-car status, my sister and I started our own direct sales company and marketed non-run hosiery. After a few years, she returned to practicing law and three new partners and I expanded the home party plan business across North America. Year six, Pelican Publishing purchased the rights to my book *Direct Sales: Be Better Than Good—Be Great!* Year eight, we sold the business and I started running singles dances for the over-forty crowd.

For the next fourteen years, I earned a decent living organizing bands and venues for Saturday night dances. It was a ton of fun and I thoroughly got a kick out of telling people that I partied for a living. Having had my how-to book published, my ego recovered from Harlequin's rejection of my manuscripts, so between organizing and partying, I resumed writing romance.

My yearning to become a romance novelist wasn't all that followed me into that career. Much like my work at the youth detention center, people I got to know and care about, died one after another. Stomach cancer took Rob and his contagious laugh into the next world, where I'm positive he's still making jokes that send his fellow deceased into hysterics.

Like nobody else, Rob could poke fun at someone so that they saw the humor in their own flaws, and laughed. His ribbing of me came with literal pokes. Often, he'd sneak up behind me, lightly poke both sides of my waist and call me spongy.

One day when a bunch of us were on a packed Skytrain headed into Vancouver, he suddenly jumped up at a scheduled stop and in a deep voice announced, "Everybody off!" Most of the non-singles-club passengers stood up and prepared to exit. Those of us who knew him roared with laughter. Everyone sat back down.

Rob met Susan at a club function. Except for their height and attractive facial features, at first consideration, they were as opposite as north and south magnetic poles. She had gorgeous long brown hair. Strand-by-strand, his hair had thinned away until his head became a shiny globe. He was gregarious and outgoing; she was shy and introverted. What, it turned out, they did have in common was lots of children and a love of wrestling each other. At least it seemed that way when a bunch of us spent a weekend at a lodge near Squamish, B.C. I still chuckle when I look at the photo of the two of them, wearing pajamas, each with the other in a leg-lock and lying on the floor killing themselves laughing.

A couple of years in a row, about two dozen of us headed to Harrison Hot Springs for a camping trip. As the organizer, I chose that area because Harrison Lake is beautiful, and if we didn't feel like cooking, we could eat at one of the nearby restaurants.

One night, after a few of us had snuck off to a local bar for drinks and dancing, I went back to the campsite early and tucked Susan's kids into their sleeping bags. About two hours later, I heard Rob and Susan outside the tent. She hated camping and in her drunken state was refusing to crawl into their tent in case there were bugs in there.

As Susan and Rob weren't big drinkers, the next morning, I teased her about having had a few too many. Laughing, she shared how as she and Rob staggered back to camp, the police had stopped them and asked if they were planning on driving. Rob responded, "I can hardly walk. How the heck would I drive a car?"

A couple of weeks before he died, Rob invited his closest friends from our club to his and Susan's place. He'd appeared frail and skinny. "Hey," he said as we walked through the door. "Don't I look great! My Jenny Craig diet's working wonders for me."

Within a few short years, cancer claimed Arnold, Arnie, Gil, Jeannie and more. Steve's love of beer was what got him. Wally's heart gave out while he was playing ice hockey. Eugene, one of my dearest friends and roommate, had a heart attack and died in our backyard.

When Eugene died, I wrote a short story about him and gave copies to the dozens of grief-stricken friends at his standing-room-only funeral. One of the kindest people to ever grace the earth, Eugene loved to make people happy.

One day, I spotted him washing his fancy red convertible while wearing a clown outfit. "Why are you dressed that way?" I asked, a chuckle in my belly. "I want to make people laugh," was his reply. I nodded and left him alone to continue his mission.

Eugene feared death and we sometimes talked about our beliefs about the afterlife. During more than one heart-to-heart, we promised one another that provided it was possible, the first to die would come back to tell the other about eternity. Forever a loyal friend, Eugene kept his promise.

A few months after he died, he appeared in my dream to warn me not to make a residence change I'd been contemplating. In my dream, we were sitting on a bench in the forest exchanging telepathic thoughts about missing each other. After a while, Eugene stood and walked toward a part in a thick hedge. "Wait, wait," I hollered. "You promised to tell me what it's like to be dead." Eugene looked back toward me, a sweet smile on his peaceful face. "It's really nice."

The next day, I shared with my good friend, Patricia Connor, that Eugene had visited me in my dream and warned me not to make the move I'd been contemplating. After telling her about his having left my dream through a part in a hedge, she asked, "Where were you?" It was an odd question, but one I was certain had a purpose.

"We were sitting on a bench in a forest," I answered.

"It must have truly been a spiritual visit," Patricia said. "When I was counseling Eugene for anxiety, his safe place was a bench in the forest."

Though I continued to sometimes dream about Eugene, and said hello when he often came to mind, he never again visited my dream in spirit-form.

It was years before I realized the connection between my childhood tantrum when I couldn't see Nana and the young tyke's tantrum when her mother left and the little girl somehow knew that her mother was never coming back. Children obviously are more in tune with their spiritual knowings than adults.

Eugene's visit via my dream is only one of many loved-ones from the eternal side who made their wishes, regrets and thoughts known to me. If we were all aware of our soul-to-soul connections with those we love, though we'd still miss them in the physical world, there'd be far fewer tears when those we care about return to the spirit world.

Having lost countless friends and a few family members to the eternal side, one summer's eve about two years ago, I sat in the backyard saying hello to one spiritual being after the other. For more than a half hour, memories surfaced and faces floated before my mind's eye. When I could no longer recount names, I stared into the darkening sky, feeling melancholic and sad.

It was then that a drop of water fell into the corner of my right eye. Startled, I glanced up at the tall evergreen overhead. The tree was crying for me; the Universe had let me know my loved-ones were close by.

It warms my heart that ages from now, when someone reads about my friends and family, my loved-ones' spirits will echo forward. As an editor and writing teacher, it brings me absolute joy to help others craft their literary legacies.

Every morning, seven days per week, it's my privilege to awake before dawn, throw on a pot of coffee and then spend numerous hours absorbed in my own or someone else's imaginings and wisdoms. It also warms my soul, that like me, one story at a time, authors around the globe are honoring their own and others' lives with far more than an inch.

About Joyce M. Ross

Joyce lives in Delta, British Columbia. She and her lifelong friend and mission partner, E. Patricia Connor, are the cofounders of Kindness is Key Training and Publishing Inc., home of the Heartmind Wisdom Collection and Heartmind Effect. She can be contacted by e-mail at info@heartmindeffect.com.

Her chapter in *Heartmind Wisdom Collection #1* is "Rainbows, Butterflies and Other Miracles" and her chapter in *Heartmind Wisdom Collection #2* is "Taming Shame & Blame." Her published works include *The Kindness Ambassador* and *Direct Sales: Be Better than Good – Be Great!*

Joyce's books and the Heartmind Wisdom Collection are available at www.heartmindstore.com and through online bookstores.

THE BEST DOG IN THE WHOLE WORLD

E. Patricia Connor

"Is that my new mommy?" I asked the Great Dog Spirit who had summoned me to the edge of the heavens.

"Yes, my angel."

We had a clear view of a woman walking on a trail with tall evergreens on either side. She caught up to a beautiful large white longhaired dog and a man waiting for her. They continued walking together.

"But she has a doggie earth angel already. Why would she want a puppy?"

"That's Batza. He's old and has been looking to the heavens and asking for us to find his human parents another doggie earth angel to fill their lives once he comes back to his spirit home."

"I'll do it! I can't wait to have a human mommy and daddy." Watching how they treated and adored Batza made me instantly love them.

"Thank you for thinking of me, Great Dog Spirit."

"You're welcome, Charlie. You and they are a match made in Heaven."

As soon as Batza's human mom walked into the barn, I recognized her. Remembering the Great Dog Spirit's instructions, I knew that it was my responsibility to make sure she picked me. I yelped and ran circles around my brothers and sister. When they dared move closer to her, I body slammed them out of the way so they would know she was mine.

"Do you want to pick one up?" The feeding woman asked Batza's mom.

"Sure!" She smiled.

I scrambled to the front of the pen, leaving my siblings loitering behind me. I felt the gentleness of her hand as she scooped me up and cuddled me against her bosom. Closing my eyes, I melted into the warmth and aroma of her. *I was home.*

"He certainly looks comfortable in your arms," the feeding woman said.

"Yes, he's adorable. When can the puppies go to their new homes?"

"In a week. Are you interested? They're going to go fast. I have a couple of people coming this afternoon. The female is not for sale, only the males."

"I have to talk to my husband, Marek, first. We lost our precious dog only two months ago. Marek's not convinced that we should get a puppy right away."

"Well, let me know. The pups will all probably be spoken for by next weekend."

After kissing the top of my head, Batza's mom placed me back in the pen. After staring at me for a long while, she and the feeding woman walked out of the barn and closed the door. I was confused. There was nothing else I could do, so I curled up in the corner. As I drifted to sleep, I heard the Great Dog Spirit whisper, "Don't worry, you did good. She'll come back for you."

When I returned from work at 5 p.m. Monday night, the house felt dark, cold and lonely. Knowing Marek wouldn't be home for a couple of hours, I thought about what to make for dinner as I turned up the thermostat and flipped on a series of lights. November in Vancouver was miserable and gloomy, and the idea of living through another winter heightened my anxiety.

Robotically, I went into the bedroom to change out of my business attire and into a sweater and sweatpants. Making my way to the kitchen, I took out the leftovers from the previous night's dinner and put them in the oven on low. Hopefully, I'd feel like eating by the time Marek arrived.

Feeling lost, my thoughts turned to the tiny golden English Lab puppy I'd held in my arms on Saturday. Looking back, I realized that I should not have gone there. But when my mother told me about the litter her friend's dog had birthed, my heart skipped and I felt the first flicker of joy I'd felt since Batza left us.

When I told Marek I was going to see a litter of puppies, he made me promise that I wouldn't come home with one. I kept my word, but it almost killed me. I hadn't missed that the rambunctious little male puppy noticed me at the exact instant I noticed him. The way he pushed his littermates aside to get my attention had made me smile. He was pretty smart for a little pup. Picking him up was my second mistake. When our eyes met, there was a connection I couldn't explain. His fur was silky soft and he had a distinct newborn puppy smell. When I held him close, he closed his eyes and snuggled into me in a way that warmed me throughout. I could tell that when I put him back in the pen, his heart was breaking too.

I couldn't argue with Marek that we were too busy to take care of a puppy. My mind realized that he was right, but that didn't stop my heart from aching for another dog companion. The sudden departure of our Polish sheepdog, Batza, had left a huge void in our lives. Our family didn't feel whole. Our house felt empty.

There was no way we could replace Batza or forget how he'd faithfully watched over us and loved us. I missed his resounding woof, the way he nuzzled up for a back scratch, and the walks we took to my favorite tree in the forest. Remembering the time he had sneakily stolen sandwiches from a tray laid out for guests, still made me laugh. It was a good thing we'd seen him stick his nose under the cloth cover and snatch another one. Otherwise, there would have been none for our company. Batza loved us; he wouldn't think we were getting a new puppy too soon after his departure. He'd be happy that we found another dog companion to warm our hearts and make us laugh.

The next evening, having had a dream I interpreted as being a divine message, I tentatively broached the banned subject one more time. "Marek, I dreamed about the puppy last night."

"Uh-huh," my husband said, a hooked half-smile on his face as he glanced away from the kitchen TV and met my gaze.

Ignoring that he was on to me, I kept going. "My dream was so clear. We were strolling with Charlie along a street adorned with Christmas decorations, looking in all the store windows."

"Charlie?" Marek asked. "Who's Charlie?"

"The puppy; that's what I called him in my dream."

Marek's hooked smile spread across his handsome face. He knew me well.

"You know how empty the house has been without Batza, can't we at least consider getting him?"

"Patricia, I don't have time to walk and care for a puppy. I'm too busy at work. And, you're gone all day."

I pretended not to notice the frustration in my husband's tone as I pleaded, "Marek, I need a dog companion. Otherwise, I get too lonely when you're working long hours, sometimes all weekend, and I'm home by myself. I haven't even been to my tree since Batza died."

My husband went mute as he looked back toward the television. I continued with my sales pitch. "You won't have to do a thing. I'll take care of him. I have an idea. Let's go to the breeder's on Saturday. She said that there was a good chance that all the puppies would be gone by the weekend. If Charlie's not spoken for, we adopt him. If he's already someone else's animal companion, I promise to drop the subject for good."

Marek shot me a doubting look, eyebrow raised and all. I didn't care. We were going back to see my puppy. There were only four days left until Saturday.

On November 19, 2005, life with Charlie began. The breeder suggested that we feed Charlie dry dog food made from lamb and rice. On our way home, we stopped and bought a big bag of dog food, a kennel, toys, and food and water bowls.

Minutes after devouring his first meal at home, the poor little guy threw up. Figuring we'd given him too much at one time, we fed him smaller portions three times a day. He was able to keep his food down, but we soon discovered that his plumbing was an issue. Worried, we took him to a nearby veterinary clinic.

After I explained the reason for our visit, the vet examined Charlie. Impressed by how well he was behaving, pride swelled in my heart. "He's such a wonderful dog," I said, certain she'd agree. "The breeder told us that he's from a superior bloodline."

Finished with her exam, the vet gave Charlie a treat as she said, "He looks like a fairly common yellow Lab to me. From what you've told me, although he seems fine, if I were you, I'd purchase pet insurance."

Taken aback, I didn't know what to say. Regardless of his bloodline, Charlie was a special dog. Batza had been healthy all of his life, so that was the first I'd heard about pet insurance.

We left the clinic with medication to calm Charlie's intestines. I should have asked for some to calm me. The silly vet had a lot of nerve telling me that my beloved Charlie looked like a common yellow Lab. He wasn't ordinary, he was extraordinary. I made a mental note not to let that vet near Charlie ever again.

Once in the car, I told Charlie not to pay any attention to what the grumpy vet had said, that she didn't know what she was talking about.

I then assured him that he was a very special dog and that Marek and I were fortunate to have him in our lives.

Though he might not have understood my words, the way he lovingly looked at me, I was fairly certain he concurred with my sentiments. Smiling, I headed for home.

I'd forgotten that a puppy demands far more attention and care than a mature dog. The energy our little munchkin exuded surpassed anything we had ever experienced. Everything Charlie did, he did with speed and gusto. His tail wagged ninety miles an hour. When he repeatedly wagged it against a hard surface, such as the kitchen floor or a chair leg, we worried that his cute little tail might bruise or break, and would quickly pick him up. After a few days, it was obvious that his tail drumming wasn't painful because he never tried to reposition himself and his tail rarely stopped wagging.

Within a few days, it became obvious I wouldn't be able to keep my promise to my husband that I'd be totally responsible for our pup's care. Charlie was a handful. Marek didn't seem to mind, however, once in a while he'd remind me of my promise and that Charlie was my dog. Though I kept my fingers crossed that my husband would continue helping, I needn't have worried. No matter how exhausted my husband was after working all day, when Charlie sat at his feet, tail wagging, playfulness shining in his big brown eyes, off to the park they went.

When awake, Charlie wanted to play. After three exhausting weeks of sleepless nights, potty mishaps and indigestion issues, we finally settled into a doable routine—four walks a day plus in-house playtime. Marek and I both sighed with relief whenever Charlie finally fell asleep.

From the moment we became a family, there was no denying that our cute little guy had a lifetime grasp on our hearts. In the mornings, with me still sleeping, after getting ready for work, Marek would walk Charlie, play fetch with him, and then place him at the foot of our bed so he could be with me. Charlie would then scurry up to me and plop himself down in the curve of my stomach and fall back asleep.

The peace, love and completeness I felt during our morning snuggling sessions translated into pure joy. I imagined that how I felt was akin to how a woman feels when nestling with her newborn. In those delightful bonding moments, our little angel became the child I never had. Daily, I thanked God for giving me such a beautiful gift.

Though most of Marek's business was local, he occasionally worked out of town. On the nights he was gone, when alive, Batza made me feel safe and protected. Big, muscular and with a ferocious bark that would terrify any intruder, I never worried about being alone in our big house. Charlie was a love dog, not a guard dog. If a burglar were to sneak into our house late at night, a delighted Charlie would likely fetch his ball in a bid to play.

At age thirteen, Batza had unexpectedly and peacefully passed away in the big flower and shrub garden in the center of our backyard. After he departed, it comforted me to stand in the garden and feel his presence. When Marek announced that he'd be out of town on business for a few days, while standing in the garden, I asked Batza to train Charlie to be more protective. Batza must have heard my plea and acted. The next day, when someone knocked on the door, sounding loud and threatening, Charlie barked and barked until I opened the door and assured him all was okay.

In the house, Charlie followed me everywhere. When I moved, he moved. He'd be sleeping peacefully, I'd reach for something or reposition myself in a chair, and he was instantly at my feet, tail wagging as he waited to be picked up. Too cute to resist, he always got what he wanted—a quick cuddle, a few minutes of play and a treat.

Personal privacy became something of the past. If I closed the bathroom door to take a shower, he'd whimper and scratch the door. If I didn't open it immediately, he'd bark until I did. Realizing it was best to take him into the bathroom with me, I'd fill his treat ball with dog biscuits to keep him occupied while I quickly showered. One morning after rinsing the shampoo out of my hair, I opened my eyes to find Charlie in the tub, patiently waiting for me to be done.

Watershed Park was where Batza, Marek and I regularly went for long weekend walks. A gorgeous urban forest with numerous trails, tall evergreens and glorious maples, the park was home to a variety of birds and small creatures. It was peaceful and beautiful. Afraid that he might take off and get lost, when we took Charlie for his first walk in the park, we kept him leashed. Charlie had a different plan. He ran as far as the leash allowed, came back a ways, took the leash in his mouth and jumped up and down. There was no mistaking that he wanted us to either run so he could, or let him go free.

"Let's take him off the leash," Marek suggested.

"Only if you're ready to run after him," I said, feeling nervous.

"He'll come back," Marek said, sounding almost convinced as he leaned down and unhooked the leash from Charlie's collar.

A bullet couldn't have traveled faster. Charlie took off, his ears flopping as he almost became airborne. Seeing how much he loved his freedom, warmed my heart. Two seconds later, realizing that he'd soon be out of sight, I panicked. "Charlie! Come, Charlie!"

Without slowing, he made a big loop and ran back toward us. Laughing with relief and happiness, I patted his head and he took off again. At that moment, I realized that his bond with us was stronger than his innate instinct to run. I could relax. We were his family and he would always return to our side.

Charlie and Marek were quick to make friends with other dogs and their guardians, and soon became part of a newly formed dog walkers group that met every evening in the schoolyard a few doors from our house.

Charlie soon earned the nickname Dennis the Menace. Like the comic strip character, he had a mischievous side. Though he mostly played with his dog friends, one evening, he spotted a man biking along the path at the far side of the schoolyard, and took off after him. I wasn't there, but according to Marek, Charlie then started chasing the bike and barking. Thankfully, when Marek called him, Charlie returned to the group.

We soon became convinced that Charlie could tell time. According to Marek, every evening around 7:15 p.m., Charlie would flop down on the grass, his eyes peeled on the path. Spotting the cyclist, he'd wait until the guy was part way down the path and then charge after him. Marek would call Charlie and he'd come back.

Curious and worried that the cyclist or Charlie might get hurt, one evening I joined the walkers and dogs. Sure enough, the cyclist entered the park at the usual time. Charlie waited until the man was a ways down the path and took off. Though a little too close to the bike for my comfort, and although the cyclist hollered a list of expletives, it seemed a harmless enough game. Still, I asked Marek not to let Charlie chase the guy anymore. It was too dangerous and not fair to the poor cyclist.

One evening, the two of them returned from their walk earlier than normal. Noting my husband's sheepish grin, I glanced at Charlie. Though he was wagging his tail, there were black tire marks and smudges all over his cream-colored fur. Marek had forgotten to leash

Charlie at 7:10 p.m. Thankfully, neither the cyclist nor the dog were hurt during their tumble. There forward, Marek watched Charlie more closely; however, they never saw the cyclist again. Though he wouldn't dare say so to me, I believe that ever a proud dad, Marek thought Charlie was the victor of the chase game.

As Charlie grew older, morning time with him remained the best part of my day. After his walk with Marek, he'd sleep beside our bed until his breakfast time. Then, he'd stand close to the head of the bed, his wildly wagging tail hitting the window blinds. If the clattering blinds didn't awake me, he'd paw the bed, pulling the covers off me, inch by inch. Even when tired after a late night, his absolute delight at having succeeded in getting me up, brought a smile to my lips.

Charlie's sunny disposition made it impossible for me to get mad at him. After he completed puppy training, Marek and I somewhat inept when it came to syncing our commands, I resorted to bribing our little angel with treats. Charlie quickly turned the tides and treat-trained me. Often, he'd ignore my call for him to come until I hollered, "Treat. Charlie, come get a treat."

Marek wasn't impressed. He was even less impressed when my best friend Joy came to live with us. Charlie had her treat-trained in a single day. Whenever in the kitchen, Charlie would sit under his jar of treats, patiently waiting for her to look his way. The instant their eyes met, he'd tilt his head back and look upward at the jar and then back at her. On the rare occasion when she didn't immediately fetch his treat, he'd sit at her feet and stare at her with his soulful black eyes. She always, always caved. No matter how often Marek and I tried to get her to limit the number of treats she gave Charlie, she simply could not say no to him. We dubbed her the Treat Queen and started breaking his treats into quarters.

Being a retriever, Charlie always seemed to have a toy in his mouth. Though we were careful not to pull too hard and hurt his teeth, we often played tug with him. No matter who came into the house, Charlie would fetch a toy and bring it to the visitor, hoping for a little playtime.

One afternoon the doorbell rang. On cue, barking loudly, Charlie ran to the top of the stairs to stand guard while Joy opened the door. It was the cable man we'd been expecting. Once certain the man wasn't a threat, Charlie retrieved one of his favorite toys, a lilac and white stuffed bunny. As Joy invited the cable man to come in, she assured him that though Charlie sounded ferocious, he was a lovely dog and wouldn't bite. Laughing, the cable man said, "Yeah, the purple bunny in his mouth kinda gave that away."

Joy and I marveled at Charlie's loving ways. Often, we talked about how while petting or hugging him, we could feel a direct connection to universal love. No matter how upset or down either of us might feel, five minutes of Charlie time would melt away our unpleasant feelings and thoughts. His seemingly spiritual essence was so potent that Joy dubbed him Love on Paws. It was his most appropriate moniker.

Charlie's companionship and unconditional love saw me through the end of my father's life. When someone would do or say something that hurt me deeply, after a few minutes with Charlie, I'd again see the goodness in whoever had upset me. His lovingness made me want to be a better person. No matter what happened, he was by my side, letting me know all would be okay. Charlie was God's love gift-wrapped in a beautiful dog.

Keeping Charlie healthy and pain free was a constant challenge. Age four forward, the poor dog was yearly afflicted with a new lifelong, sometimes life-threatening, ailment or condition. His loving nature and frequent visits made Charlie a favorite at the vet clinic, especially with his primary veterinarian Dr. Irene O'Brien.

Knowing he'd score treats, he eagerly entered the clinic and, for the most part, patiently accepted the vet's or technician's poking and prodding. The staff was attached to Charlie too, and always went out of their way to welcome us both.

With each diagnosis, I'd kiss the top of his head and promise my beloved angel that everything would be okay. His trusting eyes would meet mine, and I'd know he understood and believed me. His strong spirit and eagerness for life were essential in helping us manage his health.

Thanks to them being wrapped in cold cuts or tucked into dog food meatballs, Charlie willingly swallowed his various medications. When he developed diabetes, he sat still for his twice daily injections. Though he wasn't wild about his eye drops, he rarely turned his head away. If I forgot to give him a pill or a shot, the treats on the desk were his clue that we weren't done. My clue was his wide eyes following me about until I finally caught on.

To ensure his optimum health, we kept to a strict schedule of exercise, meal times and medicine administration. For a few years, Marek cooked a month's worth of homemade dog food at a time, ground it in a blender and then placed it in containers for freezing. Toward the latter part of his life, Charlie's health regime required that one of us stay with him at all times. As his illnesses compounded and he valiantly survived a few close calls, Joy and I renamed him our miracle dog.

Almost everyone who witnessed our vigilant monitoring and care of Charlie commented that he was one lucky dog. That is not how I felt. I was the lucky one. God had entrusted Charlie to me and I was honored to care for him. Charlie loved wholeheartedly, trusted completely and did his best to make everyone happy even when he was unwell. He was my spiritual teacher and the light in my life.

Every night, while I brushed my teeth, Charlie would lie in the hallway outside our bedroom door. Before getting into bed, I would spend a few minutes caressing him and telling him that he was the best doggie in the whole world. Before drifting off to sleep, I included him in my prayer of gratitude. After giving thanks to God, I asked the angels to watch over him.

Charlie seemed to sense when I was done praying, and would then move to his own bed on the floor next to my husband's side of our bed. Relishing in the serenity and safety I felt having my husband and Charlie close by me, I'd drift into a peaceful sleep.

The last time Charlie came home from a prolonged stay in the hospital, he didn't seem the same. He was suffering. The specialists had found a large clot in his pulmonary artery and a blockage in his heart. Over the next few days, I spoke endlessly to the specialists and his vet, asking questions and discussing possible treatments.

There was a heart operation that could save Charlie's life. However, in addition to his many ailments, he was getting on in dog years and was nearly blind. My husband and I discussed the possibility and decided our beloved angel had been through enough. He just wasn't the same; it was as if he'd given up. His gastro-intestinal issues had flared up and didn't improve with medication. He either refused food or threw it up shortly after eating. His breathing was labored and his back legs were extremely weak.

Sunday morning, as I watched him in the backyard, I knew it was time to gift Charlie back to God. The poor dog was patchier than a farmer's fallow fields. Having been in the hospital a few months earlier for a skin infection, there were large bald spots on his back. There were also freshly shaven spots on his legs and tummy where he had been hooked up to machines and tubes a few days earlier.

Wanting to be closer to me, he took a few steps, sat down, lowered his head and stared toward the middle of the garden. When I gave him a big hug and whispered into his ear that I dearly loved him, he didn't wag his tail. Deep in my broken heart, I knew he was letting me know that he couldn't do it anymore.

I reached for comfort by telling myself that he was staring at the center of the garden because angel Batza was there, waiting to escort him to Heaven. Once back in the house, I tearfully told Marek, "We have to let Charlie go. It's the loving thing to do."

Feeling healthier than he had in years, Charlie watched from the heavens as his human family grieved. His Mom was crying and crying. His Dad wasn't saying much and appeared sad and lost. Wanting them to know he was happy and well, that he could run fast and far, and eat what he wanted, he barked a few times, but only Joy could hear him.

The Great Dog Spirit came to his side. "They'll be all right. It takes time."

"I wish I could take their pain away. I love them so much," angel Charlie said as angel Batza appeared on his other side.

"When they are ready, we'll send them an earth angel puppy."

Charlie barked his agreement. They were the best human family in the whole universe. He'd make certain they chose carefully.

"Until one has loved an animal, a part of
one's soul remains unawakened."

—Anatole France

About E. Patricia Connor

Patricia and her husband, Marek, live in Delta, British Columbia. She and her lifelong friend and mission partner, Joyce. M. Ross, are the cofounders of Kindness is Key Training and Publishing Inc., home of the Heartmind Wisdom Collection and Heartmind Effect. She can be contacted by e-mail at info@heartmindeffect.com.

Her chapter in *Heartmind Wisdom Collection #1* is "Heart Connections: A Matrix" and her chapter in *Heartmind Wisdom Collection #2* is "Freedom by Angels." Patricia is the leader of the Heartmind Community Café, a meeting place where people gather to hear inspirational speakers and musicians. She feels closest to angels when surrounded by nature.

The Heartmind Wisdom Collection is available at www.heartmindstore.com and through online bookstores. Patricia's e-book *Heartmind Purpose: Identify Your Calling through the 13 Heartmind Keys* is available at www.heartmindstore.com.

HOPE

HIDDEN BLESSINGS

Rahim Valli

A five-ton truck hurled toward me, its horn blaring as it kicked up a sky-high dust storm. Too numb to react, I kept walking toward home…toward safety on the far side of the street. Brakes screeched and someone yelled in the distance. I didn't care. Entering the small shop below my family's apartment, I heard my grandmother yell, "Oh, my God! Something terrible has happened to this child! He needs to get to a hospital right away!" Snapping into action, my uncle picked me up and drove me to the hospital where my dislocated shoulder was put back in place. My arm in a sling, I was sent home to mend. I was three years old.

Without the capacity to digest or articulate the events that precipitated my catatonic wandering, memories of that day remained in a vault somewhere deep within until the "right" moment.

Some accounts suggest our lives flash quickly before our eyes just before death. Two months after my twenty-ninth birthday my life played before my eyes, except it wasn't a quick flash—it was a long, drawn out film reel that re-ran everything I'd thought, said and done, and every relationship I'd held dear…how I'd been and who I was in each. At the time, it seemed unfortunate that I didn't die afterward.

Instead, I was left amidst a crushed and crumbled comfort zone of feebly constructed beliefs and values that forced me to examine my life with unfiltered candor. I despised what reflected back. Sure, I'd graduated university and accumulated commendable leadership, work and volunteer experiences; however, I was also a self-righteous windbag with a told-you-so attitude. I was clueless when it came to taking personal responsibility, and oblivious to the impact of my words and actions on others. I was quick to dole out unsolicited advice and to criticize anyone who didn't see the world as I did. I knew everything.

The eventual collapse of that poorly constructed version of my "perfect" life plunged me into a turbulent sea of uncharted emotions. I couldn't find the words to describe the emotional pain that consumed my entire being, my soul. I yearned instead to experience this relentless turmoil in a concrete, tangible physical way.

Sure enough, a couple of weeks later, I twisted and fractured my foot while running down stairs with a bicycle over my shoulder. That excruciating self-fulfilled prophecy broke more than a bone in my foot; it busted and shattered the frail remnants of my ego, spirit and will. In a cast and confined to my parents' basement suite for eight weeks, the emotional pain I sought desperately to escape ironically became my primary companion.

Completely isolated from everyone, one by one, the sorry circumstances of my life surfaced. Three months earlier, the girl I planned to marry dumped me. As she didn't like my friends, I'd severed ties with them. My employment contract was about to expire with zero promising prospects lined up. I was flat broke and receiving demand payment notices on my student loans. Every physical pain and emotional ache acutely amplified as I wallowed alone in misery. I had nowhere to go, no one to turn to, nothing to do but wait, and think, and hate, and cry... and then think, and hate, and cry some more.

I felt tired, old, lost, naïve and disillusioned. I had been disconnected from reality for nearly thirty years. How was it possible that I lacked the basic skills to manage my finances? Where did all the money I had earned since I was thirteen disappear to? I had nothing to show for my hard work and sacrifices—nothing! As though I'd been sucker punched hard in the gut, I felt winded, paralyzed and unable to say or do anything. I had failed at love, failed in my career, failed at life. Taking stock of my flawed existence was brutal and bitter...and surprisingly humbling.

Over the next two years, I stumbled along trying to find stability. For the first time, actually fully feeling and realizing every consequence of every choice I made, good and bad. After derailing from a career I was passionate about in sustainability, I bounced in-and-out of a management job with a prominent truck rental company. After that, I became a plant manager for a small snack food venture while volunteering part-time at a local crisis center. Contrary to my family's cultural norms, I moved out of my parents' home into an apartment in the same neighborhood.

I considered further education and career possibilities, acutely aware of the limits of an undergraduate degree in a rapidly professionalizing and globalized knowledge-based economy. I explored social work and teaching as possibilities, concluding that I definitely did not want to teach in a *public* school. A short while later, my career direction prayers were answered.

I learned about a faith-based pilot initiative to train secondary school teachers at a master's level over two years, followed by a three-year employment contract. The ground beneath my feet steadied slowly as I walked cautiously toward something meaningful again. The drawn-out film reel playing in my head somewhat faded to the background, but did not entirely disappear. As I began the application process, old fears resurfaced. Could I do it? Would I be able to get my rusty intellectual gears grinding again after five years away from anything remotely academic? How would I find time to complete the rigorous, practice-based application process while holding down a full-time job and two demanding volunteer commitments?

Though I was determined to handle it all, my body started sending signs of doubt. After each grueling day, I felt uneasy and nauseous. The foot I'd injured flared up again, and I started getting painful twinges in my right shoulder. I blamed the shoulder discomfort on my poor posture. My lower right abdomen, where my appendix had been before it was removed when I was a teenager, ached and felt strangely hollow. The right side of my chest felt tight, causing breathing discomfort and intermittent chest pains. I was reaching my breaking point and hanging on by a thread. I could not afford another crash, another accident.

This time, I recognized I needed help and support. Ideally, I'd be able to find a professional who could treat all of my health needs—intellectual, emotional and physical. In the past, I'd sought help from a series of conventional medical practitioners, including a physician, chiropractor, massage therapist, and counselor. The resulting relief had been minimal and temporary.

Fortunately, a prior conversation I'd had with a friend about osteopathy and craniosacral therapy that had been tucked away for precisely this moment, the "right" moment, reappeared in my film reel. Perhaps these combined practices of gentle touch to enhance the functioning of the membranes, tissues, fluids, and bones surrounding or associated with the brain and spinal cord would afford me lasting physical relief, emotional balance and spiritual peace. With nothing to lose, I decided it was time to take my friend's advice.

Through research, I found three local practitioners and chose the one whose personality and approach aligned most closely with the help I was seeking. I especially liked that the length of a session honored a patient's individual process rather than being driven strictly by the clock. If my body had enough before the end of the slotted session, or if I needed more time to complete a process, I'd be billed accordingly. Most importantly, I wouldn't be subjected to sessions that ended abruptly. At the practitioner's suggestion, I booked three appointments.

A few days later, after filling out the appropriate intake and waiver forms and a short wait, I stepped into the treatment room feeling anxious but hopeful. The therapist began by explaining what she termed the Grounded Theory Approach. Rather than look at the answers on the form I'd completed, she preferred to put my body's wisdom in charge of the process through a hands-on physical assessment, with her taking the role of facilitator. She then asked me to stand beside the treatment table so she could place her hand on the top of my head to begin the assessment. Her palm barely touched my head when I collapsed to the floor and blacked out.

When I came to, I was sitting upright. After making sure I was not injured from the fall, the therapist gave me a glass of water and continued with treatment. Checking for the pulse of my craniosacral rhythm, she subtly palpated the membranes around my skull where cerebrospinal fluid circulates as part of the craniosacral system. After a thorough two-hour treatment, I learned that because of my intense desire to please others, I'd subconsciously accumulated the emotional burdens of a ninety-year-old man! If I wanted to heal, I needed to move myself to the top of my priority list and concentrate on my health and well-being.

Confident that I'd finally found the appropriate health practitioner and process to support my journey toward wellness, I committed to continuing treatment. I didn't know how long it would take, how much it would cost or how I would pay for it. What I did know was that if I wanted to be well, I had to heed my quest to uncover and learn my own story. I had to listen to my body and allow my personal truths to take precedence over everything else.

As memories surfaced, I better understood my shortcomings and the mental blocks that hindered my personal and professional goals.

Acknowledging and accepting each memory and resulting personality traits was tough. Each two-hour session evoked emotional and intellectual discomfort and included a few moments of physical pain. At the approach of several appointments, my apprehension and anxiety levels skyrocketed. What drove me to continue was my genuine desire to discover my personal truths by uncovering the significant events that made me who I was, good and bad. Slowly, I regained direction and control in my life, including passing the application process for the faith-based teacher program.

It was two years into my osteopathy and craniosacral therapy when I finally learned why, at age three, I'd crossed the street alone and in a trance-like state, oblivious that I was in the pathway of a five-ton truck and unable to hear the horn warning me to jump out of harm's way.

When I arrived at my appointment that telltale day, as I had numerous times before, I changed into loose, comfortable clothing and stepped into the treatment room. The familiar routine session began: debrief any life and relationship happenings, assessment with practitioner's hands on my head, then feet, then sacrum and abdomen.

As the treatment progressed, I drifted into a memory of being in a small storage room full of newly stitched and repaired clothes. I recognized it as being the home-based tailor shop that was owned and operated by neighbors who lived across the street from my family. On that particular day, I'd been playing hide-and-seek with their son Parker and had found him not very well concealed behind a small pile of clothes. When I ran over to tag him, he pulled me down beside him and coaxed me into playing what he called "dress-up" and "doctor." Convincing me that it was part of the game, he slowly placed his fingers in my mouth. The next thing I knew, he was sexually forcing himself on me as I begged him to stop. I tried to push him away, but he was older, bigger and stronger. When he finally decided he was through with me, I was allowed to leave.

It took several more sessions before additional scattered memories gradually formed a complete picture, with some memories surfacing between sessions. Throughout the months it took to capture all of the painful details, I journaled to help me remember, process and slowly heal.

Over time, I recalled that after Parker's assault, I went home. Tears streaming down my chubby cheeks, too young to verbalize what happened, all I told my uncle was that I didn't want to play with Parker ever again.

The next day, with me in tow, my uncle went to confront Parker's dad. The shop was closed so we were invited inside. Parker's dad listened to what my uncle had to say before insisting that his son would never hurt me. He then offered to watch over Parker and me to ensure that I wasn't being picked on or harmed in any way.

Scared, I tugged at my uncle's pants until he looked down and could see that I was vehemently shaking my head no. My uncle studied my upturned face while trying to decide whether to leave me there. When Parker's dad insisted that I stay and reassured him that everything would be okay, my uncle slowly turned and left. My pounding heart sank into my aching belly. I did not trust Parker or his dad.

The second my uncle was out the door, Parker's dad turned into a monster. Together, father and son viciously attacked me. I was kicked, punched, burned with a cigarette, and beaten with and penetrated with a thick wooden dowel. I lost consciousness twice. Then, while threatening to kill me if I even thought about telling anyone, they showered me with buckets of cold water. When they finally threw my clothes on the floor by my feet, I put them on without uttering a sound. I left feeling completely dazed and numb from head to toe.

While crossing the street, I'd heard muffled yelling and a horn, but both noises seemed to come from far away. I'd seen the big truck heading straight for me but couldn't reason that it might not stop. When it did stop a mere three feet from me, the driver hollered something I was too foggy to hear.

Uncovering the horrific happenings of that day led me to realize additional truths. Parker and his dad had dislocated my shoulder through the same despicable actions that derailed my life for decades. Unblocking those memories also explained why it seemed that life unrelentingly threw challenges my way, and why I was constantly disillusioned by people, circumstances and myself. Parker and his dad had stolen more than my innocence; they robbed me of my ability to feel safe and to trust.

Once aware of the childhood trauma that manipulated my head and heartstrings like a cloaked puppeteer, I gradually forgave myself for regrets and missteps, and stopped being so hard on myself for my perceived failures and relationship aloofness. Thanks to the continued support and guidance of my health practitioner, I slowly began to heal.

However, my life did not immediately begin to tick forward like a clock. As I struggled to come to terms with the gruesome details of my memories, I remained perched on a ticking time bomb, vigilantly monitoring what people said and did, readying for the next explosion of betrayal and disappointment.

Needing emotional space to incorporate the once missing painful pieces into the film reel of my life, for a time, I recoiled further away from friends and family. To fully understand the whys behind who I was and where I was career-wise and relationship-wise, I needed to spend time alone. Only through making sense of the trajectory of the past would I be able to decipher what I wanted in the future, and how I could get there. At the encouragement of an educator mentor, I also incorporate aspects of my traumatic experience into my thesis research report. Thankfully, spending time alone and writing about what had happened helped me slowly integrate the experience.

As a result of my continued emotional, physical and spiritual work, I was eventually able to open up to a few trusted confidants other than my therapist. During a conversation, one friend shared the results of a study that examined why some people are driven to heal themselves. The finding was that their healing quests were largely motivated by a desire to be of service to others and/or to have a purpose beyond themselves. As she spoke, it dawned on me that the personal work I struggled through over the past five years was inspired by a greater purpose—an opportunity to be of service.

The results of the study further clarified why a few years earlier, I chose to become a massage therapist. Having found physical, intellectual and emotional relief through the appropriate support from the appropriate therapist, I wanted to provide the same for others. Having experienced the benefits of a holistic approach, I was naturally drawn toward a career in integrated healthcare, where the body is understood as a unit rather than the sum of its functioning parts.

Reflecting further on these insights and choices, I gradually came to understand the blessings birthed in misfortune and hidden beneath suffering. Had I not fallen down the stairs and broken my ankle, it's unlikely that I would have sought holistic treatment. Without therapy, unable to trust anything or anyone, I might have spent my entire life consumed by the blinding nothingness set in motion by Parker and his dad, forever leaping between careers and mates in search of a missing something. Minus the three-decade derailment of my life, I'd be far less effective in my pursuit to help others.

As I prepare to complete the final step toward becoming a registered massage therapist, I understand and celebrate that personal work is an ongoing process. I aspire to approach each new client with my eyes, ears and heart wide-open. By paying attention to my clients' physical, intellectual and emotional clues and needs, through healing hands and words, my goal is to pay forward that which was gifted to me.

About Rahim Valli

Rahim lives in Port Moody, British Columbia. With a strong desire to help others heal via an integrated and natural health approach, he is studying to become a registered massage therapist. Rahim can be contacted by e-mail at info@heartmindeffect.com.

KOKOMO

Didi Simer

*"If there are no dogs in Heaven, then when
I die, I want to go where they went."*

—Mark Twain

After all the vehicles were parked on the ferry sailing from the main-land to Vancouver Island, British Columbia, I opened my car door. The second I did, my toy poodle, Kokomo jumped over me and leapt out. Trusting that she'd bring the ball back to me as usual, I opened the door wider and tossed her favorite yellow plastic ball along the deck. Once out of the car and the doors locked, I glanced around in search of my furry friend. I couldn't spot her.

Panicked, I repeatedly called out, "Kokomo, where are you?" as I hurried between rows of cars, occasionally bending over to see if she was walking beneath the vehicles. When I couldn't find her, I wondered, "Instead of rolling toward the back of the ship where I'd tossed it, had her ball rolled toward the far side of the ship?"

During our numerous ferry rides, I'd never noticed any holes that she might fall into. But then, we normally played fetch toward the center of the ship. *Was it possible the sides of the ship had holes to the outside that I hadn't noticed?* Reassuring myself that even if her ball had rolled outside, Kokomo was too smart to follow it into the ocean, I kept searching.

On the advice of my doctors, after I was severely beaten by a dis-gruntled worker's wife at a roofing company where I worked as an office manager, I'd spent months searching for the perfect dog for me. It had to be small as injuries to my arms and neck affected my strength, making it impossible for me to control a large-breed dog. Cute, affectionate and good-natured also made my list of preferred traits and features.

An intelligent, agile and active breed, toy poodles need frequent play which fit perfectly with my need for an animal companion to take my mind off my troubles, aches and pains. Caring for a pet that needed me as much as I needed it, would get me off the couch and outdoors.

I found Kokomo through a newspaper ad. Since the day she came home at twelve-weeks old, she'd been my guardian angel. During the attack at the office in 2008, I was beaten all over my body with a thick stick. The residual effects included short-term memory loss, migraines, ringing in my ears and dizziness. Although my dizziness was eventually diagnosed as trauma-induced Ménière's syndrome, some of the many medications prescribed by my specialists also caused dizziness. Often confused and uncoordinated, I would easily fall. Whenever I hit the floor, Kokomo was immediately by my side, tail wagging, head tilted as her shiny blackish-brown eyes stared lovingly into mine.

One day with the engine running, Kokomo in the back seat, I jumped out of my car to get a closer look at a pile of debris I'd spotted in a vacant lot, near where I lived. When I tried to get back in my car, the door was locked. My first thought was to call my son to bring me my spare keys, but my cell phone was in the car.

It was Kokomo's turn to be confused. Her eyes trained on me as I paced and fretted, she barked at me as if saying, "I want to play too. Why aren't you opening the door to let me out?"

"Come into the front seat," I said loud enough for her to hear me through the closed window.

Kokomo did as commanded.

"Unlock the door, Kokomo. Mommy can't get in the car."

Her ears went up as her expression became puzzled.

Recalling the time Kokomo and my son Ekam's golden retriever Quincy had escaped from the car by pushing the button on the armrest, I said, "Open the window, Kokomo." Of course, I had no way of knowing whether Kokomo would recognize the word "window" or if she had been the sneaky culprit who'd figured out how to escape from my car. It could have been Quincy; he was smart too. Regardless, the memory of being on my knees picking strawberries at a local farm, when Kokomo suddenly started pawing at my legs to play made me smile. My tone happier, I again coaxed Kokomo to open the window. The window dropped down. Wowed, I vowed never again to leave the keys in the car.

"Have you seen a tiny black and tan dog?" I asked a man wearing an orange vest that I assumed was a deckhand.

He shook his head.

"Are there any holes on the car deck that a small dog could fall through?" I asked, praying he'd say no.

"A few," he answered, "in case we take on a big wave."

My pounding heart skipped a beat. "Where?!"

He pointed toward the one side of the ship and then the other, before asking, "How big is your dog?"

Using my hands to demonstrate, I said, "She's a toy-poodle about a foot tall."

"I can't be sure whether she'd fit through one of the holes. You better go look."

Tears welled in my eyes as I pictured my precious baby falling to her death. While hollering "Thank you," I ran toward the closest side, spotted the holes in the side of the ship's hull and peered into the first one. Kokomo could definitely fit through. Below the hole, there was a foot-wide ledge, but I couldn't see very far along it. I checked the next hole, no Kokomo.

Making my way to the other side, I spotted the engine room. *Maybe she'd somehow gotten into the engine room.* I glanced around for the deckhand so I could ask him to let me check, but he was gone. Kokomo was clever and quick. If she'd lost sight of me and spotted a worker going into the engine room, thinking I might be in there, she'd make a mad dash so she could sneak in before the door closed.

Once, while visiting my friends Marlene and Dave in Campbell River on Vancouver Island, Kokomo started pawing their hallway closet door and looking my way. Even though I repeatedly told her there was nothing in the closet for her, she continued pawing at the door until I finally opened it.

Kokomo sniffed the shoes and then the jackets.

"There are no treats in those jackets," I said.

Seeming to understand, she went back to sniffing the shoes before tapping her paw on the boots that belonged to me.

Confused, I asked, "Kokomo, what do you want?"

She just looked up at me, her head tilted.

I closed the closet door.

Kokomo pawed the door and pawed my boots again.

It was then I finally understood. My furry little friend wanted me to take her outside to play.

Shaking her head and obviously flabbergasted, Marlene said, "I can't believe how smart your dog is. She's incredible!"

At the time, Kokomo was two years old. Having amazed me many a time, in many a way, I was no longer shocked by her intelligence. Sometimes, she seemed smarter than the drug-numbed me. Before I adopted her, I put a pot of soup on the stove to cook. A few minutes later, I decided to take a bath. When I came out of the bathroom, the house was full of smoke. Thank goodness, only the food in the pot had burned. More than once, she'd alerted me that something I'd forgotten about on the stove required my attention. Whenever she barked, I'd say, "Show me where you want me to go," and she'd lead me to the danger.

Unable to work, the mortgagee repossessed my house and I moved into a rental home with my son Jagtaran. The older couple next door, Sandra and Patrick, had lost their youngest son a year earlier. Jagtaran's offering to mow the dandy lions that had overtaken their lawn was the catalyst for a steady flow of homemade cinnamon buns from Sandra's stove to our kitchen table. It was Kokomo, however, who won both of their hearts.

When WorkSafe B.C. insisted that I enroll in a training program that would lead to employment I could handle despite my physical and emotional challenges, I chose an English as a Second Language Teacher (ESLT) course. Unable to take Kokomo to school with me, I asked Sandra to check on her.

She was ecstatic which was surprising since the couple had their own poodle. When I asked Sandra why she was so happy to take care of my dog when she had one of her own, she replied, "That's my husband Patrick's dog, not mine."

For the next several months, I caught the bus at 6:30 a.m. and didn't get home until eleven or twelve hours later. When I remarked how grateful I was for her help with Kokomo and her friendship, Sandra's response was, "You're the daughter I never had." My smile wide, I hugged her tight.

Although Patrick pretended to care only for his own dog, it was easy to see that he enjoyed Kokomo. Most days when I went to retrieve her, she'd be at the door waiting to jump into my arms.

One day, Kokomo didn't greet me when I arrived at their house. "Come here," Patrick whispered, motioning with his arm as I stood by the door. Tiptoeing toward him, I spotted what he wanted me to see. Both dogs were sound asleep in an armchair, each one's front paw resting on the other's back.

"Did you find your dog?" a lady asked as I passed by on my way to the far side of the ship.

"Did you see her?" I asked, daring to hope just a little.

The lady shook her head before saying, "Yours wouldn't be the first dog to jump over board. It's happened before."

"I forgot that there were holes on the sides of the ship on the bottom deck," I said glancing up and down the row of cars as I kept going. "I haven't parked down here for years." Since I got Kokomo, in the half-dozen times we'd taken the ferry, we'd always parked on the top car deck. But even if Kokomo had chased her ball through one of the openings, she was too smart to jump off.

When Quincy escaped from our backyard, it was Kokomo who alerted me by incessantly barking. Thankfully, the puppy was still in the back alley and I was able to catch him. Apparently, a neighbor who'd earlier visited had mistakenly left the gate open.

Another time when I was weeding my flower garden, Kokomo kept running up to and away from me. Standing, I noticed that Quincy was still in the yard. "What are you trying to tell me?" I asked Kokomo. It wasn't until she took off toward the neighbor's that I remembered I was supposed to feed the man's Rottweiler while he was away for the weekend.

The neighbor's dog was locked in the house but could get outside via a door which led to a securely fenced area of the yard. My instructions were to use the rope, which was tied to the fence on one end and the dog's food bowl on the other end, to pull his dish out, add the food, and then push it back into the yard with a stick.

Fearing that Kokomo might follow me or enter the yard on her own, when I'd fed the neighbor's dog the day before, I'd made certain that she didn't know where I was going. *How did Kokomo know that it was time to feed the neighbor's dog? How did she know it was my responsibility?* Unless she understood the conversation my neighbor had with me when he'd come to ask me for the favor, there was no way for Kokomo to know where I'd slipped off to the previous day or what I'd done.

However, Kokomo always seemed to know when something was amiss. When Quincy stole my sock off the clothes drying rack, she tattled on him by barking until I came to see what all her fuss was about. Thinking that the two dogs sometimes acted like rival siblings, I laughed.

Normally, she hated being bathed. One evening when she was filthy dirty from having chased her ball into the mud, I told her, "You can't sleep with me tonight unless you have a bath." Later when I went to brush my teeth, she followed me into the bathroom and sat beside the tub. "Would you like a bath, Kokomo?" I asked, thinking she'd run out of the room. She sat there. I started filling the tub, she didn't make a mad dash for the living-room. Surely, she'd run when I bent over to scoop her up. Nope! She wanted a bath and didn't even wiggle when I ran the shower over her or when I blew her fur dry with my hairdryer. At bedtime she stood by the bed, looking at me waiting for permission to jump up and spend the night cuddling. Having nightmares of being beaten much like what had happened when I was assaulted at work, I was more than happy to oblige. Hugging her comforted me when I'd awaken in the middle of the night, covered in sweat, my teeth aching from clenching them.

I'd long forfeited watching the news, crime shows or anything that might stimulate another bad dream. Instead, I only watched comedies and game shows, hoping to train my subconscious mind to search for the positive while I slept. As time passed, the bad dreams lessened in frequency, but not intensity. What saved me from a nervous breakdown was Kokomo's love.

Sometimes, I would wake up with my face and hands swollen, my ears ringing so loud I could hardly hear Kokomo's bark, and so dizzy I could barely stand. When I'd ask my family doctor or a specialist what medication might be causing these debilitating side-effects, the answer was always the same: "I don't know. You're on a lot of different medications, all of which you need."

Though it's impossible to know whether the cause was my head injuries or the multitude of prescribed medications I took daily, at one point, I couldn't always distinguish between what was real and what wasn't. While watching a movie about a little girl who was kidnapped, when I saw the kidnapper at a gas station, I made note of the name on the street sign and picked up the phone to call the police. Thankfully, I realized it was only a movie before I dialled 911.

Tired of waiting to get better, ignoring my family physician's and my specialist's advice, I tried going back to work but couldn't handle the physical or emotional stress. But that didn't stop me from trying to do things around my home.

A self-taught carpenter, one day I decided to turn a hallway closet into a pantry. On the fifth day of this slow-going project, the ringing in my ears and dizziness in my head intensified to the point where it felt as though I was about to collapse. Trying to use the walls for support, I bumped into the wall on one side and then the other as I zigzagged to the kitchen.

As was often the case when I was working on a project, determined to get as much done as possible, I'd ignored the thunderstorm warnings in my stomach and skipped lunch. Thinking that my blood sugar level might be low, using the counter and appliances for support, I managed to pour cereal and milk into a bowl. My sugar-fix prepared, I staggered into the living-room and flopped into an armchair.

Rather than subside, the dizziness became worse as the room started to spin. I called our provincial government nurse's hotline, 811. Unable to understand me, she told me to hang up and call 911. With the 911 operator still on the phone, at her insistence, I tried to get up to unlock the door. During my second attempt, I fell on the floor. "Crawl on your hands and knees," the operator shouted into the phone.

Unable to do that, having seen how soldiers in movies creep along the ground, I used my forearms to pull myself along the floor. Once at the door, I reached up to unlock and open it a crack. The second the door opened, Kokomo leapt over me and out the door. Seconds later, she returned long enough to lick my face, then took off again. A few more seconds later, she came back with a neighbor. The ambulance arrived shortly afterward.

The paramedics thought I was having a stroke or heart attack. Having once been a paramedic, although my symptoms were indicators, as my breathing was normal and my speech and thoughts clear, I was fairly certain that I wasn't having a heart attack or a stroke. However, I didn't argue when they insisted on taking me to emergency.

In the hospital, I was placed on an IV and given Gravol to settle my stomach and dizziness, and injected with a muscle relaxer. In the wee hours of the morning, after an ECG and blood work indicated that all was fine, the emergency doctor released me. Once home, although still a bit wobbly, when I sat on the couch and Kokomo jumped into my lap, I knew all would be okay.

As time passed, I realized and begrudgingly accepted that there were new limits to what my body could handle. Long periods of strenuous activity such as using an electric drill or saw, tightened the muscles in my neck, stimulating ringing in my ears and triggering migraine headaches. Though often frustrated by being forced to take frequent breaks, once Kokomo was by my side, I stopped fretting about whatever it was I could no longer do and instead enjoyed what I could do—hug, play and walk with my dog.

With long strong legs, a tiny body and weighing just over six pounds, Kokomo continually amazed me by jumping high into the air. Once while filling out forms at our local city hall, I placed her ball on the edge of a high counter so she would jump for it and keep herself entertained. I was surprised, when on her second attempt, Kokomo managed to get the ball in her mouth.

Amazed and impressed, a clerk measured the height of the counter—it was forty-six inches from the floor. Word of Kokomo's jumping prowess quickly spread and soon a crowd had gathered to watch her attempt the astonishing feat a second time. When she did, everyone laughed and applauded.

A people-magnate and attention-seeker, Kokomo made everyone happy. Whenever I gardened in our backyard, neighbors came to visit and play with her. Children delighted in tossing her ball, often giggling as they watched her scurry to retrieve it and then drop it at their feet before readying for the next toss. Elderly folks smiled wide when they watched the two of us playing in the park. If anything happened to Kokomo, the world would be a far less entertaining and happy place to be, especially for me.

Bending to check the last hole on the ferry deck, I spotted Kokomo's black tail. She had followed her ball out and was standing on the foot-wide ledge peering into the ferry's wake below. If she fell, I'd lose her forever.

"Kokomo, come here," I softly called. "Come to Mommy."

She turned her head to face me, but didn't move.

"Come on, you can do it," I coaxed her a little louder so she could hear me over the sound of the waves kicked up by the ferry's movement.

She inched closer and froze. Her little body shaking as her eyes trained on me.

I considered reaching for her; she was too far away.

"You want to go for a walk?" I asked, hoping that my invitation to do her favorite activity would take her mind off her ball and the perils that lurked below.

She took a few more steps and stopped.

I reached out, grabbed onto her and pulled her to safety. Crying, I hugged and rocked her as I cooed, "What would Mommy do without you?"

Afterward, I realized how fortunate it was that the ocean was relatively calm. If the waves had been five-feet-high as they sometimes were when a coastal gale bellowed across the Strait of Georgia, she might have been dumped off the narrow ledge. People say that cats have nine lives. Thanks to her curiosity, energy and playful nature, Kokomo had escaped more than that number in her first few years of life. Perhaps, my little guardian angel had someone watching out for her too.

It's been seven years since my life was forever altered. My family has been unwavering in their caring support and help. However, Kokomo is who gets me out of bed in the morning and keeps me going when I sometimes get marred in muddled thoughts, hopelessness or bouts of depression. Somehow, someway, she always knows when I need an emotional boost and will suddenly jump up on my knees, lick my face while I'm lying on the couch, or paw at my feet to get me to toss her ball. Most beneficial of all, she makes me smile, inside and out.

About Didi Simer

Didi Simer lives in Burnaby, British Columbia. She has three grown children. Didi has worked as a security officer, substitute teacher, dance instructor and as a first aid instructor. Didi enjoys cooking, gardening and spending time with her family and friends. She can be contacted by e-mail at info@heartmindeffect.com.

Her specialized vocabulary exercise book is used at Captain Meares Elementary Secondary School in Tahsis, B.C. Her poem in *Heartmind Wisdom Collection #1* is "Love Now and Then." Her chapter in *Heartmind Wisdom Collection #2* is "The Healing Power of a Puppy." The Heartmind Wisdom Collection is available at www.heartmindstore.com and through online bookstores.

LOVE IN ACTION
Stories from four *MVAfrica Mercy* Volunteers

JoJo Beattie

"Love and say it with your life."

—St. Augustine de Hippo

The eight-deck 15,572 ton *Africa Mercy* is the world's largest nongovernmental hospital ship. Docking in various ports along the coast of West Africa, the ship delivers state-of-the-art healthcare to regions where medical facilities and personnel are limited or nonexistent. The ship has five operating theaters, an intensive care unit, an ophthalmic unit, a CT scanner, x-ray equipment, a laboratory, an 82-bed recovery ward, and accommodation for the approximately 450 volunteers needed at a time to run the hospital.

Annually, 1200 people from around the globe pay their way to the vessel and fees for their onboard keep while they are donating their skills and considerable time to help others. From various walks of life—medical and dental professionals, engineers, cooks, teachers, baristas, receptionists and countless others with the skills required to run a small town—the volunteers ensure that this love in action echoes into the surrounding communities by also providing sustainability and disease prevention training. Through healthcare, education and friendship, their selfless service forever improves the lives of countless people, exemplifying St. Augustine's teaching: "Love and say it with your life."

The idea of bringing hope and healing to poverty-stricken people in urgent need of medical aid was inspired by the devastation caused by hurricane Cleo in 1964. What began as a tropical storm off the coast of Africa, moved westward and strengthened into a hurricane that pounded parts of the Eastern States and the Bahamas. A group of young survivors came up with the idea of a floating hospital. A decade later, husband and wife Don and Deyon Stephen brought the young group's dream to life.

Below are personal accounts from Canadian volunteers who served aboard the *Africa Mercy*, the third and largest vessel in Mercy Ships Charity Hospital Foundation's thirty-five years of service. The stories are only four amongst thousands that symbolize the way in which work is done aboard the *Africa Mercy*.

About Volunteer Nadine Steiner

A registered nurse, Nadine lives in Vancouver, British Columbia. She volunteered in 2013 when the *Africa Mercy* was docked in Conakry, Guinea. In addition to attending to their medical needs, she spent much of her free time educating and building relationships with her patients in the Obstetric Fistula Program. (An obstetric fistula is a hole between the birth canal and the urinary tract that occurs as a result of an unusually prolonged labor. In most cases, the child is stillborn, and the woman becomes incontinent. In addition to the physical trauma, in many cultures, sufferers endure rejection, isolation and extreme shame.)

NADINE'S ACCOUNT

Many heart-wrenching stories float through my mind when I recall the women I worked with in the Obstetric Fistula Program. Scattered throughout, are memories of devoted, steadfast families that remained by the side of women rejected by their communities. A few are of women who had to sneak off under night-cover to seek help aboard the *Africa Mercy*. Other recollections are of the horrific ordeals these women endured in order to survive as "untouchables."

In Guinea, as it is in much of West Africa, very young women are often married off to older men. The matrimonial union of these barely teenage females is negotiated by and according to the will of their fathers or other male relatives. A story that remains forefront in my mind is that of a patient's father who shared his regret for the way he treated his eldest daughter. For me, his outward sorrow reinforced that the work we were doing healed and served more than our patients; our program had a much broader reach that included helping to change the customs that perpetuated suffering.

A traditional and typical Guinean patriarch with four daughters to consider, he sought to marry them to older, more powerful men as soon as possible. After he arranged for his fourteen-year-old daughter to marry a man in his thirties, she soon became pregnant. When she went into labor, she was left on her own for three days. Fortunately, a family member realized that the baby was stuck and took the distressed girl to a hospital where she underwent a cesarean section.

Her baby was stillborn. Due to the immense pressure her body endured during the obstructed labor, his daughter was left with fistulas that caused her to leak stool and urine. Left with no child and a wife who was constantly wet and smelled foul, his daughter's husband immediately cast her off.

Certain that her father would not accept her back into his home, his daughter appealed to various friends and other family members. When it became clear that she had nowhere else to turn, she took her chances and returned to her father's house. His rage was as brutal as she had feared; however, it was directed at his daughter's husband, not her. By negotiating a marriage agreement with such a man, the father felt that he had failed his daughter. Distraught, he vowed to protect his younger daughters from a similar fate, and to secure medical treatment and provide emotional and financial support for his eldest daughter.

After sharing his regrets, this father spoke of the need to re-evaluate the traditions and values that sanctioned people from his culture marrying off their female children at such a young age. It was humbling and encouraging to hear about the transformation of a man whose influence could have an incredible impact on the way women and girls are valued in Guinea. I pray for him often.

Not every woman who received a surgical procedure was entirely healed of incontinence; however, all were grateful to the volunteers and God for the health gains they did receive. Having made friends and talked with women whose fate mirrored theirs, they spoke of feeling valued, less fearful and relieved that they would no longer be scorned, forced to live in isolation or have to beg for food.

As our fistula patients approached their discharge dates, the chaplaincy team on the ship ensured that they were celebrated at a Dress Ceremony. Each was given a beautiful new dress, jewelry, gifts and commemorative photos. At this solemn yet jubilant ceremony, many crew members and other patients gathered to sing, dance and pray. Watching their glowing faces and hearing their spoken testimonies, I knew that these women would enter their renewed lives feeling confident and blessed.

About Volunteer Nicole Moen

Nicole is a nurse who lives in Maple Ridge, British Columbia. She volunteered in 2013 when the *Africa Mercy* was docked in Conakry, Guinea. Like most everyone in North America, she'd read stories and watched programs about what people endured in war-torn countries. Once in Africa, what she thought she knew about the atrocities of war was not even close to the realities. A conversation Nicole had with a patient named Marla, rocked more than her perceptions.

NICOLE'S ACCOUNT

In the late 1990's, Marla had been a business man. As part of his work, in spite of the brutal civil war, he weekly crossed the border from his home in Sierra Leone into Guinea. When the Rebel United Front (RUF) began patrolling the border, in order to provide for his new bride, Marla continued his travels. In early 2000, following an unprovoked interrogation by the men and boys patrolling the border, he was arrested and tortured for information he didn't have. He eventually lost consciousness. When he awoke, a padlock had been shoved up his nose, hooked through a hole that had been knifed into the roof of his mouth and then locked shut through his smashed teeth.

When an aid organization in Sierra Leone found Marla, they took him to a local hospital to have the padlock removed from his face. The doctors were not able to remove it. Marla was transported from hospital to hospital, until the aid organization located a hospital in Conakry, Guinea where doctors were confident they could remove the padlock. They were able to remove it, but left him with a mangled face.

Unable to contact his family, Marla didn't know whether they were alive. Alone to deal with the residual pain and his deformities, he did his best to survive. His arrival at a Mercy Ships patient screening in Sierra Leone was the beginning of his three-year road to recovery. Through a series of several surgeries, the doctors placed a metal plate on the roof of his mouth, rebuilt his crushed face and reconstructed his nose using a flap from his forehead.

A week before we closed the hospital in Sierra Leone, Marla had his last surgery. When we welcomed him aboard, he was smiling and happy to be on the ship and eager to have the surgery that would give him two nostrils for his reconstructed button nose.

When I walked into the recovery unit after his surgery, Marla called me over so that he could demonstrate how he was able to breathe through his nose. He was going home with two nasal trumpets in place to hold the airways open and could remove them in a few weeks.

Witnessing his excitement as he thanked God for his wonderful new face, was inspiring. Although he had experienced the worst of humanity, throughout his recovery, he praised God for his blessings. My faith had never been tested in such a horrific manner; yet, I sometimes hesitated about sharing the gospel. Watching Marla lift his hands in praise will forever be my reminder to be bold and brave in the sharing of my faith and to always give thanks.

About Volunteer Brian Drebert

Brian is a registered nurse from Vancouver, British Columbia. He volunteered in 2013 when the *Africa Mercy* was docked off the coast of Conackry, Guinea. Now married, Brian and his wife volunteered together in 2015 when the ship was docked in Tamatave, Madagascar. The following is a post that he wrote after the second month of his initial service.

BRIAN'S BLOG POST

A few days before I left for Africa, I posted an Ernest Hemingway quote on my blog. Maybe you read it. If not, here it is:

"All I wanted to do now was get back to Africa. We had not left it yet, but when I would wake in the night, I would lie, listening, homesick for it already."

To be completely honest, I'll admit that I didn't really understand or relate to this quote at the time. How could I really? I would even go as far as to say that I didn't imagine myself ever feeling that way. Regardless, it sounded deep...so I used it.

The other night, I was lying awake in my upper bunk tossing and turning the night away when I finally understood what Hemingway meant. With just less than four weeks left in this field service, the reality that I will have to leave this place that has started to grip me so tightly, has set in. Funny, the transition that has taken place within me from when I first arrived. Initially, I was unsure how I could cut it out here for two and a half months, and now I'm having a hard time imagining leaving.

It seems like with the passing of each day, my heart has continued to soften towards this land and its people. The love that I initially felt incapable to offer, seems easier to give with each passing day. I'm finding that there is something to be said for "practicing to love." Just like anything else, after a while it starts to become easier...maybe even natural.

I will miss how "real" this place feels, and in turn, how "real" it makes me feel. Life as we know it just seems stripped down out here, raw even. The sun is hotter, the air more humid, the streets more dusty, the traffic more chaotic, the smells more strong, the sidewalks more cracked, the buildings more aesthetic, the people...more people. The struggle to survive...more. Everything seems more...ironically, there is even more joy, especially my own joy.

For myself, this "joy" has been birthed out of doing. Feeling like I'm making a difference and ultimately finding more meaning in my own life. I think these are all things possible back home, just seems like life tends to get in the way. I guess that's the challenge, figuring out how to navigate life leaving room for doing things that bring meaning and ultimately joy.

Eventually I will leave Africa...but I don't think it will ever leave me. I pray that the challenges it's given me and the lessons I've learned will never be forgotten. I know that I will miss it though, because I miss it already...

About Volunteer Jasmine Bursey

Jasmine is a hairstylist from Guelph, Ontario. She was twenty-two years old when she volunteered in 2014. Her story is about a woman who entered her shop when the *Africa Mercy* was docked in Pointe-Noire, Republic of the Congo.

JASMINE'S ACCOUNT

Her head held high, a woman walked into the ship's salon and told me that it was her sixtieth birthday. She removed her hair net and immediately began fiddling with her hair, which I assumed was usually perfectly coiffed. She explained how she liked it cut, and added that it didn't need much work because her stylist at home would *fix it* when she got back. She just wanted to feel good on her birthday. She was picky, precise and particular. *Not* a hairstylist's favorite.

Our chitchat quickly turned into a more personal conversation. She shared that since the passing of her sweetie three years earlier, she had been traveling the world with different organizations. She filled her time with tsunami relief, attending to the poor in crisis areas, tornado cleanup, and now here she was on a ship on the west coast of Africa. She found it hard to be away from home. At least her kids were happy that she wasn't at home feeling depressed.

As I listened, my respect for her grew and I quickly regretted that I let her attitude bother me at first. I realized that this woman was not afraid of hard work. She wanted to be of use. She longed to make her deceased husband proud; to feel alive and make a difference in this world.

Between each snip, I noticed her eyes begin to brighten. She sat more upright, and as she relaxed, the corners of her mouth turned upward. I asked if her hair was how she liked it. With a grin she said, 'Don't tell my stylist, but if you were in Colorado….'' We both smiled. She apologized for her initial abrupt approach, explaining that she always found it hard to try a new hairstylist.

She gleamed when she saw herself in the mirror and I could tell she was ready to celebrate. As she gathered her things, I heard God's soft whisper, "Pray for her."

"Can we pray together before you leave?" I asked.

Delighted, she dropped what she was holding. Hands joined, we closed our eyes and prayed. "Thank you Lord for this woman's sixty years on earth. Protect her family while she's away doing Your work. Shower her with blessings for the acts of service she is doing." Opening my eyes and looking at her, I finished with, "May you feel His peace and the warmth of His love. Amen."

Tears streamed from her eyes. "Thank you," she managed to say. She opened her arms and gave me a hug, holding on for an extended moment. It felt like a hug of gratitude, an embrace of joy. I caught her eye as she walked out the door; she alternated between smiling and crying.

I prayed again. "Thank you, Lord, for the opportunity to fulfill the Divine appointment with which You have entrusted me. I know this is the reason I came to the *Africa Mercy*. When I share my gifts with others, I feel lighter and see them as fuller. Blessing and praying with them has healed me. Moreover, I get to enhance the beauty of others that God has created. I rejoice as I watch them see their reflection in the mirror when their hair appointment is finished. God made us perfectly in His image."

Mercy Ships Charity Hospital Foundation follows Jesus's 3000 year old model of love in action. As humans, our lives revolve around love. No matter our circumstances, we all want to be loved, to share love, and to learn to love ourselves. More than an organization, Mercy Ships is a global family of people from all walks of life working together to help bring hope and healing to those in need. The more we demonstrate love through humanitarian deeds, encouraging words, friendship and prayer, the more peaceful and positive our world.

Four core values of Mercy Ships

- Love God.
- Love and serve others.
- Be people of integrity.
- Aim for excellence in all you say and do.

*"At the center of the universe is a loving heart
that continues to beat and that wants the best for
every person. Anything we can do to help foster
the intellect and spirit and emotional growth of
our fellow human beings, that is our job."*

—Fred Rogers,
Presbyterian minister,
television personality,
songwriter and educator.

About JoJo Beattie

JoJo lives in Victoria, British Columbia. She is an artist with a passion for human rights and for helping to give others' a voice. JoJo is the Public Relations Coordinator for Mercy Ships, Victoria. She can be contacted via info@heartmindeffect.com.

About Mercy Ships Charity Hospital Foundation

Mercy Ships uses hospital ships to deliver free, world-class health care services, capacity building and sustainable development to those without access in the developing world. Founded in 1978 by Don and Deyon Stephens, Mercy Ships has worked in more than 70 countries providing services valued at more than one billion dollars, and with more than 2.35 million direct beneficiaries. Website: www.mercyships.ca

SELF-
ACTUALIZATION

I AM POSSIBLE

Hema Subramanyam

"Hi, Manni. I'm moving to Canada!" I excitedly announced, addressing my cousin's wife Lakshmi by the Tamil name for sister-in-law.

As she moved about their kitchen, she smiled before saying, "Oh, I didn't know that you had a work assignment in Canada. When did that happen?"

"No, Manni. I am not going on any work assignment. I am moving to Canada."

She stopped and shot me a look of disbelief hedged with horror. "Why are you leaving Hyderabad? Why Canada?"

Joining us in their kitchen, her husband said, "Lakshmi, don't worry; she must be joking. Why would Hema leave her family?" My cousin's alarmed expression told me that he wasn't happy about my decision.

I was shocked. I assumed that they would be happy for me and would want to celebrate my brave, bold move to North America. My intention was not to hurt the people I loved most in the world. After my mother died, my cousin and Manni had quickly become my closest family. I usually shared everything with Manni. The obvious hurt in her gold-flecked brown eyes told me that it was a mistake to keep it a secret that I'd applied for my Canadian permanent residence status.

"Well, are you moving?" Manni demanded to know.

"Yes," I said. Unprepared for their reaction, I sheepishly tucked in my chin and said nothing more.

Shaking his head, my cousin's eyes locked on mine. "I do not understand why you want to uproot yourself. You are doing fine here."

Knowing it was always best to keep quiet when another was upset, I did. With each of my cousin's interrogating questions, I thought about what my answer would be…later, when he calmed down and Manni appeared less sad.

"You are not all that young, Hema," my cousin continued.

Exactly! Being in my late-forties was a reason to go, not a reason to stay.

"Besides, what will you do in Canada?"

I don't know what I will do in Canada, which is one of the reasons I am going. I want adventure and to explore the world.

"Do you have any friends?"

I don't have any friends there yet, but I will make some.

"Do you have a job?"

I do not have a job, but I will find one.

"Do you have a home?"

I do not have a home there, but I will find somewhere even if it's only a temporary place. The details that concerned him did not concern me. *How would it be an adventure if I already had all those things in order?* Life had a way of working out in my favor, and it would this time too.

Still, my cousin's concerns were valid. I was a single, middle-aged woman going by myself to a country I'd never visited. I didn't know a single soul and was clueless about what I was going to do career-wise. Yet, I was excited, not afraid. I would figure out everything once I was there. I had researched the country online and chosen Vancouver, British Columbia, for my new home. I loved everything I read about the city. No matter what anyone said, I was moving to Canada.

Over the next few months, I shared my plans with other family members, friends and coworkers. With the exception of my two best friends, people seemed shocked by my decision. Almost everyone's reaction was surprise followed by an interrogation as to whether I'd lost my mind. A few expressed sentiments akin to pity. It took a while for me to recover from the unexpected reaction of my friends and family, but when I reflected calmly, the reason became clear.

A big country with an even bigger population, India lived simultaneously in several planes. What was true for one community and culture might be completely alien to another. When India was a British colony and the period following its independence, bright young people (mostly men) from wealthy families went to Cambridge or Oxford to complete their higher studies. Gradually, the desired education and residence destination switched to the United States of America.

Influenced by their parents' desires and ambitions, from a very young age, almost every child in India wanted to study, work and live in the States. In fact, family pride and societal status were intrinsically linked to making it "big" in USA and living happily ever after. Though this status-conscious achievement goal didn't uniformly apply to all regions of the country, it was a primary success indicator within large cities, including Hyderabad where I lived.

Priding itself in academic brilliance and professional achievement, almost everyone in my community aspired to attain at least a master's degree from a foreign university. Young adults choose careers based on current trends, demand and the attached status. Their leaving home to become a medical professional, engineer or computer scientist, or a financial, business or managerial expert was expected and commonplace. Year after year, Hyderabad had the esteemed distinction of having the highest percentage of people immigrating to the United States either to attain a higher education or pursue a career. Practically every household had at least one immediate family member who was either studying or working in the States.

The last thing anyone expected of undereducated, single, not-so-young me was that I'd choose Canada to immigrate. Not that they had anything against the country; most people didn't know enough about the nation or people to form an opinion. They simply could not fathom why I'd chosen Canada over its coveted neighbor.

My final week in India was busy; my last day, heartbreaking.

As I traveled about the country on a work assignment, between writing project reports, I reviewed my must-do-before-I-leave list. Though excited, I was a tad nervous about moving to the other side of the planet. Shoring my nerve was that I'd traveled extensively abroad and within India, had lived on my own for many years, and was accustomed to doing things by myself.

Even though I could afford the luxury of hired help, I preferred to be self-sufficient. However, there were a million things that needed to be done and some tasks were not easily accomplished. For instance, having decided to take only two suitcases, I fretted about what to pack and what to give away. Thankfully, my worry turned to joy when I donated my nearly new and barely worn sarees, shawls, handbags and accessories to an old age home run by nuns. Grateful, the sisters blessed me.

Being able to open a Canadian bank account from India and immediately transfer funds alleviated my access to money concerns. Disappointingly, however, a neighbor couple to whom I had lent a substantial amount of money, promised to return it before I left and didn't. Though I suspected the husband and wife were happy that I was leaving and had no one to follow up with them, I was sad to lose my trust in them and their friendship. When Dad was alive, he used to say, "When you lend someone money, don't expect it back. That way, you won't have any rude surprises." He was right. Being angry or resenting their betrayal served no purpose.

Most distressing of all was that Manni and my cousin became increasingly distant and unavailable until it felt as though we were strangers. When they didn't volunteer to see me off at the airport, I was hurt. Having lost both of my parents years earlier, my cousin, his wife and their three kids were my family. Though I had other relatives and friends nearby, I wasn't close to them. My very best friend lived outside the city. Being isolated was partially due to how much I hated to ask anyone for help. Used to being independent, I seldom reached out in a way that indicated I needed and wanted their support.

Rather than concentrate on my disappointment and hurt feelings, I put my energies into preparing to move. Most disconcerting was that though I kept searching the Internet for short-term accommodation, I found none. Finally, I googled "People who immigrated to Canada from India in the past year." That search led me to an active online forum where recent immigrants were sharing information on jobs, housing, schools, cities, etc. Ah, the miracles of modern technology that helped people connect across the world!

I posted a query asking for help and suggestions for finding a place to live in Vancouver. Within days, I received a response from a gentleman who had recently moved to the Lower Mainland region. As I was single and female, to ensure my safety and a smooth transition, his advice was that I live with an Indian family in an area where there were plenty of Sikhs who spoke Punjabi. That place turned out to be Surrey, the second largest city in British Columbia and only a half-hour commute from Vancouver. Thankfully, he made the arrangements and assured me that when I arrived, my new home would be ready for me to move into.

The final few days before my departure were stressful. It was mid-summer in India and the temperature hovered around 40°C. Prone to migraine headaches when under stress, especially if it's also hot, I worried that I would get sick. Fortunately, I didn't.

Most international flights leave India around midnight. After learning that I was leaving that day, an old friend came to wish me good luck. Shocked that Manni and my cousin weren't seeing me off, he insisted on driving me to the airport.

Waiting for my flight, from their accents, it was easy to tell which of my Indian travel companions had spent considerable time in the United States. When the lady next to me enquired about my destination and I told her that I was moving to Canada, her entire response was, "Oh."

Having booked my flight well in advance, I had only one stopover in London, England. Overcome with exhaustion, I fell asleep the minute we were airborne. Though I vaguely recall a flight attendant tapping me on the shoulder during the meal service, I was too tired to eat or drink. I slept blissfully and didn't wake up until ten hours later when we landed in London, England.

While sitting at my departure gate for my flight to Vancouver, a couple sat down across from me. I was surprised to see that the man had a turban and the woman was wearing a traditional salwar kameez. It was the first hint of what would soon be the only cultural shock in my entire move.

The flight from London to Vancouver was pleasant and uneventful. Having emigrated from Bangladesh thirty years earlier, my taxi driver from the airport to Surrey provided me with a list of newcomer dos and don'ts. Toward the top of his list was that I should never accept even water from a stranger in case they slipped drugs into my drink. Receiving wisdom generally reserved for teens and university students made me feel young.

As though I were family, my new landlords in Surrey welcomed me with a warm smile and a delicious home-cooked Indian meal. My basement suite was spotlessly clean and the fridge thoughtfully stocked with a week's worth of food. I was overwhelmed by their kindness and generosity.

While exploring the city, I was shocked by the number of Sikhs wearing their traditional attire and by the number of *gurudwaras* (Sikh temples) in Surrey. I felt as though I had been magically transported to a city in the state of Punjab. From a cosmopolitan city in South India where most people were fluent in three or more languages, Punjabi being not one of them, I was surprised when person after person spoke to me in Punjabi. This had never happened to me in India, making it seem strange that it was happening in Canada. Some people were mildly offended when I politely told them that although I spoke four different Indian languages, I didn't speak Punjabi.

Within a short while, I was convinced that what I'd heard about Canadians being open, accepting and polite was true. Making friends was easy. Discovering that people from almost every part of the world had made this culturally diverse country their own, made me feel welcomed and happy.

Finding suitable employment was challenging. Working below my abilities at a variety of unfulfilling jobs, I occasionally considered moving back to India. Eventually, I solved this conundrum by starting my own business.

Though leaving my good friends' basement suite was emotional, after I'd been in Canada for three years, I moved into a beautiful apartment in downtown Vancouver. Located in the heart of the multicultural metropolis and within walking distance of my place was a luscious green 1000-acre oasis called Stanley Park. Almost entirely surrounded by the Pacific Ocean, the public park contained gorgeous bays, a nine-kilometer seawall for cyclist and pedestrians, and evergreen trees tall enough to shake hands with the sun and moon. Set against mountains that were snowcapped in winter and peaked inside fluffy white clouds the rest of the year, for me, Vancouver was heaven on earth.

Though the closed-minded attitudes of some dampened my spirits when I was preparing for my move to Canada, I know that if they were alive, my parents would have wholeheartedly approved of my decision. My father encouraged me to follow my heart. My mother named me Hema, a Sanskrit name meaning "golden." Mythically, Hema was the daughter of the ice mountain and a goddess. No wonder I felt like a blessed goddess when I moved to the beautiful city at the lap of the mountains. Neither was it surprising that the business that I chose to do in Vancouver revolved around gold.

The year after I emigrated from India, to clear a backlog, the Canadian government closed the files of thousands of immigrants who'd applied for permanent residency. The following year, the age of immigrants deemed desirable was drastically lowered. Had I decided to immigrate even one year later, it is quite plausible that my application would not have been approved. As *they* say, timing is everything.

I continue to heed the desires of my heart. At times, this proves to be the right thing to do; other times, not. Regardless, I have no regrets. I never meant to be a rebel, but neither do I apologize for taking a stand or for acting on my dreams and ambitions. No matter the odds, the challenges, or the doubts of those who don't share my visions, I proudly strive to be the best I can be. As *I* say, I am possible.

> *"Nothing is impossible, the word itself says 'I'm possible!'"*
>
> —Audrey Hepburn

About Hema Subramanyam

Hema lives in Vancouver, British Columbia. She enjoys people and nature, and has traveled extensively. A business woman who heeds the desires of her heart, Hema is a shining example for entrepreneurs everywhere. Hema can be contacted at info@heartmindeffect.com.

LEARNING TO DANCE IN RAIN

Deborah Nelson

Sitting in my new surroundings after downsizing, I paused to reflect on my sixty-two years of life, especially how proud I am of my children and their accomplishments. Though we don't always agree, which is normal with parents and children, my hope is that they understand that I truly and deeply love them and who they are. Thanks to lessons hard learned by me, their journeys have vastly differed from mine. However, glimpsing my life today, no one would ever know what my journey has been.

I was born the last of three children. My brother was five years older than I, my sister thirteen years. I wasn't an afterthought; my brother wanted a baby brother. When I was born female, he implored, "Mom, take her back where she came from." It was an often told family story that stung.

As was the norm in the fifties, my mother was a stay-at-home mom, and my father was the authoritative master-of-the-house. Under his rule, children were to be seen and not heard. No one dared question him.

Though Mom was spunky, determined and loving, by the time I was ready for school, her high-spirited energy had disappeared. When it came to my father, she simply did what he wanted…expected. With the exception of his son, nothing anyone did was right and nothing accomplished, was good enough.

One day when I was seven and doing homework in my bedroom, I heard my mother scream and then a thud, thud, thud. I ran to the top of the stairs leading to the basement and watched her roll down the last two stairs before her head hit the concrete hard.

I froze. "Mom, are you okay?"

She didn't move.

My brother at high school and Father at work, it was up to me to do something. I ran down the twelve stairs and touched her shoulder. Her eyes were closed. Again I asked, "Mom, are you okay?"

She moaned and turned her head slightly.

She was alive. Maybe she needed a doctor.

"Mom, who should I call to drive us to the hospital?" Only a couple of neighbors had cars and the men would have taken them to work.

"No, I'll be okay in a minute. Just let me lie here."

I wanted her to be *okay*, so even though her eyes looked dazed, I waited.

After a few minutes, Mom rolled onto her side and looked up at me. "I have to get the laundry done," she said, trying to get up. She didn't finish her sentence with "or your father will be mad," but I knew it was her unspoken concern.

Most days, I wished my father wouldn't come home. That day, I prayed it would be soon.

When she was ready, I helped Mom limp over to the washing machine. My stomach in knots, I watched as she took out the clothes one at a time and fed them through the wooden wringer to squish out the excess water. Leaning against the washer for support, she looked ghostly pale.

Once all the clothes were in the basket, I carried the heavy load while Mom used the bannister to pull herself up the stairs to the main floor. Obviously in pain, Mom slowly passed me items of clothing as I stood on my tiptoes and stretched to hang each on the clothesline. Once finished, we headed for the kitchen. Father would expect his dinner on the table at six.

I was setting the dining room table when the front door opened and closed. Father was home. Always either grouchy or blatantly withdrawn, when Mom didn't greet him at the door and ask about his day, he'd know something was wrong and demand to know what.

Standing in the kitchen doorway, the newspaper in his hand, he watched as Mom hobbled between the counter and the stove.

"You're limping," he said with a shrug.

"I caught the heel of my shoe on my skirt and fell down the stairs," Mom explained.

"Oh, that's great! Another expense," he barked. "Now I'll have to pay to have your shoe repaired."

I was shocked. He wasn't the least bit concerned about Mom, just money.

Never given an allowance, at age eight, I took a nine-block paper route in a neighborhood littered with apartment buildings. Without a bike of my own, I borrowed my brother's. It was too big for me and the straddle bar in the middle made it difficult for me to reach the pedals.

As I had to make several six-block trips to the "shack" to get more newspapers, when he hired me, I could tell that the manager thought I'd soon give up and quit. When I piled the papers high above the wire frame of the oversized basket it was tough to balance the bike, so I pushed it.

One day, the bike basket full of newspapers, a policeman stopped his car so I could get across the busy street. Smiling, I pushed my bike into the first lane where he was and checked for traffic coming from the other direction.

Suddenly, my bike and all the newspapers went flying as I hit the pavement. Still gripping the handlebars, I tried to figure out what happened.

Jumping out of his car, the policeman asked, "Are you okay?"

I nodded. My papers were everywhere and the wheel of my brother's bike was mangled. Feeling a stinging burn on my thigh, I noticed that my pants were ripped. I was going to be in big trouble. Father would be mad about the expense of fixing the bike and my pants. "I have to finish delivering the papers," I said to the policeman, trying to right the bike while surveying the damage.

After assuring me it would be okay if I didn't finish delivering the papers that day, the policeman put my bike in the trunk of his car.

Thinking of how often my mom kept going when she didn't feel well, I hesitated. However, not wanting to argue with the policeman, I agreed to pack it in for the day.

Leaving me alone to fret, he went to tell the shack manager what had happened. When he returned, he drove me home.

Mom was glad I wasn't hurt badly and thanked the tall policeman for bringing me home. When she later relayed what had happened to my father, I watched in horror as his brown eyes darted back and forth. He was calculating how much it was going to cost to fix the bike and my pants. Thankfully, he didn't scold me for being careless; nor did he ask if I was okay.

Desperate for Father's approval, I deliberately excelled at almost everything my brother was praised for doing. It was for naught. My accomplishments were ignored.

Anxious during written exams, my elementary school grades were average, sometimes below average. I wanted to do well, but was paralyzed by fear, especially when the teacher asked me a question. *What if I gave an incorrect answer and my classmates laughed at me?*

I dreaded physical education classes. Exposing my arms and legs meant I was forced to lie about the bruises left by Father's belt. No one questioned my claims that I'd fallen or that I bruised easily. Not even the teachers.

Taking Mom's lead, to avoid the immutable emotional abuse aimed at female family members, like her, I withdrew into a shell, seldom saying anything when Father was present. When tension ignited and fueled by him became unbearable, to escape his wrath or my parents' fighting, I hid in my closet. I kept a flashlight in my private sanctuary so I could read. My closet was my vacation from a frightful reality, my safe place.

The eldest, my sister often expressed her wish that my brother and I hadn't been born. In particular, she viewed me as a nuisance and pest. If I didn't comply with her requests, she would either punish or neglect me.

One day after school while visiting my sister in her bedroom, I spotted a pretty figurine. Thinking our mother would like to see it, I picked up the ornament and headed for the kitchen where Mom was making dinner. As I reached the last step, I heard my sister coming down the stairs. Without warning, she grabbed onto my long blond hair and yanked me back up the eighteen wooden stairs. My feet knocked out from under me, my lower back repeatedly smashed against the hard stairs, sending waves of excruciating pain up my spine. Once in her room, with me trembling, crying and rubbing my back, she grabbed the figurine and put it back on the shelf. It was then that she told me that the ornament was a gift from her boyfriend, whom our parents didn't like.

When I was six years old, one night while my brother was babysitting me, unable to sleep, I got out of bed and went to his room where he was doing homework.

"You're supposed to be sleeping," he said, and then looked at my feet. "You know you're not allowed to walk around barefoot."

He didn't seem mad, so I moved closer to him.

"If you don't go back to bed, I'll shoot the *rocket* at you," he warned as he glanced toward what looked to me like a harmless plastic toy.

I walked around the desk.

He grabbed and dropped the rocket on the floor and stepped on it, shooting a straight pin at my foot.

"Ouch," I hollered.

Reloading his weapon, he shot me again.

Still wanting to be with him, I didn't run away. For the next few minutes, with one hand on the desk and the other braced on the wall, I jumped up and down, trying to keep my feet off the floor to avoid getting hit.

He missed me a number of times before a straight pin went deep into my foot. Unexpectedly painful, my knees buckled. I fell on the floor and broke off the bottom half of one of my front permanent teeth. The nerve exposed, my tooth started to throb. I cried. Without comforting me, my brother told me to go back to bed.

I picked up my tooth and did what I was told.

When my parents came home, my father gave me the strap for getting out bed and for being barefoot. My brother just watched and smiled.

In addition to my newspaper route, to make certain I had pocket money, I took every weekend babysitting job offered and saved as much as I could. When the dad of three kids I babysat became overtly friendly with me, I was confused but grateful for the fatherly attention. My father never complimented anyone but my brother, so when this man thanked me for taking care of his kids and told me what a wonderful job I was doing, I glowed.

When this man's attention turned amorous, at only eight years old, at first, I was too surprised to protest or voice that his lingering hugs and kisses on my lips made me feel yucky. When able to find my words, I shook my head and begged, "No. No. No." The tall heavyset man ignored me. I was too young and innocent to fully understand what was happening to me, too intimidated by adults to stand up for myself.

I told my father what was happening and that I did not want to babysit for that family again. Father shrugged off my claims, saying I didn't know what I was talking about and inferring that whatever happened to me, I brought about myself. I was confused. *How could I not know what I was talking about when it was happening to me? How could I be responsible for someone else's behavior?*

For the next several years, my pleas for the man to leave me alone were unheeded as he repeatedly violated me. With each violation, I felt more and more powerless and less and less human. But nothing I said mattered. I didn't matter. I was nothing.

Father's refusal to believe or rescue me left me feeling lost, lonely and further convinced that because I was a female, apart from pleasing men, I simply did not matter. Hating that I had been born into such an unfair and uncaring world, I withdrew and became silent.

It wasn't until later, when the man's relationship with his wife deteriorated to the point where it was likely they would divorce, that I was finally not required to babysit for this couple.

In my mid-teens, I became interested in boys. Following Mom's lead, I placed males on pedestals. The idea that I was lovable never entered my mind.

Trapped in my need for approval, when a boy I was dating continually insulted and degraded me, I took it. Often, I was also subjected to insults from female schoolmates who were jealous that I was dating a particular boy. Not only did I not know how to stand up for myself, I was somewhat convinced that I must be deserving of ill treatment.

At age fifteen, when I started working as a receptionist at a car dealership on Saturdays, I was an easy target for the full-time staff. Knowing I wouldn't complain, they repeatedly assigned me work that was theirs to do. Allowing others to take advantage of me became a pattern that I repeated in my first full-time job as a records clerk for the airlines. When asked to do something, I did it without question, often working hours of overtime to complete tasks not in my job description.

At nineteen, I married a used car salesman from the dealership where I still worked on Saturdays. Finally, someone wanted me. Finally, I could escape my parents' house, my father's emotional abuse and the unhappiness that permeated our home.

Ten years my senior and of a different nationality, seemingly intrigued by me, my husband initially treated me with respect. Grateful, I happily paid the majority of our expenses while he struggled to make sales at the dealership.

A year into our marriage, once a week he'd stay out all night. Each time I questioned where he'd been, his excuses were borderline believable. Though it was unfathomable to me that he might be cheating, after a conversation with a girlfriend, I hired a private investigator to follow him.

The investigator confirmed that my spouse was indeed having an affair. When I asked my husband about what I'd learned, he admitted to having had several affairs because I wasn't fulfilling his sexual needs. Accepting the blame, I wondered why he didn't just teach me how to please him. However, unable to trust him, a short while later, I filed for divorce.

Emotionally drained, I wondered about my ability to recognize love, and what it was to truly give and receive love. I had a vague notion that if I was ever going to attract genuine love, I needed to believe in myself. Unfortunately, I couldn't visualize how to achieve this elusive goal.

After divorcing my husband, I moved into an apartment and worked three jobs. Learning to survive on little sleep, the only personal time I allowed myself was Sunday mornings, when I did laundry and shopping.

Five years later, my work associates introduced me to a male friend of theirs and we all went bike riding. When this man and I started dating, I fell back into pleasing mode. Ignoring my wants, I decided it wasn't "normal" to *want* to be on my own. When he asked me to marry him, though my instincts told me to say no, the little voice in my head screamed, "You must keep him happy and do whatever he wants." We married a year later. I quit my part-time jobs but continued working full-time.

Years of babysitting led me to believe that motherhood wasn't for me. My husband wanted six kids. We remained childless until my doctor advised me to give my body a break from birth control pills. Contraception became my husband's responsibility. Once again, I had no control over my own body or life. Having witnessed the lack of interaction and teaching in the homes where I babysat for mothers who worked full-time, when I became pregnant, I agreed to quit work when the baby was born.

Our lovely daughter gave me someone to love, who in her own way, loved me back. Intent on doing all the little things for her that weren't done for me, I absorbed myself in motherhood. Two years later, our second daughter was born and life became taxing. Jealous of her baby sister, I read to my eldest while nursing the baby, baked with her when the baby was sleeping, and took them both for daily walks. Still, she seemed unhappy, which broke my heart.

Rather than help, my husband disengaged. He traveled on business more often. When home, under the guise of needing quiet time, he cut us off emotionally and physically by retreating to a room downstairs. Though I knew what he was doing was wrong, having been raised by an emotionally unavailable father, I accepted it. As he claimed having a son would make him happy, I reluctantly agreed to have another child.

Six weeks into my pregnancy, knowing something was different, maybe wrong, I went to my gynecologist. He informed me that I was carrying twins. A thousand fears exploded in my head. My marriage was faltering. There wasn't enough of me to keep both of my daughters happy, how could I keep four kids content? What if my husband and I got divorced? I couldn't rely on him to provide financial support when he refused to provide emotional support. How would I feed four hungry mouths? Not knowing what else to do, I asked the gynecologist for an abortion. He refused my request. Unless my husband gave his permission, the doctor wouldn't perform the operation. Rendered powerless, I followed through with my duties.

In the first week of the ninth month, my stomach at maximum expansion, I underwent a cesarean. While I was unconscious, my gynecologist and husband decided to cauterize my fallopian tubes. Regardless that the doctor may have been trying to do me a favor, it infuriated me that I was sterilized without being consulted.

Once home with the twins (a boy and a girl), still recovering from major surgery, life was a hectic marathon for me. My husband remained uninvolved with the children and in the daily upkeep of the house. With the twins nursing on different schedules, and determined to remain engaged with my three and five-year-old so neither would feel left out, I ran all day and sometimes all night.

When the twins were two, my husband decided he wanted a change and left us. Though he provided some child support, it wasn't enough. Having been out of the workforce for seven years, I had to take a job that paid minimum wage, the majority of which went toward childcare.

We agreed that as our children resided with me, I would receive sixty percent of the proceeds from the sale of our family home. Before the house sold, my husband decided he wanted fifty percent, not forty. Able to afford a good lawyer, he won. It was one more battle lost among too many to count.

The constant strain of juggling my job, house work, cooking and helping my children cope with their father's exit, left me in a constant state of exhaustion. I worried constantly, especially on alternative weekends when the kids stayed at his place. My fear that he wouldn't provide the emotional nurturing they needed proved founded. Numerous times, I drove an hour each way to pick them up when they called and asked to come home early. As time passed, they didn't want to spend any time at his place. In her teens, rebelling against my rules, my eldest daughter moved to her father's. She returned home within a couple of weeks.

During this time, I met a man who was a year older than me and had never been married. He enjoyed interacting with my children, often drawing pictures to go along with stories he made up to entertain them. He eventually moved in with us, which helped financially. For three years, life was good. Then he started his own business.

A few years later, explaining that his business needed an influx of cash, he asked me to secure a mortgage on my house. Raised to be supportive of my mate, I did. Busy with work, running the house, caring for my children, and trusting his judgment, initially, I didn't ask to look at his business records. However, once the mortgage money was in the bank and I found the time to go over his books, I was shocked to discover that his suppliers hadn't been paid and that he was making substantial monthly payments on his new truck. When his business failed, as interest rates were twenty-four percent and I couldn't make the payments, the bank foreclosed on the mortgage and I lost my house.

Devastated but determined, I vowed to find a nearby rental home so that my children wouldn't suffer the heartache of leaving the community they'd known since birth. It wasn't easy, but I found a suitable home.

Wanting a career that would support my family without any help from someone else, I returned to school and dedicated myself to obtaining my bachelor's and then master's degree in psychology. For the next several years, I worked full-time during the day and scoured textbooks in the evening, often working on papers and assignments into the early hours of the morning.

During the eighth year in our rental home, the landlord decided to sell the house. It was the twins' graduation year, a time when the stability of a familiar neighborhood was of utmost importance. Though it was more expensive, we moved to a new home. Being forced to move made me even more determined to complete my education, which I did.

Unhappily coupled, at my request, though it took him a year, my partner moved out. A short time later, my eldest daughter asked if she and her young son could move in with me. She'd been living five hundred miles away in Calgary, Alberta, so I was shocked to learn that she was leaving her husband and wanted a fresh start. Though sad that her marriage didn't work out, I was proud of her for having the courage to make such a momentous move. They lived with me for nearly a year. It was wonderful seeing my grandson every day.

While working full-time, over the next few years I built my psychology practice into a viable business. Now grown, all my children have left home and embarked on their own lives. My twin daughter works for the government in Yellowknife. Last year, my second oldest daughter completed her master's in marine biology. My eldest daughter and grandson still live nearby in Vancouver, British Columbia. She's gainfully employed and a terrific mother. My son completed his Bachelor of Computer Science degree, and is currently designing educational games for children. Equally heartwarming, he treats women with respect.

I'm proud of all of my children…and myself. Despite being physically, emotionally, and sexually abused and bruised, and against what sometimes seemed insurmountable challenges, I persevered. I know that my example as a mother helped my daughters and son realize that men and women are equal. Although it often required me to work two full-time jobs at a time, I'm pleased that I was able to put a decent roof over my family's head and help with the cost of my children's schooling.

I've come to know that, regardless of circumstances, when one truly desires to make positive changes in their life, the possibility exists. Though it might take years, by clarifying and setting goals, anyone's dreams and ambitions can be accomplished, one step at a time. For me, the first step was realizing that I needed to recognize and boost my self-worth. Though it took a few failed relationships, the second was taking back control of my destiny by getting the education needed to live the life I desired.

In my counseling practice, I teach my clients that although "poor me" ponderings might be justified, even comforting in the moment, in the long run, self-pity keeps one stuck in muddy despair. As adults we have the power to choose. One can remain mired in childhood mistreatment, or use these resentments as a road map for change.

Though my father viewed jewelry as a frivolous waste of money, I didn't. At age thirteen, having saved money from my bike route and babysitting, I proudly purchased gold earrings. Saving for this treasured acquisition was a crucial stride in my path toward independent thinking and action. As the youngest child, my needs and wants were often ignored or ridiculed. One of my primary parenting goals was ensuring none of my children ever felt left out or inferior. It irked me that my father and brother viewed women as second-class citizens and treated my mother and me with disrespect. As such, I raised my kids to view both sexes as being equally deserving of proper treatment, consideration and reverence.

If you truly desire to make changes, believe that there is something better in store for you. Focus on how you want your life to unfold, and pursue your goals with steadfast determination. Remember, inaction breeds hopelessness, while action breeds the hope that fuels positive outcomes. Facing one's fears and tackling one's dreams leads to liberation, increased confidence and happiness.

Since getting my degree and starting my psychology practice, I've set aside a portion of each paycheck for traveling. I've been to the Caribbean, Panama, the South Pacific, Alaska, and Mexico. Having learned to fully engage in life regardless of whether I have a partner, I sometime travel alone. What I discovered is that free of anyone else's desires and demands, I can do what I want, when I want.

I also joined a Flamenco group because this dance doesn't require a partner and allows me to passionately and freely express my creative self. It's very healing and life-affirming. I haven't closed and bolted the relationship door. However, I now open it with seasoned caution and from a peaceful place born of self-love and confidence.

I hope you make the decision to break free of the emotional and circumstantial chains strangling your dreams. Make a list of all those things that you have always wanted to do, and begin to do them. Regardless of whether you do it on your own, or with the help of a good counselor, make now the time that you move out of your comfort zone and into your joy zone. And one day, you too will learn to dance in the rain until the sun shines.

*Positive change is possible when you have the courage to
dare and refuse to give up.
Always remember that you are deserving of happiness.*

—Deborah Nelson

About Deborah Nelson

Deborah is the proud mother of four grown, wonderful and caring children. She holds a Master Degree in Psychology and is a registered professional counselor. She can be contacted at info@heartmindeffect.com. Website: www.deborahnelson.ca

LOST & THEN FOUND

Lisa Walker

*"Love is what we are born with. Fear is what we
learn. The spiritual journey is the unlearning of fear
and prejudices and the acceptance of love back in our
hearts. Love is the essential reality and our purpose
on earth. To be consciously aware of it, to experience
love in ourselves and others, is the meaning of life.
Meaning does not lie in things. Meaning lies in us."*

—Marianne Williamson

"I talked to your birth mom today," my husband Larry announced
as I walked through the front door after finishing my shift at the
hospital one late afternoon. He took my arm and had me sit on the
ottoman in front of him, our knees touching.

I stopped breathing as a dozen thoughts swirled in my head. I wanted
to know everything at once. I had written to her years ago. When she
didn't respond, I gave up, disheartened that I'd never know anything
about my birth mother beyond the information in the adoption records.
Without telling me, acting on a heartfelt hunch, my husband had called
her that day. She took his call and talked openly with him.

Catching my breath, I blurted out, "What did she say? Tell me
everything!"

He told me that my birth mother's husband had opened the letter
I'd sent. As he was unaware of my existence, the news took a toll on
their already rocky marriage. Her husband was out of town that day,
which was why she was willing to talk with Larry. She was young and
scared when she gave birth to me. It was a different era and she didn't

have the guts to go against societal norms and keep me. Though she loved me, she just couldn't do it. She had searched for a family to take me and was thrilled to find my adoptive parents at a local Lutheran church. As they already had an adopted son, my birth mother felt that it was a perfect family for me. After giving me up for adoption, she became a nurse, married and had children. She thought of me often.

Mesmerized, I double-checked with my husband that my birth mother had actually said that she loved me and thought of me often. When he assured me that she had, my heart filled with a serene joy. These were the words I had longed to hear for most of my life. A sense of being born emerged from deep within. Like a beautiful butterfly trapped inside a cocoon, I was finally free of the last strands of darkness. There was a woman out there that had given me life and handpicked a family to love me. Once she was certain of my safety, she let me go. She had never forgotten me.

I have two brothers who are also adopted, an older and a younger one. We have completely different stories and backgrounds. We always knew we were adopted. Every year our parents gave each of us a gift celebrating the anniversary date our adoptions became legal. We were loved and wanted.

When young, I occasionally wondered about the woman who birthed me, but it really wasn't much of a concern. What did gnaw at me was feeling disconnected. Though a physical part of my family, I was emotionally detached. Mom did the best she could; still, I didn't feel seen, heard or valued. I didn't matter. I worked hard to be the best daughter, the best sister, the best student. It was to no avail. My brothers got the attention, not me.

I could hear the resentment and anger in my voice. I hadn't intended to aim my anger at my sister-in-law. But the second I heard "Disneyland" my head exploded.

My younger brother, his wife, Melinda, and I were gathered at the kitchen table the morning after my adoptive mother's death. I don't know why I brought up the painful incident at that moment. Perhaps it was because Mom's passing nixed any chance of me ever truly feeling like a valued member of our family.

For the past year, since my ailing mom moved to the east coast to be closer to Melinda and my brother, I traveled to Pennsylvania from

California every few weeks to visit her. In the early morning, I would sit at the kitchen bar and chat with Melinda while she made my favorite coffee drink.

I cherished these intimate moments with my lovely sister-in-law. Living thousands of miles apart from one another, now that the reason for my visits was gone, I knew that I would deeply miss us sharing our deepest secrets and ponderings about the true meaning of life. I could already feel the loss of our special relationship in my arms, heart and stomach. *Why couldn't I feel the loss of my mother?*

I took care of Mom before she went to live with my brother and Melinda. I rarely did anything without thinking of her. Wanting to love and connect with her, I worked hard to please her. Deep inside, more than anything else, I wanted her to be happy. If she was happy, I was happy.

As she aged and became increasingly confused at times, my workload increased. Working full-time, when she moved to Pennsylvania, it was a huge relief to hand over the responsibility to my sibling and his wife. Now that Mom was gone, instead of feeling the grief of losing her, I felt abandoned.

All Melinda had said was, "I don't remember you being any part of the Disneyland trip."

"Really? That's because I wasn't included!" I snapped. "Going to Disneyland was my idea. Then you all chose to go on a weekend when I had to work. I take that back, I was included. Mom called to have me watch the dog while the family was away!"

"I didn't know going was your idea," Melinda said, sounding sorry.

I immediately regretted bellyaching about what likely sounded trivial to her. But it wasn't trivial to me. Being discounted during the planning of the Disneyland trip further fueled my sense of being an outsider in my own family. I was always the first to think of others and offer a helping hand. "Lisa will do it!" repeatedly rang through our house like a family motto. *Why was it that no one ever put me first?* The role of familial helper didn't bring me any closer to my goal of belonging. It did, however, keep me very busy and distracted from what ached within, my *primal wounds.*

I learned about the concept of primal wounds when I told a lady I met at a church function that I was adopted. An adoptive and foster mother, she was well-versed on the loss children experience when taken away from their birth mother. She could see the profound differences in the children that came to her via adoption or foster care. They were more fearful, angry and distant despite her attempts to comfort and nurture them.

At first, I resented her inference that I was wounded. *How could this be true when I was welcomed home from the hospital by a loving family?* However, haunted by my lack of connection with my adoptive mother, I bought the book she recommended, *The Primal Wound* by Nancy Verrier.

Learning about the perinatal bond between a natural mother and her child and the complex effects of separation on adoptees was somewhat helpful. Apparently, as separation occurs at a preverbal time, and is later received and processed by each relinquished individual in unique and abstruse ways, adoptees process and react in various forms. Good to know; however, the book left me wondering about whose feelings the author was trying to assuage—mine, my adoptive mother's, or both?

I later read the book *Adoption Healing* by Joe Soll in which the author explains the adoptee's experience in a simple and direct way: "They lose it all. They lose the smells and tastes and sounds and places and people with whom they are familiar…all of their favorites. Everything they have ever known is gone and changed forever."

What Mr. Soll wrote made sense to me. I had lost all of my favorite things on the day that I was born. I wasn't worthy of my birth mom's love. She'd given me up! No matter how much my adoptive mother loved me, I couldn't truly connect with her. I had lost everything the day I was born.

Feeling it was crucial that I share this new found information with my older brother, I poured my heart out in a letter telling him my insights regarding my life as an adoptee and what it had been like being raised in a somewhat crazy family setting. I gave him my copy of *The Primal Wound.*

He didn't share my sentiments and wrote back, "Being adopted is just a small piece in the big pie of life. It's no big deal to me!"

After reading his letter, I wondered, "Where do I go from here? Is it my job to simply move on and never look back?" I couldn't ignore what I'd learned. Nor could I ignore the new thoughts and feelings reading the book elicited. It was no longer okay to survive my way through life. I wanted to thrive.

One day, Mom and I were sitting in the kitchen chatting and catching up. It was a beautiful spring morning and I was enjoying our conversation. Then she told me how happy everyone was about my brother's friend who had been a surrogate and had just given birth to twins.

"It's nice that everyone's so excited about these new twins. Are you even aware of the incredible loss that just occurred for them?" Sounding harsher than intended, I finished with, "I wonder how those babies are really doing without their original mom!"

"What do you mean, dear?" Mom asked. "They are perfectly fine! They're loved and well taken care of."

I tried to explain what I'd learned about primal wounds, saying that although the twins were reunited with their genetic origins, they would forever suffer the loss of being disconnected from their birth mother. I'm not sure she totally understood what I was saying, but the next words out of her mouth totally surprised me.

"Would you like to see your adoption papers?" Mom asked.

"Yes!" I said without hesitating.

A while later, when Mom handed me the papers, I went to sit at the kitchen table in a lovely patch of sun. Taking a deep breath, I read that my birth mother's name was Barbara, that she had named me Cynthia Susan, that I had a half-sibling who was born in Florida early in 1952 and, like me, he was given up for adoption. There was also a letter that Barbara had written thanking the attorney and the adoptive parents for all that they had done for her. In it, she wrote that she'd moved to San Francisco and was looking for work.

For a bittersweet moment, I imagined my tender-hearted birth mom planning my future. A few minutes later, curious, I asked Mom, "Were you worried about how I would turn out given that my birth mother had two out-of-wedlock pregnancies?"

"Oh, no, Lisa," she said with a smile. "I brought you home and made you mine."

For the first time, I was truly grateful for the incredible love and commitment of my adoptive mom. She'd openheartedly claimed me as her own…signed, sealed and delivered. Through tantrums and insensible shenanigans, she'd never wavered in her love, not once.

Still, I longed to look into the eyes of the woman who had given me life. I craved a simple conversation and to feel her physical presence, even if for only a few seconds.

A year later, I hired a detective to find her. Though I'd been born during a time when adoptions were private, closed and anonymous, she located my birth mother. She lived in the Midwestern United States with her husband and ninety-nine year old mother. Wanting to follow my heart, not someone else's outdated birth plan, I wrote Barbara a letter about my life, thanked her for what she had done for me, and sent it off with a few pictures. Knowing that it might be our only contact, I kept the letter simple and loving.

When I didn't hear back, I told myself that I fully accepted and respected her decision not to respond. I had found her, connected, and was ready to let go. My happiness would never again depend on having a connection with my birth mother. Of that, I was certain. Being happy was mine to claim and was exactly what I was going to do. It was my life and I intended to live it fully.

It wasn't a coincidence that I dedicated my working life to caring for newborn infants. As a nurse, every shift represented a return to *the scene of the crime*—my birth. Whenever attending deliveries, most of which had heartwarming outcomes, I felt fortunate. I loved caring for the tiny, helpless and amazingly tenacious beings at such a vulnerable time in their lives. However, whenever I admitted a baby being placed for adoption, my heart shattered.

As she was being prepped for delivery, one young woman who was giving her newborn daughter up for adoption the next day, asked me if she could spend as much time as possible with her baby. I hesitated. This was not normal procedure. She must have noticed the concerned look on my face, for she explained, "When I hand her over to her adoptive parents tomorrow, my time with her will end."

Later, as I sat at the end of her bed and watched the tender exchange of love, I wondered, "How could this be the right thing to do? Wouldn't holding her baby in her arms and staring into the wee infant's beautiful trusting blue eyes make it more difficult to say good-bye?"

The next day, I watched from the nursery window as the young woman was wheeled out. Like a gentle waterfall, tears flowed from her eyes as she wrapped her empty arms around herself. I cried too, shedding tears for her…and for me. *Had my birth mother cried for me? Would my life have felt less empty, less lonely, if she had held me for just a little while?*

A short while later, Byron Katie's process "The Work" tied up the dangling strings of my broken heart. I had explored many healing avenues, taken many personal development courses and read countless self-help books. Each new insight I uncovered brought me closer to my goal to feel valued, not discarded. However, it wasn't until I participated in "The Work" at an intimate three-day conference in Fairfield, Iowa that I faced my darkness.

Byron Katie teaches that when we are clear about and accept that *what is, just is*, it becomes what we love. When we fight reality, we lose one-hundred-percent of the time. As this message kept repeating over and over in my mind, I realized that in order to truly feel alive, I would need to fully and completely embrace all of my emotions, happy and sad. I was finally willing to grieve the loss of each mother.

As part of my healing process, I chose to see each woman in a new light and from a loving perspective. When I did, I saw their inner beauty. It had always been there, but had been blinded by a self-created veil of fear, deep inner feelings of unworthiness, and overpowering anguish.

Instead of denying or stifling my grief, I welcomed the large warm tears that slid down my face in enormous amounts. I felt the pain of loss and accepted the truth of it. Allowing my feelings to move through me, prepared me for the next wave of emotion. For many hours, the pattern was emotional swell, rinse my heart and soul with tears…repeat. As I said a simple hello to each troubling aspect of my life with deep respect and acceptance, I was able to slowly say good-bye to what ached.

Over time, in the darkness of my story I began to see the light. I started to view being adopted as proof of my worthiness. I am now aware of my own wants and desires. I no longer feel the need to seek validation by always doing and caring for others without reciprocity. By having the courage to find my way through the sorrow and hurt, I found my true self and experienced peace.

Since that day on the couch when Larry told me what he'd learned about my birth mother, life has been an incredible journey. I have faced challenges with openness and gained incredible wisdom and inner growth. Pieces of me are no longer missing. I now accept Barbara's path as being aligned yet separate from mine. I have claimed happiness, love and joy.

"Owning our story can be hard but not nearly as difficult as spending our lives running from it. Embracing our vulnerabilities is risky but not nearly as dangerous as giving up on love and belonging and joy—the experiences that make us the most vulnerable. Only when we are brave enough to explore the darkness will we discover the infinite power of our light."

—Brené Brown

About Lisa Walker

Lisa lives in California with her daughter and son-in-law. She has enjoyed a long successful career in nursing and is a certified professional coach. In her words, "I have learned that it is not what happens to us that is important. It is our thoughts and actions about what happens to us that is key in our lives." Lisa can be contacted at info@heartmindeffect.com.

PERSISTENT RESISTANCE

Louise E. Morris

*"Only if you resist what happens are you
at the mercy of what happens."*

—Eckhart Tolle

I bit into my third slice of vegetarian pizza. The crisp bottom of the thin crust was baked a golden brown, just right to hold the marinara sauce topped with fresh roasted tomatoes and red peppers, bitter black olives, sweet white onions, slivers of pungent garlic, and sliced button mushrooms, all nestled into a melted bed of succulent mozzarella cheese. As these appetizing morsels met in my mouth, I noted that the subtle hint of oregano and olive oil were the perfect complement to this festival of flavors.

I shouldn't be eating this third slice. I promised to only eat two. I'm not even hungry. Why did I eat so fast? Why can't I control myself? What's wrong with me? Well, at least there's no meat on it, and the lycopene in the tomatoes is good for me. I'll walk an extra half hour tomorrow.

Did I enjoy that third slice? No! I was too busy berating myself, too busy trying to resist temptation. In the few minutes it took to eat this delicious gift from Italy, my thoughts went from self-shaming to justifying.

What other pleasures were being ruined by negative self-talk? Berating myself and making excuses didn't just happen when I was enticed by taste or aroma. I scolded myself while eating anything that wasn't considered diet food. My struggle wasn't with physical hunger; my nemesis was emotional hunger. Comfort eating was a well-ingrained habit with roots in my childhood.

For the first year of my life, I suckled canned milk through a rubber nipple. Afterward, I'd double up from excruciating pain caused by intestinal spasms. After fifty years on earth, I was still cramping and moaning—physically and emotionally.

When will I learn? Why can't I control myself? I was doing fine. I'm gaining back all the weight I worked so hard to lose. Why do I return to the same habits that make me feel unwell and unwise?

Over the years, I spent countless time and money on books and courses as I tried to overcome what I viewed as my ego's self-destructive tendencies. This journey of self-discovery opened my eyes to the most vital understanding of humanity—we are not alone—I was not alone.

Encouraged by this awareness, I dared to share my struggles and fears with a few others. Whenever I tentatively raised the subject in a group, people would nod and smile reassuringly. Some approached me afterward, usually alone, and humbly disclosed similar experiences. Though, like me, a few struggled with their weight, there were a myriad of flaws my new-found friends were trying to fix. What amazed me was that all of these kindred souls were attempting to improve themselves or something in their lives—in secret!

Our commonality of having suffered alone, of having waited until our failures and pain reached an intolerable level before we dared to expose our flaws to the scrutiny of family, coworkers and friends, made me realize another truism. Our struggle for perfection was at least partially rooted in our need for validation from others. As Eckhart Tolle wrote in *The Power of Now*, "The ego's sense of self-worth is in most cases bound up with the worth you have in the eyes of others."

Still, I wondered, "Why were so many of us ashamed of our imperfections? Why were we working so hard to resist our addictions?" There had to be more behind our perpetual self-perfection pursuits. Surely, our fear of other people's opinions wasn't all that motivated us. Once out of the I'm-flawed closet, perhaps being able to speak about our darkest fears without being interrupted, judged or dismissed helped fuel our ceaseless journey to be better.

As Bruce K. Alexander stated in his book *The Globalization of Addiction*, a lessening with "the stigma of addiction" is evident by the influx of many more addictions. He further explained that the reason "people identify themselves as addicts quite openly" is because "whereas today's popular media terrify us with images of the most dangerous drug addictions, they usually reassure us with good humored portrayals of addictions to food, consumer goods, sex, religion, television, video games, and so on."

What Alexander wrote made sense. If being addicted to something had become an accepted and laughable societal norm, then there wasn't any valid reason for hiding our flaws. However, as he went on to explain, "…addictions that do not have drugs or alcohol as their objects are more prevalent than drug addictions and just as dangerous in severe cases" leaving people feeling guilty, depressed and/or filled with self-loathing. Apparently, even though behavioral and non-alcohol/drug addictions were widely accepted as being normal, unpleasant feelings kept us *addicted* to self-discovery in pursuit of perfection.

Was there any way to become happy with one's self, flaws and all? I was beginning to doubt it.

Perhaps it wasn't our flaws that kept me, my new-found friends and the majority of society unhappy with themselves. Maybe rather than being the cause of our discontent, our imperfections were symptomatic of something deeper. If true, our seemingly collective inability to make permanent self-improvements would make sense. There would be good reason for why we want to change—but can't.

Often, my willpower did prevail in keeping bad habits at bay, only to have them return. Why did they persist? Why did I return to habits that made me feel immature, unhappy and out-of-control, especially— remarkably— after months of feeling healthy, peaceful and in control? As Deepak Chopra and Rudolph E. Tanzi mentioned in their book *Super Brain*, "The best moments are merely a prelude to a relapse."

Chopra and Tanzi also stated that, "The secret to beating any fixed habit is to stop fighting with yourself, to find a place inside that isn't at war." *Easier said than done.*

One of their many strategies that did somewhat help me was, when reaching for a third slice of pizza, do so without self-recriminations and useless rationalizations. Enjoy it. Stop the chatter. But be aware of what you are doing.

As a result of following their advice, I had fewer negative thoughts going through my mind while eating, and for a while it did curb some of my overeating. However, my old habits slowly returned and I reverted to eating myself sick.

Throughout my perfection pursuit, I often felt discouraged because I knew better than to overeat. Having an open, curious and critical mind, I valued the vast amount of available research. I understood the detrimental long-term effects of stress on the body and that excess weight was a stressor. Because of this knowledge, I worried about what would happen to me if I never changed my eating behavior. My concern heightened when I was diagnosed as having type 2 diabetes.

The Canadian Diabetes Association (www.diabetes.ca/research) reports that "more than 20 people are being newly diagnosed with the disease every hour of every day." *Every hour of every day!* I obviously had a lot of company, but I wasn't happy about it.

The only report I wanted to be associated with was one I read about in *The End of Diabetes* by Dr. Joel Fuhrman: "Our studies found that people in their midlife who began living a positive balanced lifestyle, and stuck with it, can live a long and healthy life." He also reported that "…type 2 diabetics can become nondiabetic, achieving complete wellness and even excellent health."

In my quest for a healthier lifestyle, which included the usual integration of a more nutritious diet and improved exercise program, I began adding strategies to prevent stress-induced overeating to prevent the overeating that caused stress.

It was normal for me to sleep for five or six hours each night. When menopause arrived and disrupted my sleep pattern, I sometimes slept for only three or four hours. Constantly exhausted, I was unable to fully connect with my family, friends, coworkers and my students. Neither could I battle my ego and unhealthy habits. I made poor choices, especially about what I ate. My energy spent at work, the rest of the day I ran on empty.

For a long while, I wasn't aware of how being tired was interfering with every aspect of my life. I didn't notice that I was too tired to plan, make decisions or follow through with any of my intentions. What did help me to realize that sleep-deprivation was negatively affecting my life was changing jobs. After sixteen years of teaching elementary school, at age fifty and with my menopausal hormones in tow, I took a position at a secondary school.

The transition to teaching teenagers was challenging for the first couple of years. However, it was one of the best decisions of my career. The dual role of educating and guiding my students with special needs as they built their life skills was rewarding and humbling. Many of them had difficulty focusing, staying on task and dealing with conflict, created problems for themselves rather than looking for solutions, and could not sustain their motivation and stamina throughout the day—all of which were amplified when they were tired.

Research by The National Sleep Foundation (www.sleepfoundation.org) found that, "...lack of sleep affects mood, and a depressed mood can lead to lack of sleep." They also determined that, "When you are sleep deprived, you are as impaired as driving with a blood alcohol content of .08%..." Reading their findings made me realize that incidents needing intervention by administrators and counselors in our schools would lessen dramatically if our students got more rest.

I also read a report by the National Sleep Research Project in Australia (www.abc.net.au/science/sleep/facts.htm). They found that, "Feeling tired can feel normal after a short time. Those deliberately deprived of sleep for research initially noticed greatly the effects on their alertness, mood and physical performance, but the awareness dropped off after the first few days." I woke up. Like my students, if I wanted to be emotionally and physically healthy, I needed to get more sleep.

It took more than a year for me to train myself to get one extra hour of sleep a night. I started by going to bed fifteen minutes earlier than usual. When that felt natural and I actually slept for the extra quarter hour, I went to bed an additional fifteen minutes early. Eventually, by increasing my time in bed in small increments, I was able to sleep between seven and eight hours per night. Aware of the importance of sleep, whenever tired, I took a short afternoon nap or headed for bed earlier than usual. Waking up well-rested made it much easier to follow through with my intentions.

At the same time as I was working on getting more rest, I was also becoming increasingly aware of my thinking. In my chapter "Out, Out—Damn Thought" in *Heartmind Wisdom Collection #1*, I wrote about how much of my life had been spent "attempting a multitude of tactics to gain mastery over my shortcomings." Writing my story opened my eyes at another level—my strategies were usually short-lived; there was always something happening in my life that interfered with my new routine and resolve.

My constant transformational relapses led me to a deeper level of self-exploration. I learned what Captain Jack Sparrow in the movie *Pirates of the Caribbean* referred to when he said, "The problem is not the problem. The problem is your attitude about the problem."

I had spent years analyzing myself. Repeatedly and creatively tried to change my thoughts, attitude and behavior from negative to positive. Though a testament to my perseverance and willpower, and although there was definitely more contentment in my life as a result of all my inner-work, the answer to the one question my friends and I kept asking eluded us.

Why, when everything seems to be going so great, when our lives are under control, when we feel proud and confident, when our weight is down, when our finances are up, when our relationships are loving, and when we have resisted our flaws and addictions and achieved our goals, do we return to our same old familiar and unwanted habits?

And each time we returned to our old ways, we did so with even more guilt and shame added to our already heavy emotional baggage. *We had failed again when we knew better.*

As Robin Sharma wrote in his *Little Black Book for Stunning Success*, "Every time you don't live your values, the Integrity Gap widens." Reading this triggered another momentous paradigm shift for me from which there was no going back. Being tired, depressed, or whatever reason or excuse I had, when I didn't live up to what I believed was my 100%, I knew so at a deeper level. As Sharma explained, our bodies feel this imbalance for us, and guide us to the realization that something is not up to par…that we need a more nutritious diet and life…that we are not living to our potential…that we are not fulfilling our purpose.

Unlike Maya Angelou who said, "I did then what I knew how to do. Now that I know better, I do better," my story was different. *Or was it?* For years, I felt ashamed because I knew better but kept sliding back into my old ways. I was a fraud. Who was I to think I could help people when I couldn't even help myself. Yet, I had a loving relationship with my family, had several close friends, achieved a master's in education, and enjoyed my drive to work each morning. I must have done something right to have all these blessings in my life. Still, deep down, I didn't see myself as being successful because I kept looking at what I didn't have, and what I didn't have was the ability to change familiar habits, especially my eating habits.

In *The Hunger Fix*, Dr. Pam Peeke discusses the weight management dilemma, which she summarized in the winter 2012 edition of *Prevention* magazine. In her practice, she noticed that dieters had pleas that were "…eerily similar to the cries for help from [her] patients with hard-core drug or alcohol addictions." As a result, she now teaches that we can stop getting "False Fixes—anything (like food) that leads to short-term reward in association with self-destructive behavior, followed by feelings of guilt, shame, and defeat." She also explained the power of the following question when asked before you eat, "Is this healthy?" Apparently, this activates a part of your brain that can help you overcome addiction. It was a simple solution that did help. However, I continued to slip back into old eating habits.

In *A New Earth*, Eckhart Tolle wrote, "...unless you know the basic mechanics behind the workings of the ego, you won't recognize it, and it will trick you into identifying with it again and again." According to Tolle, "Once the ego has found an identity, it does not want to let go." He further explained that "...for so many people, a large part of their sense of self is intimately connected with their problems."

I had always believed that the road to happiness would occur when I understood and healed every travesty of my life. Not so, according to Tolle who also wrote, "Once you know how the basic dysfunction operates, there is no need to explore all its countless manifestations, no need to make it into a complex personal problem." His wise words caused a paradigm shift for me. I stopped strategizing and mending myself, and practiced what Eckhart Tolle referred to as "watching the watcher."

As I became more aware of how I was reacting to my body and mind, something amazing happened—I stopped thinking there was something wrong with me, and quit blaming myself for my setbacks. My mind grew quieter and more peaceful. Still, from time to time when I'd revert back to unwanted eating habits, I would berate myself.

Why, even when we are moving towards an authentic life, when we are more positive and content, when we are beginning to realize our purpose in life, do our relapses persist?

It was difficult to make lasting changes. As John Baker explained in *Life's Healing Choices*, "A lot of our character defects are like old shoes—they're comfortable." I was fairly convinced that he was right; however, I wondered if there might be a hidden force that was more powerful than our will and intelligence that caused people to choose the same old shoes and pathways. Then, I heard Dr. Joe Dispenza speak about the relationship between the brain and the body. Impressed, I bought his book *Breaking the Habit of Being Yourself*.

Dispenza explained that it is difficult to change one's thinking because "...5 percent of the mind is conscious, struggling against the 95 percent that is running subconscious automatic programs." He further explained that the brain wants to maintain the status quo, to continue functioning as it has since birth. According to him, our thoughts produce chemicals that surround our cells. Over time, as our cells die and divide, they want more of these thought-produced chemicals. The result is that trying to make behavior changes on a conscious level is like trying to swim against a current that is easily pulling you down a river. Though it was comforting to learn that it was my brain, not my lack of willpower, that caused my numerous behavior relapses, I was thankful that Dispenza also stated that it is possible to build pathways, other currents. According to him, "Learning new responses forms new neural pathways in the brain." And one day, with enough positive responses, this new way of thinking and feeling will be the main current pulling you along the river.

Encouraged by Dr. Dispenza, I began to incorporate his main strategies for reprogramming one's brain—visualization and rehearsal. It was exciting to know that by visualizing my behavior as I wanted it to be, I could influence my brain to get on my change team. By rehearsing desired outcomes, I could practice new thoughts and actions that would build new cells and pathways. As Dr. Dispenza explained, "If you can influence your brain to change before you experience a desired future event, you will create the appropriate neural circuits that will enable you to behave in alignment with your intention before it becomes a reality in your life…you will install the neural hardware."

However, having spent much of my life analyzing my experiences, I initially found it difficult to be *aware* of my feelings and how my body was reacting, often reverting to the familiarity of self-analysis. According to Dr. Dispenza, this kept me in high-frequency Beta mode, which over long periods of time can cause illness. By analyzing everything, I was unknowingly keeping myself stuck in the past and making myself sick. With this in mind, to decrease my body's level of high-frequency Beta brainwaves and increase more healthful low-frequency Alpha brainwaves, I started meditating. In a deep state of meditation, the body can rest and heal.

Years of reading and incorporating what I learned has greatly enhanced my sense of well-being. I am no longer stuck in the past and slave to old behaviors that did not serve me. When I occasionally slip, I remember Eckhart Tolle's wisdom: "Practice bringing consciousness during ordinary circumstances, and be ready for the bad days." By analyzing less and being in the present more, I am no longer unwittingly stuck in the past or chasing an elusive happy future. The chatter in my head has quieted. I have moments of exhilarating nothingness where I am one with the universe, and closer to God than I'd once thought was possible.

Having experienced it in an absolute sense, I now know why so many of us obsess about our flaws—we want them gone so we can experience peace. Peace that is quite attainable when we: abandon self-criticism in favor of envisioning that we have already attained what we desire; observe rather than react or judge; and reprogram our brain, one positive thought at a time. Habits can be changed.

> *"... eventually, suffering destroys the ego—*
> *but not until you suffer consciously."*

—Eckhart Tolle

About Louise E. Morris

Louise lives in Langley, British Columbia. She holds a Master in Education. Her teaching focus is on quality education for all students. Her interests include dancing, tennis and reading. Louise is available to talk to groups and can be contacted via info@ heartmindeffect.com.

Her chapter in *Heartmind Wisdom Collection #1* is "Out, Out—Damn Thought!" The Heartmind Wisdom Collection is available at www. heartmindstore.com and through online bookstores.

THE KASHMIRI FLUTE
Call to the Divine Feminine
Rehana Nanjijuma

*With heartfelt thanks, this story is dedicated
to my dear family, friends and mentors.*

Jogging for Freedom — Vancouver, Canada, 2003

The wind howled. I pushed my feet into my Nikes and sprung onto the carpet of crisp leaves at the trail's entrance. Propelled by a potent inner-fuel, I yearned for each step. The sound of trickling water from a nearby creek floated between the trees. After stopping to lace-up my sneakers, I switched to the soft bark mulch trail and looked up at the canopy of trees protecting me from the rain-clouded sky. I inhaled a deep breath of crisp Vancouver air and sighed. Freedom was waiting just ahead.

Jogging broke the bubble that encased and separated me from the world. As though obscured on the dark side of a two-way mirror, I could clearly see the reality of other people, but they could not see me. I anxiously breathed in, yearning for the oxygen of the familiar forest to clear the air within this suffocating sphere. My gut churned, desperate to release droplets of the festering feelings overwhelming me. As deadlines and expectations piled up, the clock just seemed to tick faster. Constantly, I worried, "How will I get all my homework done? Without enough sleep, how will I make it to work and then university awake?"

The only way to deflate the pressure was to jog as fast as my ever-strengthening legs could carry me. Quickening my pace, I tuned into the sound of my windbreaker rhythmically swishing back and forth amid the near silence within the depths of the forest. I willed and waited for the welcomed sensation that would melt the fatigue of that day's commute to and from the beautiful University of British Columbia campus.

Thanks to my single mom's dream to provide her children with a peaceful home, we moved to a forested Vancouver neighborhood halfway through my undergraduate studies. Though I cherished our new spacious townhome, I wished it were closer to the University of British Columbia so that I didn't need to carry what felt like my entire life on my back: lunch, gym clothes and humongous textbooks. Although grateful to have a privileged life, in spite of how organized I was, the daily grind of university plus a fun part-time job at a photo lab left me wondering how I would manage it all. I felt something was missing.

Twenty years old, an idyllic desire glowed within me. I yearned to be a part of global change. What I wanted was to help people to live healthy lives and find creative ways out of poverty. My feet pounding on the forest floor, I wondered, "Do I even have space for this dream when what I need to do is focus on making it through my classes?" I knew the truth inside my heart—I needed to listen to this call to bring my purpose to life. I refused to be stuck inside a story that didn't quite feel like it was mine.

Raindrops dripping on my lashes, I pulled my blue hood over my head, wishing that the gushing rain could wash away my stress. Frustrated, I quickened my pace. *Why do universities treat us like numbers, mere customers of a business transaction?* Students were expected to perform like acrobats, bounding through multiple rings, sometimes of fire, to get an education. *What for? Isn't the real point to gain knowledge and skills we can use to leave the world better than we found it?*

Even though my family's and friends' intentions were genuine, they didn't understand my inner-struggle. How could they? They were on their own respective journeys. I was trapped inside my bubble, alone. They were seemingly unable to know what it was like to be me. How was I supposed to juggle the demands of excelling in university, emotionally supporting my mom, mentoring my ten year old sister and working a part-time job? *I don't remember signing up to be a Superwoman in the making!*

"How do women do it?" I wondered, envisioning women arriving at parties beautifully dressed, holding onto a successful husband with one hand and carrying a freshly baked gluten-free apple crumble in the other, their perfectly-poised children following behind them. The image made me feel like taking a nap on the spot. *Is this what I actually desire?* My stomach growled out loud in protest.

The rain stopped as I ran through a clear patch. Now a striking blizzard of colors in the setting of the sun, I called out to the sky, "I cannot do all the things I should or I will internally burst and turn gray before I am thirty." Sweat dripping down my back, I quit running. The guilt of not being everything to everyone weighed heavily in my heart. What I truly craved was to be seen, not to be Superwoman. Who got to decide the *shoulds*, anyway?

I walked over to the oldest fir tree on the trail, placed both hands on its sturdy trunk and stretched my calves. Inhaling deeply, I soaked up the sweet serenity the forest offered unconditionally. Finally, I exhaled my remaining drops of angst. In the silence, my inner-voice beckoned me to break free and find a way to make a difference in the world.

A blue-feathered bird on a nearby branch inched toward me. Pausing, it watched me deeply inhale and exhale. Its presence brought a grateful smile to my lips. *This bird understands my unraveling inner-journey.* The cooling fall evening air left goose bumps on my arms as I walked up the hill toward home. The urgency to answer my questions was absorbed by the earth beneath my feet. Hallelujah for endorphins.

Fish out of Water — Kabul, Afghanistan, 2003

"This is our chance Soraya," I exclaimed, looking out the window at the brewing dust storm. "Come on, before our housemates return from work."

Soraya, my roommate and confidante, chimed in, "Some music and a little dancing!"

Eager to melt the memories of cross-cultural faux pas moments in my day, I nodded eagerly before shaking my head in disbelief. "I really tripped up today. When a male Afghan colleague smiled shyly and said, 'Welcome to our guest, our Canadian intern,' I naturally extended my hand to greet him without waiting for him to offer his hand first. His warmth instantly evaporated. I could tell by his awkward noncommittal handshake that he was thinking, 'You should have waited for me to reach out first.'"

"I know. A similar situation happened to me," Soraya empathized. "Our supervisor mentioned that men usually initiate handshakes in this culture. It is hard to shift our ways because it's all new to us."

"Let's shake it off!" I called out, rolling my shoulders, ready to get the kinks to dissolve into beads of sweat. I was relieved that Soraya also liked to dance to decompress without feeling compelled to speak much at the same time.

Soraya and I spontaneously spun around the room to the beat of a Middle Eastern song playing on a laptop. We'd be lucky if the electricity held out. Normally, it came and went during the evening.

Outside our window, the forming windstorm swept up a swarm of dust particles speckled with garbage. The frenzied swirl outside mimicked our grooving to the music inside. In our second-floor room, the windows closed to keep the flying dust out, Kabul's burning 113°F dry heat was hotter and more oppressive than anything I'd ever experienced. Sweat dripped down my temples and soaked my t-shirt as I enjoyably released the uncertainties of the day.

When we spotted two little girls and a boy curiously watching us from their upstairs window next door, we smiled and waved. Soraya then discreetly drew the curtain, leaving only a sliver of sunlight to shine onto our olive green carpet. I gave her a thumbs up.

It was essential that we be mindful of the conservative cultural norms of the country we were visiting, and tricky to respect that which we didn't fully understand. While in Kabul, our social lives would mostly be within the four walls of our comfortable guesthouse, which was totally reasonable as a measure for maintaining the safety and security of our young international group. Confined and unable to jog, I hoped dancing would become the way I would reconnect with myself daily.

As I shimmied around the room playfully, I called to Soraya, "I feel freer within myself here than I do at home in Vancouver." Soraya just smiled unperturbed by the paradox.

When the windstorm's howl ceased, silence ensued. I dropped into a spinal roll and then a squat. Rising slowly, I unfurled my neck. Yearning for even a hint of a breeze, I moved across the room and opened a window. The air motionless, I announced, "Time for my second three-minute shower today." Towel in hand, I slipped out of our room, leaving Soraya to her stretches on the floor.

As warm water spluttered from the showerhead onto my face and body, calm washed over me. I was thankful that I let myself dance so spontaneously, grateful for the welcomed sacred pause. Being a social extravert in most moments was too much for me. Turning the tap to blast cold water onto my burning muscles, I consciously relaxed my calves, thighs and shoulders, as I sank into my grounded feet.

I was surprised that my sojourn in Kabul was helping me connect to my joyful self rather quickly. I exited the shower room, loudly humming my favorite new Cheb Khaled song. Spotting my housemates trickling in from playing volleyball in the courtyard with our security guards, guesthouse manager, and cook, I continued humming without caring if they heard me.

On my way back to the room, my sense of peaceful elation was momentarily disturbed as I glimpsed outside the window and noticed the security guards with Soviet-style Kalashnikov rifles at the front gate. It was a strong reminder that I was in war-torn Afghanistan.

A few seconds later, I stopped to glance at my reflection in the mirror just outside Soraya's and my bedroom. A welcomed but unfamiliar look had settled in my eyes; there was a sparkle, a presence. *Is this me?*

Standing there, I marveled at why I came to this place. Albeit a traumatized part of planet Earth, Kabul was propelling me to step into a new rhythm. I was astonished by the constant challenges people faced every day—threats to personal safety, destroyed roads, open sewers, airborne fecal matter, intermittent electricity and challenges to human rights. Although the instabilities and hazards provoked fear in me, surprisingly, I also experienced a sense of brewing courage.

Momentarily free from the North American rat race, I had the capacity to breathe, no longer suffocated, in spite of wafting airborne fecal matter. While in Vancouver, with all its relative opportunity and luxury, I felt restless. In Kabul, though unnerved by the constant uncertainty, my work project triggered my conviction to act...to speak up... to illuminate the truth of the local women's unheard voices and needs. My actions trumped my fears. I voiced opinions and followed my gut to make things happen, including locating a highly-skilled, street-smart interpreter who spoke Pashtu, Dari and English, Fershta. I also helped nurse my newly arrived housemates with critical moments of acclimatization when their bellies and lungs got hit hard by the changes in food, water and air. I felt an authentic me awakening.

As I hit the pillow that night, fatigued from the heat and my body relaxed after the shower, stark images of Kabul appeared in my mind's eye like a slide show. I watched as the sandy-beige homes on a hillside at the outskirts of the city appeared. Their roofs flat and their windows small, they blended into the dusty road. *How do old women and young girls climb up to their houses at the peaks with large containers of drinking water towering atop their heads without falling?* Dirt particles skipped in the welcomed breezy moments, settling into every corner of every street and building, and pore of every being. Seeing green, I thought, "What a pleasant surprise to see trees from one of the viewpoints in the city." Kabul had been a world of paradoxes since the moment we landed, brimming with determination to *do good* with the local Afghans who'd suffered years of war and instability.

Sitting up in bed so we could make eye contact, I said, "You know, Soraya. I do feel kind of outside myself here. I barely recognize myself in a mirror. And that's before I cover my head with a chiffon scarf." It was new for me to daily wear a scarf on my head. I chuckled. I sometimes ask myself, "Who am *I* to be here?"

"Why not you, Rehana? You are carrying yourself taller. Could you be noticing your real strengths?"

Soraya's reflectiveness and Zen were exactly what I needed in a friend; she understood me. Smiling, I changed the subject, "Isn't Fershta amazing?"

"I know, it's hard to believe Fershta's family had to leave their home in Kabul to prevent being forcefully displaced like most of their neighbors."

Recalling my conversation with Fershta, I shook my head. "I was blown away when she joined us for tea at the office and calmly told us her family's story of migration."

"She's an open book," Soraya said. "It must have been challenging and disillusioning; yet, I heard a tinge of knowingness in her voice. It seems as if she had no doubt that everything would eventually work out okay. She certainly has chutzpah."

"Today, Fershta and I heard a lot of stories from other Afghan women who were forced to move to refugee camps in Pakistan." I was curious about her family's story but wanted her to initiate sharing it," I confessed. "She shared it boldly, although in her unassuming way."

"While making us laugh too!" Soraya added.

"She's refreshing. Maybe it is *because* of her experiences that she finds the courage to laugh her way through hardship?"

"Maybe resilience isn't something you *have* or *don't have*," I said, expanding on Soraya's train of thought. "Perhaps it is something that grows from within. Regardless, I was wowed by her faith. She reminded me that we are all being taken care of." I smiled.

"Yes!" my good friend agreed. "I felt Fershta's gratitude in spite of all that she's been through."

"She knows we are all exactly where we need to be, wh—"

"While being sheltered, nourished and safe." Soraya finished my sentence.

Lying back on my bed, I glanced through a slit in the curtained window and noted the sparkle of a pristine star. Feeling blessed to have heard real people's stories and for being guided by earth angels like Soraya and Fershta, my eyes welled. How sweet it felt to be grateful. *Could I bring this feeling home with me to Vancouver?*

"Rehana, we are here together to learn our own lessons. It's no accident," Soraya said, her voice heavy with sleep as her eyelids shut.

Soraya really listened to what I said and understood what I left unsaid. Thankful for her friendship, I stared longingly at the glittering stars before closing the curtain. Welcoming a peaceful rest, a slight smile on my lips, I closed my eyes to let the dreams begin.

Pinning Down Peace — Kashmir, Pakistan, 2006

Just before dawn on a Sunday morning, as I lay in bed in a cat-like curl, looking forward to a day off after a month of soul-clutching training, I heard the mystical sound of a flute. Assuming I must be imagining the soothing sound, I envisioned the melody floating over the dusty mountain peaks and newly planted vegetable fields next door to our camp. *Maybe I am dreaming.* I closed my eyes tighter and stretched out for just a little more sleep.

Did I really need to be this far away from those I love? Did I need this to belong to something greater? Was I finally free of the sense of unrest I was so determined to run away from in Vancouver?

The melodic sound of the flute faded beneath the distinct rhythmic sound of my running shoes hitting the pavement. My heart beat faster. *No, not again!* I struggled to fully awake, but couldn't as the images in my dream sharpened and my pulse quickened. Running like mad, familiar toxic bubbles churned in my tummy and fear pulsated in my temples. My muscular arms swished back and forth against my royal blue windbreaker. Filled with emotion, my belly protruded. I wondered, "Will I ever be free? No matter how much my family loves me, my friends care for me and support me, I run to escape feelings I can't explain. Being in this place makes me want to run even more. I wish I could feel relaxed, be free of the heavy slop boiling inside my core."

Watching myself—tall, determined, pulling more mileage than I realize—I'm aware that only running brings me peace. It is all too familiar. *If I chose Kashmir intentionally, why did I still feel the need to run?* This was a place to learn, to be part of a cause that mattered. My running should be done.

Sitting up with a jolt, I threw off the lilac floral duvet. Glancing at my sleeping roommate, I blurted out, "I've gotta get out of here!" Feeling some relief from having voiced my fearful desperation, I flopped back down, pulled the covers over my head and fell back asleep. The remnants of the nightmare fizzed close to the surface of my awareness.

I had chosen to go to Chakhama Valley, a remote village in Kashmir, Pakistan. A mere eleven months earlier, a 7.6 magnitude earthquake had destroyed homes and much of the infrastructure, and claimed thousands of lives. I was 6,554 miles from my family home in Vancouver, a five-hour drive from the nearest city, and one-and-a-half hours from the only town with a general store that catered to expatriates, and thankfully, had cell phone service.

When I arrived, one of the first things I did was reach down to touch the brown earth with my hands. It was musty and dry. Scooping up a handful, I could feel the great loss this place had suffered, the gravity of being close to the India-Pakistan temporary ceasefire line. The village was home to many tribes, none of whom were accustomed to foreigners. Like the villagers, our revitalization staff was mostly mountain bred, culturally and linguistically diverse people from other parts of Northern Pakistan. Then there was me—one of a countable number of North American women working in the remote valley.

The women's residence was a prefabricated aluminum building with shoebox-sized rooms with two beds and an airplane-sized bathroom. Repurposed from an old ship, the bathroom included a cubicle for bucket showering. My roommate, Anoushka, and I shared our close quarters amicably. Though I didn't ask her to, she took to being a big sister to me. Her protectiveness sometimes felt overpowering.

Eleven months into my year-long commitment, the morning sun gleamed into my eyes through the spaces between the apple blossoms outside my window. Lying in bed, I listened to the call to prayers that, like clockwork, happened precisely at sunrise and sunset. Anoushka opened the squeaky sounding bathroom door and shot me a look of victory. Through the slits of my half-opened eyes, I observed her satisfaction at having claimed the bathroom first. I smiled my congratulations. *Today is mine to create. I am open to what the day will bring.*

Twenty minutes later, I stepped outside into the cloudy and rainless morning. I had chosen to wear beige cargo pants and a pink longsleeved loose cotton shirt that covered my thighs and was long enough to respect the more conservative dressing norms for women. Trail runners completed my fashion statement. As the fresh morning balm-like mist touched my eyes, I fully awakened.

Shireen, my boss, met me at the camp gate for a walk. As a newly discovered soul-sister, she cared about my growth. Our deep connection was unexpected and welcomed. For many years, I had known that a wise woman would one day materialize in my life. *Was Shireen my anticipated sage?*

"Did you have tea?" she asked. "I made real coffee. Would you like some?"

"Smells good," I said, sniffing the scent of freshly brewed Ethiopian coffee beans. "Maybe later. My travel mug of orange pekoe tea and three bananas on toast with peanut butter will hold me over for now." Surprised by a feeling of happy ease, I took a deep breath before saying, "This morning has the feeling of home away from home."

It was Shireen's turn to be surprised. "Wow! Sounds like you've definitely settled in here!"

"In some ways," I said. The words 'settled in' sounded far too permanent. Not wanting to draw attention to ourselves, we passed by the neighbor's fully planted fruit nursery in silence. It was uncommon for the local women to wander about unless they had a purpose, like collecting water or firewood.

As we approached a waterfall gushing from the mountainside, I was awestruck by its beauty. Though it was March, the mountain chill lingered as we headed down the mountain on jagged gravel pathways.

The smell of burning garbage and human loss was palpable. A rumbling thunderstorm brewed in the distance.

Maintaining a respectful volume, Shireen whispered, "I hope the neighbors don't think that we are here on behalf of the housing reconstruction engineers. I wouldn't want anyone to think that we're checking up on them on a Sunday."

Nodding, I glanced at the soft pink blossoms clustered on an apple tree beside the tumbled mountain road that served as our path. "What a paradox—beauty and devastation."

"I know." Shireen shook her head. "Since the monsoon rains started early this year and lasted almost six months, none of the infrastructure repairs have gone according to plan."

"What can we do but surrender to the force of nature," I absently said as my eyes followed the outline of the sharply pointed mountains that shaped and defined the valley. Seconds later, dirt-brown mud sliced through the green mountain flora and sent large chunks of rocks tumbling across the river 9,000 feet below. I gasped as my hand shot to my forehead and my eyes opened wide. Silence soon followed, save for the lull of the river below seeking a new path. The heavy air smelled like a pungent cocktail of life and death. Mixed with smoke from open cooking camp fires, was the smell of goats, sheep and baking flat bread, roti.

For a long moment, I stood there, my mouth gaped open. *What did I really come to this place for? How could I possibly make a difference when nature was so much stronger? No wonder I wanted to run, and run and run.*

As if sensing what I was feeling and thinking, Shireen interrupted my thoughts with an encouraging remark. "Rehana, can you believe that you've almost made it to your eleventh-month mark here?"

I had to admire her finesse as my mood lifted. "Time has flown! Every day brings something fresh and positive, in spite of the frustrations outside of our control. I've grown too, though I confess that some lessons were harsher to learn than others. For instance, taming my ego not to care who gets the credit for work done and instead focus on what's best for the program. Thankfully, I trust that you and the Divine know the truth."

"Rehana, never doubt how much I appreciate you." Her gaze thoughtfully held mine as I blushed. "How are you surviving the boot-camp quarters?"

"I'm managing, in spite of feeling squished. Sometimes, I want to scream at the top of my lungs. I'm sure Anoushka occasionally feels the same way. We oscillate between appreciating and irritating one another. There isn't enough solo time or sufficient space. I so miss jogging. Going on more walks like this one would be just the rejuvenation I need."

"How about spending more weekends in the city? I know you can't jog there, but at least you can zone out, go shopping at the bazaar and maybe even meet other people."

Shireen's concern was visible in her raised eyebrow and heartwarming smile. "I do go into the city," I assured her. "Still, I feel isolated socially and the work is a constant test of perseverance. I have to trust myself before cultivating it with others. It's imperative that our local colleagues believe we are here to give voice to their impact, to support them and to learn from their work."

"Building trust in ourselves is key, and establishing it with others is our deepest challenge." Shireen agreed.

"What's most difficult for me is getting past my own fear of uncertainty so that I can flow with the culture change." My forehead creased with the weightiness of my truth. "Though many of the customs are foreign to me, I respect the many cultures here. I definitely resonate with their family mindedness and hospitality."

"I get it," Shireen assured me. As we passed by two of the model houses—projects that our engineers and architects had rebuilt for orphans, widows and their children—she half-jokingly asked, "Rehana, besides the desire to cultivate guts of steel, what really brought you here?"

Knowing Shireen was referring to the spicy, oily local food, I snickered. "My guts are being tested, though nowhere close to solidifying into steel. Daily, I suffer with digestion discomfort."

"Is it the food, or could the pull of escapism be the cause of your indigestion?"

Noting the glint of humor in her eyes, I smiled.

"Don't worry, I share your tendency toward escapism," Shireen said as we reached a field of tall grass and exchanged devilish glances. Laughing, we raced through it. She beat me to the other side.

Catching up with her, I took deliberately long breaths as I dug deep for the courage to share the truth about why I'd come to Kashmir.

Sensing my need for a heartfelt conversation and connection, Shireen's gleeful smile faded flat.

Pushing past my fear of opening up, I took a final deep breath and said, "In all seriousness, I've been searching for something that I know can only come from within. I feel like I came here to prepare myself for the crossroad I find myself at now."

Still nervous, I folded my arms protectively across my chest. "At first, I told myself I came here to feel satisfied that I could master something that was new and challenging. But since being here, I've been listening for my true voice—one that I somehow muzzled for a long, long time. What I am searching for is to be valued. Though my achievements are important to me and though I appreciate genuine praise…they only take me so far…then nothing."

"You're valued not just for your skills, but also…no, especially for your strong and loving spirit.

"Thank you, Shireen," I said, smiling through collecting tears. "I feel like I've been running in circles my whole life. That's the reason that I'm drawn to places like Kashmir; the adrenalin-filled existence is just another form of running."

Glancing at the threatening sky, I realized that our minutes outside were numbered. "Kashmir is the completion of a big circle!" I announced, the words rolling off of my tongue without forethought. My eyes widened in surprise. *Did I say that?*

The look in Shireen's eyes foreshadowed what she was about to share. "Rehana, I really admire your integrity. Whether you realize it or not, you've got it!"

I smiled gratefully. She saw *me*, not just what I'd achieved. It was exactly what I craved and was starting to feel from the inside. "And I will continue to do my best while here," I said, a warm sense of peace spreading within. In that moment, I knew I was ready to return home.

"Shireen, it just clicked for me. I no longer need to wait for one more achievement to accept myself. It's time to make choices for my health. I need to create a fulsome life in a space where I can fully express myself, meet new people, and dress and dance as I please. I need to be where I can embrace all parts of myself without restrictions. I want to make a difference. To do that, I need to create my own healthy constellation where I can blossom at will and dance to my own rhythm."

"And, you will," Shireen said as we reached the campground and nodded hello to the security guards. "The time has come for you to freely paint your own canvas, to experience life in a way that will fulfill you."

"Thank you, Shireen. For your friendship, your mentorship, for being you." Chuckling, I added, "I have a feeling my future-self will thank you too!"

"You're welcome." Shireen smiled and opened her arms for a bear hug. Feeling incredibly grounded, I made my way to my shoebox-sized temporary home. I hadn't "settled in" to life in Chakhama Valley; I had *settled into* me. No more did I need someone to appreciate me. I felt my own successes. In Kabul and in Kashmir, I had done enough to make a positive difference. I had done enough running. I was enough.

The Dance of Purpose — Ottawa, Canada, 2008

From blossoms to tulips, within six months, I found myself welcomed by spring in Ottawa, Canada. It was breathtaking. My new buddy Natasha and I easily jogged along the flat banks of the Rideau Canal. The blue birds chirped cheerfully. A rainbow of tulips in magenta, yellow, red and orange blanketed the ground. The water clean and clear, I noticed the steady reflection on the canal of my curly locks under a baseball cap and Natasha's long ponytail swishing back and forth.

Natasha looked to me to teach her the jogging basics. I hadn't run for more than two years. In the end, technique didn't matter. With many stories and global adventures to share, our times together were more fast-paced walks, interspersed with occasional jogging bursts. Like the flowers, our conversations were varied and colorful.

"Wow, Rehana. Your turquoise capris remind me of Northern Pakistan," Natasha commented.

"Oh, yes, I love this *Ferozi* shade. It makes me feel at peace." A sudden gust of wind pulled my attention skyward.

"I want to make the pasta you shared with me and my husband Salim. What made it so good?" Natasha asked.

"Sun dried tomatoes, cranberries and walnuts are the magic." *My mom must have hiccupped as I revealed her secret recipe.*

"How did you survive in Pakistan when you couldn't jog, cook or dance very often?"

"Small moments of joy and movement saved me. I often sang to myself, sometimes to the goats. Occasionally, I hung out with local families. I learned to laugh at myself. When possible, I went on long walks. Just before I left Kashmir, my roommate and I *attempted* to make an apple crumble in a frying pan."

Laughing lightly, I recalled how when I'd returned from that walk with Shireen in Chakhama Valley, Anoushka had come running outside to ask me to help her finish baking. As there was no oven in our compound, I was intrigued and heartedly agreed to help. The scent of cinnamon wafted through the community aluminum shed-like kitchen as we pressed and then cooked oatmeal, ghee and brown sugar into a frying-pan and boiled the apples in a saucepan.

"When we served it, the crispy base and apples literally crumbled into a zillion pieces. There's more than one way to make a crumble, and there was more than one way to keep sane. When challenged by an absurd situation, I'd tell myself, 'I can do this. There is always a way.' It was a blessing that I found comfort in these connections and creative ways of calming and caring for myself. In the end, though, no matter how much I sang or journaled or meditated, there was no denying that I had to choose a healthier and safer place to live and work."

"Did you feel that you were meant to be there?" Natasha asked.

Nodding, I gazed at a mushrooming sepia rain cloud wooing me into a contemplative trance. "For the twelve months I was there, I often wondered what kept me in the Kashmiri valley of vulnerability. At times, I struggled to resist the urge to leave, the push and pull from within. Eventually, it became clear that I went to Kashmir to face a deep need to trust myself unconditionally."

Natasha smiled her understanding before saying, "Run! It's raining."

I tilt my head westward. "Yes, let's go! The Bridgehead Coffee house is the closest."

We entered the warmth of the cozy local coffee shop. Natasha ordered us lemon teas while I dried off with paper napkins. As we sank happily into a soft brown leather couch, I continued answering the question she'd earlier asked. "I think the reason I was drawn to Kashmir's harsh environment was to discover my own boundaries, and to realize that I can *choose* to feel fulfilled by *accepting* rather than trying to *prove* that I am valuable.

"When this realization clicked, head-to-toe...mind, heart and soul...I felt the shift. On some level, I had been drawn to the distant mountain ranges, continents away from Canada, to learn and grow. Away from the comfort of everything familiar, I could discover my strength...my vulnerabilities...my limiting emotions.

"Being there, allowed me to get to know myself on a deeper level, to feel my own worth, and to realize that it's up to me to choose and define what success means to me. In Kabul and in Kashmir, the unanticipated and enlightening soul-to-soul connections I made with a few extraordinary women led me to realizations that grounded me."

Smiling, I waited for my good friend to comment. Content, Natasha savored her tea while I shared what I had been excited to tell her all week. "Last week at the Dalai Lama documentary, I bumped into a unique lady named Raffiun. She's like an Egyptian Goddess. Natasha, you'd love her. Her presence reminded me that I am exactly where I am meant to be."

"She sounds spiritual and wise," Natasha offered.

"She is! The second we met, I had the feeling that we were already well-acquainted, that we must know each other. But, from *where* or *when*? She spoke like no one else, a living history book anchored in contemporary knowledge, from a time beyond ours. Her message that we are all interconnected resonated deeply. It brought me a sense of comfort."

Natasha smiled, "She sounds like the type of person you would attract, Reh. Are you going to meet again?"

"Yes, at the Green Door restaurant on Thursday to talk about the Dalai Lama's book. Our conversation will be intriguing, I'm sure. Just being in her incredible presence, listening to her extraordinary and simple stories, reminded me of how my journey of running and running away is connected to a bigger purpose."

"When the student is ready, the teacher will appear." Natasha cited the proverb often attributed to Buddha before asking, "Reh, sometimes when we're talking more than we're jogging, rain or sunshine, I feel grateful for our time together and the stories we share."

My smile stretched from ear-to-ear at my friend's kind words. "Five years ago, I could not have imagined sharing my jogging time with anyone, or that doing so would give me a sense of pure joy that I hadn't even known was missing."

"That reminds me, Reh. Salim and I tried a Zumba class at our gym. We were in stitches, laughing our way through it. At the same time, we both thought and then said, 'Rehana would love this!'"

"Ah, thanks for thinking of me. I went a while ago and could give it a try again for fun. I just heard of this fusion dance-form called Nia. Apparently, it embodies elements from nine diverse movement forms, including jazz, yoga and even tae kwon do. I think it would be both grounding and freeing." Imagining what Nia would feel like, I felt bubbles of excitement rising in my core.

"*Nia* means *purpose* in Swahili!" Natasha said, reminding me that she was the master of languages.

"Cool! I have a sense that Nia will help me feel the joy of movement. Though this may sound strange, I also have a feeling that when I evolve into my next adventure, wherever that might be, Nia will lead me to a new community of like-spirited people."

"It sounds like you could have found the perfect dance for you."

"I hope so," I said, as the rain stopped and a streak of sunshine beamed through the window. Blinking back tears of contentedness, I thought of my many blessings. I was grateful for those I'd worked with, learned with, mentored with and laughed with. Thankful that when I looked in the mirror, I actually felt worthy of all of my blessings—my loving family, my divine and beautiful friends, my education, all the privileges of living in Canada. Perhaps I had to travel to distant lands to fully appreciate the clean air we breathed, the drinkable water that flowed freely from our taps, that we fell asleep and awoke feeling safe.

In that beautiful moment, I knew it was time to let go of guilt I felt for having left my family behind when I chose the winding journey that transformed me. One experience, one friendship at a time, the fears and doubts had gradually dissolved, revealing a woman I liked, a woman I trusted.

My journey forward will unveil turns, dips and peaks as I discover new communities and friendships to light my way. I don't jog anymore. Instead, I choose to dance, to walk with a friend or by myself. What better way to travel than grounded on my dancing feet. I trust that my steps are being divinely guided.

About Rehana Nanjijuma

Rehana lives in Vancouver, British Columbia. She is ethnically Gujerati (Indian) and her family's history is rooted in East Africa and England. She loves to immerse herself in diverse cultures and learn new languages. She holds a Master of Public Health in health promotion from the University of Alberta.

She is passionate about mindfulness and yoga, and enjoys painting, singing, and walking in nature. She strives to build inclusive communities at work, when volunteering, and at play. Rehana can be contacted via info@heartmindeffect.com

However Far Away You Are

Jennifer Marie Luce

Take a breath,
Before we say goodbye.
Take notice.
With each breath
Deep
Deep
Deeper
Into a sense of self.

The place where there is no breath
So calm
And sweet
Delicate

Beyond my senses,
Deepening into my consciousness.
Awareness.
Of all that is,
All I am,
All there ever has been.

Away to a place of no regrets,
And no returns.

Forward we go
Until there is no longer.
Stronger we become
With each breath of life
Each pause
Of ignorance or awakening.

You choose.

Recommended Reading

Alexander, Bruce. *Globalization of Addiction: A Study in Poverty of the Spirit*. United Kingdom: Oxford University Press, 2010

Baker, John. *Life's Healing Choices: Freedom from Your Hurts, Hang-ups, and Habits*. USA: Howard Books, 2013

Cameron, Julia. *The Artist's Way*. New York: Penguin Putman, 2002

Chopra MD, Deepak and Tanzi, Rudolph E. Super Brain: *Unleashing the Explosive Power of Your Mind to Maximize Health, Happiness, and Spiritual Well-Being*. USA: Harmony, 2013

Dispenza, Joe. *Breaking The Habit of Being Yourself: How to Lose Your Mind and Create a New One*. USA: Hay House, 2013

Dooley, Mike. *Infinite Possibilities*. New York: Atria Books/Beyond Words, 2010

Dyer, Wayne. *Change Your Thoughts, Change Your Life –Living The Wisdom of the Tao*. USA: Hay House Inc., 2007

Dyer, Wayne. *Excuses Begone!* USA: Hay House, 2009

Fuhrman, Joel. *The End of Diabetes: The Eat to Live Plan to Prevent and Reverse Diabetes*. USA: HarperOne; Reprint edition, 2014

Ghabi, Joseph P. *The Blueprint of Your Soul*. USA: Free Spirit Centre, 2009

Hay, Louise L. *You Can Heal Your Life*. USA: Hay House Inc., 2004

Hill, Napoleon. *Think and Grow Rich*. USA: Ballantine Books, 1983

Jaffer, Taslim. *Tuesday Tasks: 52 Activities Designed for an Entire Year of Creativity.* Canada: Let Me Out!! Products, 2013

Jaffer, Taslim. *What If …? 52 Questions Designed for an Entire Year of Self-Discovery.* Canada: Let Me Out!! Products, 2014

Jones, Lola. *Things are Going Great in my Absence: How to Let Go & Let the Divine Do the Heavy Lifting.* USA: Lola Jones, 2013

Katie, Byron. *Loving What Is: Four Questions that Can Change Your Life.* USA: Three Rivers Press; Reprint edition, 2003

Kindness Is Key Coauthors. *Heartmind Wisdom Collection #1.* Canada: Kindness Is Key Training & Publishing Inc., 2015

Kindness Is Key Coauthors. *Heartmind Wisdom Collection #2.* Canada: Kindness Is Key Training & Publishing Inc., 2014

Kuntz, Ted. *Peace Begins With Me.* Coquitlam: Ted Kuntz, 2005

Lincoln, Dr. Michael J. *Messages from My Body – Their Psychological Meaning.* USA: Talking Hearts, 2013

Naess, Inger. *Colour Energy.* Vancouver: Colour Energy, 1996

Peeke, Dr. Pamela. *The Hunger Fix: The Three-Stage Detox and Recovery Plan for Overeating and Food Addiction.* USA: Rodale Books, 2013

Redfield, James. *The Celestine Prophecy.* New York: Warner Books, 1994

Ross, Joyce M. *The Kindness Ambassador and the Sugarholic Prosecutor – 13 Keys to Living the Live You Were Meant to Love.* USA: Balboa Press, 2012

Segal, Inna. *The Secret Language of Your Body.* New York: Atria Books/ Beyond Words, 2010

Simmons, Robert and Ashian, Naisha. *The Book of Stones.* Vermont: Heaven and Earth, 2005

Soll, Joe. *Adoption Healing ... A Path to Recovery.* USA: Adoption Crossroads; Second edition, 2000

Tolle, Eckhart. *A New Earth: Awakening to Your Life's Purpose.* USA: Dutton/Penguin Group, 2005

Tolle, Eckhart. *The Power of Now.* Vancouver: Namaste, 2004

Tully, Brock. *The Great Gift: For Someone Special.* Canada: Influence Publishing, 2013

Verrier, Nancy Newton. *The Primal Wound: Understanding the Adopted Child.* USA: Gateway Press, 2003

White, Ellen G. *Education.* USA: Ellen G. White Estate, Inc., 2010

Walsch, Neale Donald. *Conversations with God.* New York: Putman, 2002

Recommended Music

Hagan, Denise. *For Those Who Hear.* Rosa Records, Sneezer Publishing, 2006. www.denisehagan.com

Singh, Ranj. *Found a Way Home.* Via CD Baby or ITunes. www.ranjsingh.com

Recommended Websites

www.beautifulchorus.com
www.blogtalkradio.com/joeygiggles
www.brocktully.com
www.callanish.org
www.deborahnelson.ca
www.denisehagan.com
www.drmeelainling.com
www.eckharttolle.com
www.eden-valley.org
www.letmeoutcreative.com
www.heartmindeffect.com
www.heartmindstore.com
www.kindnessiskey.com
www.maytawee.ca
www.mercyships.ca
www.mooji.org
www.peacebeginswithme.ca
www.proctorgallagherinstitute.com
www.ranjsingh.com
www.sleepfoundation.org
www.tranquiltouchservices.ca
www.wrongwaytohope.com
www.youngadultcancer.ca

3